A Guide to Dynamics
of Feminist Therapy

A Guide to Dynamics of Feminist Therapy

Edited by
Doris Howard, PhD

A Guide to Dynamics of Feminist Therapy was simultaneously issued by The Haworth Press, Inc., under the title: *The Dynamics of Feminist Therapy* and simultaneously published as a special issue of the journal *Women & Therapy*, Volume 5, Numbers 2/3, Summer/Fall 1986, Doris Howard, guest editor.

Harrington Park Press
New York • London

ISBN 0-918393-37-X

Published by

Harrington Park Press, Inc., 12 West 32 Street, New York, New York 10001
EUROSPAN/Harrington, 3 Henrietta Street, London WC2E 8LU England

Harrington Park Press, Inc., is a subsidiary of the Haworth Press, Inc., 12 West 32 Street, New York, New York 10001.

A Guide to Dynamics of Feminist Therapy was originally published as *Women & Therapy*, Volume 5, Numbers 2/3, Summer/Fall 1986.

Cover design by Marshall Andrews.

Library of Congress Cataloging-in-Publication Data

A Guide to dynamics of feminist therapy.

   Reprint. Originally published: The Dynamics of feminist therapy. New York: Haworth Press, 1987.
   Papers presented at the Tenth National Conference of the Association for Women in Psychology, held in New York City in 1985.
   Includes bibliographies and index.
   1. Feminist therapy—Congresses. I. Howard, Doris. II. Association for Women in Psychology. National Conference (10th: 1985: New York, N.Y.) [DNLM: 1. Psychotherapy—congresses.   2. Women—congresses.   3. Women's Rights—congresses.   W1 W0433V v.5 no.2/3/WM 420 G9466 1985]
RC489.F45D96   1987   616.89′008042   86-33616
ISBN 0-918393-37-X

CONTENTS

A Guide to Dynamics of Feminist Therapy

FOREWORD

We are pleased to introduce this special issue of *Women & Therapy*, guest edited by Doris Howard, coordinator of the Tenth National Conference of the Association for Women in Psychology. The papers in this issue were all presented at that conference. They are particularly important because they emphasize ethnic and global issues.

The title of the issue, *The Dynamics of Feminist Therapy*, is also important. "Dynamic" is a wonderful word that is beginning to lose its meaning through overuse, despite its relatively modern origins. Coined in the 19th century, from the Greek word *dynamikos,* or "powerful," it first came into use in English as a scientific term.

"Dynamic" was an adjective that described physical forces that were effective. As such, it was usually opposed to "static." Later, this whole field of inquiry began to be called "dynamics,"—that is, the study of "forcefulness," and "forces," and "power." Thus, this issue of *Women & Therapy* is appropriately called *The Dynamics of Feminist Therapy*, because the articles analyze the power, the effectiveness, and the forcefulness of a therapy designed for women—a therapy of change, the opposite of static, or of status, or of the state, or of the status quo.

The word lying behind *dynamikos,* or "powerful," is *dynamis,* or "power," and behind that is *dynasthai,* a verb meaning "to be able." Simply said, feminist therapy is a dynamic therapy because it enables.

The next issue of *Women & Therapy* will have no special theme. Since we began our editorship, many articles have been submitted, and sent to our hard-working editorial board members for review. The next issue will reflect their selections from among the articles that have been submitted. Please continue to send in your manuscripts. We welcome submissions from new authors as well as experienced ones.

Esther D. Rothblum
Ellen Cole

PREFACE

This volume is the product of the Tenth National Conference of the Association for Women in Psychology (AWP). AWP was organized in 1969 by a group of women who wanted to collaborate in pursuing their interest in feminist issues. AWP has been in the forefront of feminist psychology for sixteen years, and the conferences have provided a forum for the most recent thinking in feminist psychotherapy, research, and teaching. The articles in this volume are consistent with that tradition.

I coordinated the 1985 conference with this volume in mind. The 1985 Coordinating Committee organized the conference around the theme "The Future of Feminism." The committee also chose ethnic issues as a major focus of the conference. Some of the finest articles included here are by and about women of color or about groups other than Caucasian.

For many years, women in the mental health sciences have been struggling with the development of the concept of feminist therapy. A major focus has been the attempt to blend various theories of therapy with the goals of feminism. Several articles in this volume address these theoretical formulations. What is feminist therapy? What is its basic structure and theory? The work is far from over. In the year 2000, we will still be arguing about the relative merits of Freud, Sullivan, and others, in connection with feminist therapy. But what we do know, and will know, is that feminist therapy deals with the equality, assertiveness, and empowerment of women, with the elevation of consciousness about sex-roles and sex-typing. We know that it is an egalitarian system that has no place for sexism, racism, or classism within its parameters.

What is most exciting about the literature on feminism, whether in research, psychotherapy, or teaching, is the thinking, the speculation, the transcendence over accepted formu-

xv

lae of the past. This collection reflects that thoughtful examination of feminist issues. Some of the articles address issues or particular groups of women that are frequently overlooked. A few articles were written by graduate students, who are important members of AWP and other feminist organizations. Other authors are clinical social workers and nurses, as well as teachers and psychotherapists, reflecting the interdisciplinary membership of AWP.

The articles in this volume are important contributions to the literature on feminist therapy and research. I regret the lack of space that limited the selection. There were many other articles worthy of inclusion. I and the individual authors are grateful to The Haworth Press for this opportunity to reach a larger audience than the conference registrants.

I would like to thank all those who gave me much needed support: my friends and colleagues; my family, especially my son; the Association for Women in Psychology; and the New York chapter of AWP which helped to make the conference and this volume possible.

Doris Howard, PhD
New York, New York

I. DYNAMICS OF FEMINIST THERAPY

As a result of the women's movement, therapists are beginning to change their attitudes about and manner of interacting with female clients in order to incorporate the changes taking place in society. Feminist therapy in particular has attempted to establish an egalitarian relationship between therapist and client and to conceptualize psychological distress in light of societal discrimination and sex role socialization. Some feminists have argued that the ultimate goal of feminist therapy is social activism and institutional change. The first section of this volume focuses on issues directly facing feminist therapists. The articles cover a wide variety of topics ranging from criticisms of conventional therapy to models of change.

Traditional psychodynamic therapy interprets therapist self-disclosure as inappropriate and indicative of countertransference. Yet this model of restraint and hierarchical power was not present in early psychoanalytic thinking. In the first article of this volume, *Miriam Greenspan* provides an analysis of therapist self-disclosure from a feminist perspective. Rather than advocate the role of the therapist as the "distant expert," she views self-disclosure as the natural process between two individuals who are establishing a bond. By providing her clients with feedback about her feelings, the feminist therapist is allowing for a more egalitarian relationship. She can use her own experiences, struggles, and emotions to educate, raise consciousness, and provide an empathic style, all of which can be vehicles of change.

Clearly, the therapeutic relationship is not the only source of possible misuse of power. Patriarchal power can be modelled between fathers and daughters, teachers and students, husbands and wives. The second article in this series focuses on

1

the properties of marital relationships. *Gwendolyn Gerber* has conceptualized a Relationship Balance Model to illustrate how individuals in a couple influence the properties of a relationship. She argues that therapists cannot effectively change a client's behavior without considering possible repercussions on the couple's relationship. This would seem particularly vital for female clients, who are struggling to change major roles at home and at work, yet who have been socialized to pay primary importance to the "success" of their marriage.

In the past decade, increasing numbers of women have entered professions traditionally reserved for men. Although these women may be regarded by society as successful and self-confident, there are important issues faced by any group that is entering new roles which counteract societal stereotypes. *Jeanne Parr Lemkau* discusses themes presented in therapy by women in male-dominated professions. She describes how the isolation experienced by these women and the sex role-specific conflicts may result in internalized failure and self-blame. The feminist therapist is thus an ideal source of support and a role model of effective coping.

So far, the articles in this section focus on the congruence between the feminist therapist and her client who may be challenged by similar life stresses. How does a feminist therapist intervene most effectively with clients who are different from herself in important respects, such as ethnic and minority status, sexual orientation, age, or life experience? *Beverly Greene* discusses feminist psychotherapy when the therapist is white and the client is black. By focusing on black women's experiences in both the heterosexual and lesbian communities, she illustrates the issue of race among feminists. Thus, white therapists need to learn about black culture and confront their own—and society's—racism. Given the emphasis in professional training on identifying individual and familial factors that affect our emotions and behavior, how do white therapists intervene with black clients whose distress is the result of white oppression? Finally, Greene describes issues confronting black lesbians, a "minority within a minority" who have received little attention by feminist scholars and therapists.

In the next article, *Harriet McCombs* presents a model of adjustment to describe the cultural/environmental experiences of black women. This model interprets the experiences of individual women in a collective framework, since black women's collective herstory bears a crucial relationship to their personal lives within the context of the white dominant society. As black women seek to affirm their identities and disassociate with the mainstream and alienating culture, the feminist therapist may play an important role in facilitating lifestyle change. Thus, the therapist herself must disassociate with the mainstream professional training and its whitewashed assumptions in order to gain the sensitivity to assist black women in their redirection and empowerment.

The next article focuses on yet another issue of lack of conguence between therapist and client: the feminist therapist and male client. *Zoya Slive* illustrates how principles of feminist therapy can be applied to male clients. With case examples she describes how men are products of traditional sex roles and ways in which they may desire the flexible options now available to some women. She discusses how men may seek new roles as fathers, spouses, and employees. Finally, Slive presents ways in which the feminist therapist can facilitate such change.

As feminists have established guidelines for therapy, there has often been a critique or even abandonment of traditional psychoanalytic theory. Feminists have offered reconceptualizations of Freud's principals ranging from the penis to the mind. In contrast, *Mary Hayden* describes psychoanalytic thinking before it was influenced by patriarchal values. She states that her goal ". . . to reclaim the radical social critique and revolutionary agenda which has always been inherent in the psychoanalytic method." Thus, "political Freudians" debated many issues of concern to feminists today. Hayden advocates that contemporary women regard psychoanalytic principles as resources to probe their own thoughts and emotions.

The Latin term for family referred to the number of slaves owned by one man. The current "pro-family movement" has urged a return to the nuclear family. What are the implications of family therapy for feminists? *Michele Bograd* provides a feminist analysis of family systems theory and family therapy. Thus, she states that women's roles in the family have not been critically assessed by family systems theory. The terminology and interpretations in family therapy may reflect patriarchal values. The mother may be "blamed." As an alternative, Bograd presents a model of feminist family therapy that attends to the larger societal context of inequality of power.

As the United States prepares for increasing numbers of elderly people and as women continue to outlive men by seven years, we can expect to see large numbers of elderly women, mostly widowed and impoverished, by the turn of the century. There has been little emphasis on the treatment of elderly women. *Martha Banks, Rosalie Ackerman,* and *Elisabeth Clark* describe issues facing the treatment of elderly women in family therapy. As they state, elderly women are faced with "agism, sexism, . . . negative conceptions of mental illness . . . medical problems . . . social losses . . . lack of power, depersonalization, . . . neglect, and dependency." They discuss aspects of family therapy in geriatric psychiatric and medical institutions, issues confronting family members of elderly women, and related moral, ethical, and legal issues.

Should Therapists Be Personal? Self-Disclosure and Therapeutic Distance in Feminist Therapy

Miriam Greenspan

Most therapies, however much they differ in philosophy and methodology, share a common injunction against therapists revealing themselves as people to their clients. I will argue that the therapist's ability to disclose her feelings, beliefs and experiences as a person can be a profound therapeutic tool. The disciplined and skillful use of self-disclosure helps women in the empowerment process which is at the heart of feminist—and all good—therapy. This tool is especially useful in working with depressed women and in breaking through certain kinds of therapeutic impasses which are related to the therapist's denied or unexpressed countertransference feelings. Overall, it serves to strengthen the therapeutic alliance in an egalitarian therapy relationship and is thus especially important for the development of feminist therapy.

Self-disclosure has remained completely untapped as a therapeutic skill precisely because it has been designated taboo in virtually all schools of therapy. Before we address how this skill can be used, let us look at the arguments against it.

The traditional psychoanalytic interpretation of the therapist who talks about herself in therapy is that she is losing her professional boundaries and burdening the patient with her countertransference feelings. These feelings are supposed to be discussed only in the therapist's supervision. The therapist who airs them with a patient is thought to be "acting out" in a way that is detrimental to the patient and to the therapeutic

Miriam Greenspan is in private practice at 27 Moraine Street, Jamaica Plain, MA 02130.

process. Often, this grave faux pas is interpreted as a consequence of the therapist's "overidentification with the patient."

As a trainee in psychology in a psychoanalytically-oriented program, I remember being told that a serious professional never makes personal statements because such statements interfere with the emergence of the patient's transference. According to this line of thought, patients transfer their early needs for intimacy and approval to the therapist. The therapist's job is not to gratify these wishes but to intentionally frustrate them. In this way, the patient's transference is encouraged to surface and can be examined in the course of therapy. Prospective therapists were cautioned to avoid even the most routine friendliness.

In short, the message in my training was: patients may want us to respond to them as regular human beings, but we must avoid the temptation to do so. In this male model of therapy, the personhood of the therapist is seen as an unwanted intrusion in the therapeutic process. The ideal therapist is disciplined, distant, unemotional, immaculately in control—in short, culturally masculine. He possesses a body of wisdom about transference which is the key to unlocking the door to the patient's unconscious. He sits outside this door, unruffled and cool. He is Father Knows Best.

In my book, *A New Approach to Women and Therapy* (1983) I call this the "Nobody Home" school of how to be a therapist. Not the therapist's compassion, but his distance and neutrality, are thought to be the absolute requirements for therapeutic work. This model of therapy banishes the therapist's self-disclosure because it is deemed destructive to two major elements of traditional psychotherapy: (1) it erodes the therapist's role as Distant Expert; and (2) it interferes with what is thought to be the major substance of therapy, the patient's transference.

Feminist therapy has, of course, challenged this line of thought and the practices that go with it. It has re-examined the role of the therapist and the nature of the therapeutic relationship. It has questioned the notions of professionalism which many of us have inherited from our traditional training. We have seen this to be an eminently masculine model of therapy in which the therapist is yet another patriarchal figure, the Expert whose superior knowledge cures the passive, powerless and unknowing patient. In feminist therapy, the ideal of an all-powerful, distant, patriarchal expert has given way to an ideal of two women working together in a much more egalitarian, empathic, and responsive way. We know that these more "feminine" characteristics are not only acceptable but powerful and crucial attributes of a good therapist and a working therapy relationship.

But what about this notion that being a personal therapist discourages the client's transference? In my own experience of revealing myself in therapy, I have not found this to be the case. The transference is still evident and still examined in therapy. However, it tends to be more of a positive transference than in traditional therapy. And it coexists with the client's natural feelings towards me as a human being. The transference relationship coexists with the real bond that unites us in our work together. It is true that the transference relationship does come to assume a somewhat less grandiose, center-stage position in therapy. It remains a crucial aspect, but certainly not the whole story. Concomitantly, the real relationship of two adult women is accorded a new value. In return for this shift in the balance of transference versus real relationship there is a dissipation of the often combative quality that characterizes traditional therapy. The therapeutic alliance, which is really the basis for all the work of therapy, is strengthened.

Most feminist therapists seem to be at ease with the necessity for the feminist therapist to share with clients her beliefs about how women's problems are influenced by social conditioning and social structure. Nevertheless, we remain divided on the matter of whether the therapist should go so far as to reveal her feelings to her clients. There is a suspicion that to do so is to abuse the considerable power we have as therapists, however egalitarian the relationship may aspire to be. This is certainly an important suspicion and one that deserves some attention.

Undoubtedly, there are instances in which the self-disclosure of the therapist may be detrimental to the client. I can think of at least three such instances: first, as therapists, we must guard against talking about ourselves as a way of emotionally unloading in a relationship that is safe for use precisely because we have considerable power in it. Clients are very vulnerable to our words and behavior. They are not served well if we are using them as a kind of captive audience for our feelings.

Second, as therapists we must be careful about giving advice, albeit well-intentioned, to clients. As a result of my book, *A New Approach to Women and Therapy,* I tend to receive numerous phone calls from clients who are in the midst of difficult impasses with their therapists. One such client told me recently that her therapist advised her to get a divorce and has been angry with her ever since because she is unable or unready to do so. Because we are trying to develop an egalitarian style of therapy relationship, we may find it tempting to engage in advice-giving the way we might with friends. But this is precisely where a knowledge of our power as transference objects is very important. Any suggestion we make is laden with enormous meaning for clients; it is not likely to be taken casually. Depending on the nature of the transference, the client may feel intruded upon or dictated to, experiencing the advice as a mandate rather than a suggestion. Or she may feel that she is obliged to do as the therapist says in order to take care of her. I am not saying that we should *never* make suggestions. Suggestions in the form of sharing information about resources or in the attempt to avert self-destructive behavior can be very important. But we must be careful that our suggestions are not an insistence on the client's compliance.

Third, as therapists we must certainly guard against being sexually seductive with clients—male or female—under the misguided assumption that sexual feelings are a natural expression of affection or that anything goes in an egalitarian relationship. Sexual seductions in feminist therapy are no less abusive than they are in traditional therapy.

The use of self-disclosure as a therapeutic technique requires a great deal of care. It must be accompanied by the therapist's awareness of the potential for abusing her power or of disclosing herself as part of some unconscious hidden agenda of her own. As with all other interventions, the therapeutic use of self-disclosure depends a great deal on the skills of good timing and effective communication which are so much a part of the art of good therapy.

With these provisos in mind, how might therapists go about revealing themselves in therapeutic ways?

Let me state at the outset that as therapists we are, in fact, revealing ourselves all the time, whether we do so deliberately or not. Even the most distant therapist is, despite his judgment and training, leaking his personality into the therapeutic process. The perfectly neutral, non-personal therapist is entirely a myth. This is all to the good, as far as I'm concerned. I believe that much of the benefit that comes from the traditional masculine model of therapy derives from the fact that therapists have a hard time completely suppressing themselves as persons. If indeed this were our therapeutic ideal, we would do well to program computers to be therapists. They are infinitely more dispassionate than human beings. (One of my clients once told me that he read a study which documented the use of such computer-therapists. The study concluded that computers were better at the skills of asking pertinent questions and mirroring back patients' feelings than their human counterparts. I suppose that this client was angry at me at the time he offered this information.)

My point here is that, particularly where female therapists are working with female clients, the therapist's feelings are very much a part of the process, even when they are not intentionally expressed. As women, we are trained to have exquisitely sensitive emotional antennae: to be able to detect and respond to others' emotions even when they are not being expressed directly. Therapists do communicate feelings indirectly, just as clients do. We do so through our body language, our comments, our choice of what to pursue and what to ignore, our choice of how and when to nod our heads or smile. And our clients are savvy to this. They are intuiting, monitoring and responding to our cues. Clients probably know a lot more about what we feel than we are willing to let on. So the question is not "do we express our feelings?" but "*how* do we do so explicitly and intentionally rather than covertly and indirectly?"

Let me turn to four examples. The first two illustrate the use of self-disclosure as a technique in helping depressed women to feel more empowered.

Like so many other women, Nadine* came to therapy be-

---

*All names and identifying characteristics of clients have been changed to insure privacy.

cause she was depressed. She had a history of chronic, low level, off and on depression for the better part of her adult life. Nadine was 35, an intelligent, sensitive woman and a therapist. Her knowledge of diagnostic categories and of current psychiatric theories of depression fueled her deeply held conviction that she was suffering from a clinical disorder which was organically based and for which she needed medication. This is not the place to discuss the etiology of depression in women. Let me just say that in my view depression in women is often a consequence of women's social position which breeds the powerlessness, internalized rage, and self-hatred which most women feel and which are the major ingredients of depression. Nadine's self-diagnosis was a form of self-blame masquerading as insight. As most depressed women do, she blamed herself for being depressed. She believed her depression to be the mark of her particular brand of craziness. Being a therapist, she understood that her depression hid a great reservoir of rage which she carefully suppressed except for a few explosions per year. These made her feel even more pathological. She figured that her rage had no business being there and doubted her perceptions of the people at whom she was angry. She preferred to think that there was something wrong with her rather than to accept the validity of her anger.

Nadine was a perfect example of what I call in my book "Woman as Patient." Her self-blame and shame masquerading as insight actually held her depression in place. She was trapped in a typical female double-bind: the feeling that neither her anger nor the depression which masked it were legitimate. The double-bind made her feel "crazy" and impotent.

There is a great deal about "Woman as Patient" in my book. Suffice it to say here that no woman's therapy can be effective without a transformation of her consciousness from that of a patient with a disorder to that of a person whose problems are rooted in the reality of woman's social subordination, a person who has some power to change her way of dealing with that reality. In twelve years of practicing therapy I have seen that the use of self-disclosure in this process of consciousness-raising is not only helpful but sometimes necessary.

It was easy for me to empathize with Nadine's anxious depressions, her profound belief that if she wasn't perfect she was awful, the difficulty she had letting herself feel good about her strengths and accomplishments, and the self blame which locked all of this into place. Depression is a place I know intimately from my travels there as a teenager and a young adult. The effective use of self-disclosure to help alter Nadine's consciousness was largely a matter of allowing myself to share that empathy with her, as well as to share my feminist insights into my own depression.

After several months of working with Nadine on her depression, I let her know that I too had been depressed off and on for a good ten years. I told her that for me, depression was a kind of adaptation to my identity as a women and as a Jew. As a woman, I had learned that anger was not feminine but powerlessness was. As a Jewish woman and the child of survivors of the Holocaust, I had learned that suffering was an inescapable attribute of Jewishness. In some way, I had grown up feeling that it would be a betrayal of my ancestors not to continue the tradition. I wondered if Nadine had ever understood her depression as a kind of adaptation rather than as a pathological condition?

Nadine was amazed to hear that I had ever been depressed at all, much less that I would admit it to her. She was even more amazed to learn that, once depressed, I had overcome it without the aid of drugs. A traditional therapist might say that my self-revelation was a way of putting Nadine's positive transference to good use. She saw me as the Healthy Therapist and herself as the Sick Patient. After my disclosure, this line began to break down. She began to let go of the idea of her depression as a pathological condition. Her shame about it began to recede. Without the shame holding it in place, she was able to look more closely into the depression as well as to feel more powerful about overcoming it. She began a process of locating some of the features of her life as a Catholic girl that had taught her to be a martyr/saint, to efface her own feelings, needs and desires and to repress the anger she felt at all of this. The repression of her anger, her sexuality, and her self-respect was part of a process of living up to the best "saintly" model of womanhood that she had learned. Her depression was, in part, a way of suffering to prove her goodness. For a Catholic girl she had received the message that feeling good was bad and feeling bad was good.

The best work that Nadine did in working through her depression was expedited by my disclosure of depression in my life. More than anything else, this disclosure seemed to permit her to look at her depression without shame. Overcoming shame is probably some of the hardest work a client and therapist can do together. No genuine freeing self-exploration is possible as long as shame bars the way. Working with shame, as some of us probably know, can feel like swimming through molasses. When the client lets go of it, the therapeutic push can be rather dramatic. It was in Nadine's case. She is now medication-free and not depressed.

My second example illustrates how self-disclosure can be used to help further the process by which depressed women begin to permit and validate their anger.

Jane was 40 years old, bright, talented, a teacher and writer. On the surface she was in control of her life, but she too was depressed. Her depression was clearly connected to her relationship with her mother, a woman whose life was poisoned by the most severe form of depression one can imagine. From the time Jane was a teenager, her mother had been recurrently hospitalized, given several rounds of ECT and otherwise psychiatrically treated for depression that would not go away. When her mother is depressed she is like the living dead: nonfunctional, she simply lies in bed and refuses to eat. She is non-reachable, totally dependent and yet totally remote. For the past twenty years, Jane has played the dutiful daughter, trying unsuccessfully to save her mother. She lives in terror of being swept away by an out-of-control illness such as her mother's. The contemporary theory of depression as biochemical in nature and genetically transmitted has further bolstered her fear. She believes that she has avoided her mother's fate only by remaining single, childless and a professional, and by living 2000 miles away, i.e. by being as separate emotionally and geographically as she can be from her mother's life. Yet she still doesn't *feel* separate from her mother. Her own life often feels gray, dismal and grim, full of suffering and empty of joy. When her mother becomes depressed, so does she.

In working with Jane, I felt an odd sort of empathy. Though my own mother has never been acutely depressed or hospitalized, she was chronically depressed for the first ten years of my life. As a survivor of the Holocaust, the sole survivor of her family, my mother's depression was not only understandable;

it was almost inevitable. Nevertheless, as a child it left me without a certain kind of nurturance. It bred in me a deeply felt need to parent my mother, to save her from something that happened before I was born and over which I was powerless. Jane reminded me of myself and of other children of survivors: her tremendous, overburdened sense of responsibility for her mother's condition, accompanied by cycles of immense guilt and resentment; her difficulty separating herself from her mother's pain, her psychosomatic fears. Jane's mother was a victim not of the Holocaust but of her life as a woman.

I communicated my empathy with Jane by telling her that she reminded me of myself, forever trying to save my mother and failing at it. I told her that growing up I had always felt that I had no right to be angry at my mother. How could I be angry at someone who had suffered and lost so much? Still, I had to go through a period of allowing my anger at my mother, even if I felt it was a terrible betrayal, before I could let go of it, accept her life and my own.

Intellectually, Jane knew that she harbored a great deal of anger at her mother. But she rarely allowed herself to feel or show it. Then one day in therapy she spent the hour crying and screaming "Why don't you die, mother! I want you to die!" It was a turning-point session, the beginning of a process of allowing her anger to emerge and really separating from her mother. I believe it was expedited by the "permission" Jane felt was granted to her when I revealed my anger at my own mother.

The third example touches on the controversial issue of the disclosure of the therapist's feelings towards the client, in particular, the disclosure of the therapist's angry feelings. I am intentionally avoiding the use of the term countertransference here because I believe that the entire concept of countertransference, as presently defined, is misleading. By most definitions, the therapist's countertransference is considered to be induced by the client, the necessary complement of his or her transference (Moeller, 1977). It is as though by some immaterial osmosis beyond the therapist's control, her feelings are wrung from her by the client. The client is in the paradoxically all-powerful position of being responsible for the therapist's feelings. This is an unfortunate idea that goes along with a model of therapy in which therapists are not held unaccountable for their end of the relationship. Therapists often talk of their angry countertransference as though this anger were a predictable, legitimate and necessary reaction. This tends toward a kind of blaming logic which I believe can have some very deleterious effects on female clients who are already blaming themselves for their own feelings and everyone else's.

Nevertheless, it is common enough for therapists to develop angry feelings towards clients. Take, for example, a phenomenon quite common in the long middle phase of therapy—those sessions in which the client appears to be hopelessly stuck in past patterns. Sometimes it seems as though the client is on what I call a "stubborn streak"; consistently passive or passive/aggressive in therapy, she appears to be holding on to her resistance almost to spite the therapist. To the extent that our egos as therapists are invested in the client's progress in order to validate our own sense of competence, we will find ourselves angry or resentful. Because this anger is often difficult for us as women and as therapists, we may tend to deny or avoid it. If we do so, we run the invariable risk of turning it into distance. Clients who are attuned to our feelings will intuit the anger we deny. Furthermore, there is nothing more guaranteed to get up the ire of most clients than a distant therapist. The angrier/more distant the therapist becomes, the angrier/more passive-aggressive the client becomes. The therapeutic alliance is more and more eroded. If we are not careful, we have all the ingredients for a full scale vicious cycle and therapeutic impasse.

Before it reaches this point, telling the client about your feelings of frustration, helplessness or anger can have a surprisingly beneficial effect. Of course these declarations must be carefully worded so that they do not appear to be blaming. For instance, I often make statements such as

> I am not holding you responsible or blaming you for this, but I think you should know that when you are this stuck I feel frustrated and a little bit angry. It seems to me that the more I try to reach out to help or to get closer to you, the more you pull back and refuse my help. I sense that there is a kind of stubbornness in you, as if you were saying, "Damn it, I'm just not going to move or let you near me." Do you feel that?

These kinds of statements and questions can have remarkable results with clients who feel so powerless and such low self-esteem that they cannot imagine that they would have an impact on anyone, much less a therapist who is sometimes perceived as invulnerable. There is usually some relief or gratification in finding out that their intuitions about their therapist's anger were valid. Since many women in therapy tend to doubt their perceptions and worry about being "crazy," this can be enormously therapeutic. The transaction models a way of expressing anger which is compatible with and futhers closeness. Again, since many women experience anger as rejection or abandonment, this can be important learning. Finally, this kind of transaction also models a way to let go of anger rather than to hold on to it, turn it into distance, passive/aggression or depression.

My last example has to do with self-revelations that arise from the simple fact that therapists are also human beings subject to the ineluctable pain of life. Three years ago, I had a son who died in infancy. Clients with whom I worked during this period and asked how I was doing saw me crying and heard me sharing the greatest sorrow of my life. There wasn't even a question for me about sharing these feelings. I knew that I simply could not have worked at all if I had denied them. It was difficult for many of my clients to see me so vulnerable. Several of them told me how guilty they felt at having such seemingly "petty" problems in the face of my grief. This then became another issue to work on in therapy: the importance of validating their own pain, even if there was other or greater suffering in the world. The reality of my life as a vulnerable human being hit home with enormous impact. I think that most of my clients were surprised to see that I could cry about my son and then move on with the work of being their therapist; that it was possible to be this vulnerable and this strong at the same time. In every case but one my clients were appreciative of my honesty and openness. Most told me that they felt privileged to be let in at this time of my life rather than shut out. In most cases, my vulnerability led them to make breakthroughs in exposing their own. New issues were identified and old issues seemed to be worked through with greater ease.

It has never been clearer to me that there is really no conflict at all between examining the transference that my disclosures evoke in my clients and also being a real human being who shares a supportive, respectful bond. Sharing my sorrow deepened that bond and strengthened the therapeutic alliance.

The use of self-disclosure is not always easy or successful. There are some potentially difficult consequences of the therapist's revelations. But even these can be used to advantage. Sometimes, for instance, a client may find herself feeling resentful about the therapist's taking up even a minute of her therapeutic space. This kind of feeling must be respected. One must be able to judge when and with whom this kind of technique is most effective. Sometimes this may mean minimizing such disclosures with certain clients. On the other hand, there can be a great benefit from examining the client's resentment and/or guilt when the therapist does express herself. Sometimes, for instance, a client may imagine that now that I have revealed myself to her, she has to drop her business and take care of me. She now sees me as a Victim rather than her Rescuer. She resents my switching roles on her. Confronting and exploring these various feelings can often be challenging and fruitful work for the client. She may come to realize how much she sees herself and other women as Victims and therefore how much she yearns for an all powerful Rescuer to save her. She may begin to let go of this fantasy and appropriate her own power as a person. This is the stuff of which feminist therapy is made.

To end, let me return to the two key arguments against therapeutic self-disclosure. The first had to do with the need for therapeutic distance; the second with the need to work with clients' transference. These are still important in feminist therapy. But the use of the therapist's self-disclosure radically redefines both of them. Therapy with a personal therapist sets up rather different transference patterns than therapy with a distant therapist. The emotional withholding of the remote therapist is bound to elicit the client's anger. The client feels deprived of contact or nurturance. The traditional therapy patient learns to accept this deprivation as a condition of the work and is continually working on her anger about it all. But a therapy based on the gratification of at least some part of the client's wishes for contact tends to evoke the fears of intimacy which get in the way. Working with a client's responses to my self-disclosures is one of the best ways I know for working through the clients fears of closeness in a relationship.

In other words, the personal therapist does not do away with professional distance; she redefines it from a feminist perspective. Therapeutic distance is not a matter of withholding our emotions, it is a matter of using them. In using the feminine strengths of empathy, intuition, compassion, vulnerability and self-expression, we integrate them into a workable therapeutic relationship. This kind of distance depends on the therapist's knowledge of herself, her feelings and her boundaries. It means knowing how to use the empathic bond that unites women in the therapy relationship; but also knowing its limits. It demands the therapist's awareness of what feelings the client evokes in her and the control not to act on these feelings by becoming more and more hostile or remote. The key to proper professional distance is not in adhering to some male-defined role of pseudo-neutrality, but in looking inward and continuing our own journeys of self-exploration. This is a model of using ourselves as instruments of change rather than ignoring that we are persons. It is a model of both distance and closeness, separation and intimacy, strength and vulnerability. We do not have to be male-style therapists to do good work. We can be ourselves.

REFERENCES

Greenspan, M. (1983). *A New Approach to Women and Therapy.* New York: McGraw-Hill.

Moeller, M. L. (1977). Self and Object in Countertransference. *International Journal of Psychoanalysis, 58,* 365–374.

The Relationship Balance Model and Its Implications for Individual and Couples Therapy

Gwendolyn L. Gerber

Therapeutic change in one person who is in individual or couples therapy is frequently followed by increased problems in the relationship and with the spouse. These disruptions may occur even when the person has changed in a positive way, and experiences increased self-confidence and self-esteem. This is because a seemingly simple and positive therapeutic change in one person does not take place in isolation from the relationship as a whole. It brings about pervasive changes in all dimensions of the couple's relationship.

The kind of relationship which is established by a married couple is dependent on the personality characteristics of each marital partner. Thus, when one partner changes in some important aspect of his or her personality, there will also be changes in the way that partner functions within the marriage relationship. Unless the spouse is able to accommodate the change, this will lead to increased conflict and discord in the marriage.

The "Relationship balance model," which has been developed by the author (Gerber, 1985), can be used to specify the ways in which the properties of the relationship are based on the properties of the individual members of the dyad. If one

Dr. Gerber is Associate Professor in the Department of Psychology at John Jay College of Criminal Justice, The City University of New York, and is also engaged in the practice of individual and marital therapy in New York City. She has been doing research on sex-role stereotypes and the way in which people perceive relationships between women and men, and is the author of several articles in this area.

The author wishes to thank David Brandt and Ruth Shapiro for their helpful comments on a earlier draft of the manuscript.

Requests for reprints should be sent to Gwendolyn L. Gerber, Department of Psychology, John Jay College of Criminal Justice, CUNY, 445 West 59th Street, New York, New York 10019.

of the marital partners changes in the course of therapy, the model can be used to predict the changes that are likely to occur within the relationship.

Of central importance in conceptualizing opposite-sex relationships are the personality traits which have been found to be stereotypic for women and men. The "masculine" personality traits emphasize the enhancement of the self through autonomy and self-assertion; the "feminine" traits emphasize the enhancement of the group through concern for others and a focus on maintaining group harmony (Bem, 1974; Rosenkrantz, Vogel, Bee, Broverman & Broverman, 1968; Spence, Helmreich & Stapp, 1975). Thus, a person who is high in masculinity would be characterized as "dominant," " assertive" and "competitive." A person who is high in femininity would be characterized as "sympathetic," "compassionate" and "sensitive to the needs of others" (Bem, 1974).

The Relationship balance model describes characteristics of the marital relationship which are based on these sex-role stereotype personality traits (Gerber 1985). According to the model, people conceptualize a marital relationship in terms of three major principles, called the "Relationship balances." These principles consist of "Positivity balance," the "Satisfaction balance" and the "Leadership balance." The Positivity balance reflects the extent to which the husband and wife are similar in the number of culturally-valued personality traits they possess. The "Satisfaction balance" reflects the degree of satisfaction that is experienced in the marriage. The "Leadership balance" reflects the extent to which either the wife or the husband is the leader in the marriage. Since all three Relationship balances are based on the proportion of feminine and masculine traits which characterize the husband and wife, they are all interdependent.

The Positivity balance indicates the extent to which the wife and husband are seen as similar in the social desirability of their personality characteristics. The scales which have been developed to measure masculinity and femininity measure only socially desirable traits (Bem, 1974; Spence et al., 1975). Thus, the social desirability of a particular spouse's characteristics is determined by the sum of his or her feminine and masculine traits. When the wife has more positive feminine and masculine traits than the husband, she is seen as having more culturally-valued traits than he. When the husband has more positive feminine and masculine traits than the wife, he is seen as having more culturally-valued traits than she.

The Satisfaction balance indicates the extent to which the couple is happy or unhappy with their marriage. It is based on the balance between those traits which are concerned with task performance and those traits which are concerned with the enhancement of satisfaction within the marital dyad. It is computed by comparing the total number of feminine traits within the dyad as a whole (the wife's femininity plus the husband's femininity) with the total number of masculine traits within the dyad (the wife's masculinity plus the husband's masculinity). Both the instrumental (masculine) and expressive (feminine) traits have been shown to be necessary for a group, or marital dyad, to maintain its equilibrium (Parsons & Bales, 1955). The instrumental traits facilitate group functioning with regard to task performance; the expressive traits facilitate the maintenance of group functioning and harmony. When the total number of feminine traits in the marriage is greater than the total number of masculine traits, marital happiness is high. When the masculine traits are greater than the feminine traits, marital satisfaction is low.

The Leadership balance reflects the relative power which is exercised by the husband and the wife in the marriage. A person's power is dependent on the level of her or his self-assertive traits and also on the extent to which the other person is willing to accommodate. Thus, the husband's power is computed by summing the two sex-role "stereotypic" traits—the husband's masculinity plus the wife's femininity. The wife's power is computed by summing the two "nonstereotypic" traits—the wife's masculinity plus the husband's femininity. When the sum of the two stereotypic traits is greater than the sum of the two nonstereotypic traits, the husband is seen as the leader in the marriage. When the sum of the two nonstereotypic traits is greater than the sum of the stereotypic traits, the wife is seen as the leader. When the summed stereotypic and nonstereotypic traits are equal, the husband and wife share the leadership equally.

The model was tested in a previous research study (Gerber, 1985), in which subjects were presented with a brief description of a married couple and were asked to rate the wife and husband on a number of different measures (Gerber, 1977; 1984). It was found that each of the three Relationship balances correlated with the characteristic of the marital relationship which was predicted by the model. The Positivity balance was correlated with the relative social desirability of the husband's and wife's personality traits, the Satisfaction balance was correlated with marital happiness, and the Leadership balance was correlated with the relative power of the wife and husband.

In this study, the expectations that people have about marriage were also examined using the three Relationship balances. The Positivity balance showed an inequality, in which the husband had more socially desirable characteristics than the wife. This meant that the husband was expected to possess more of the valued personality traits than the wife.

The Satisfaction balance showed an equality, with the total number of feminine traits (for husband and wife combined) equal to the total number of masculine traits. This meant that the marital dyad was expected to be in a state of equilibrium with regard to task performance and the maintenance of group harmony.

The Leadership balance showed an inequality, in which the husband was more powerful than the wife. This suggests that people continue to have the traditional expectation for marriage in which the husband is the leader and the wife is the follower (Safilios-Rothschild, 1976). Since the husband was expected to be more powerful than the wife, the sum of the two "stereotypic" traits was found to be greater than the sum of the two "nonstereotypic" traits. Thus, when sex-stereotype was maintained in the traits attributed to the wife and husband, male leadership was also ensured. This suggests that stereotyped male-female characteristics, in which the man is high in masculinity and the woman is high in femininity, may be substantially concerned with ensuring male dominance, as several investigators have proposed (Henley, 1977; Lewin, 1984; Porter & Geis, 1981).

In applying the Relationship balance model to the practice of therapy, the therapist does not need to have the client fill out a scale. However, if the therapist keeps this model in mind, and is aware of the principles that people use to conceptualize relationships, it will help to understand the meaning of various changes in the marriage relationship and to communicate these to the client. Since the model formalizes some of the intuitive assumptions that people make about relationships, clients are generally able to understand the principles that are involved.

In my own practice of therapy, I worked with a couple whose marital difficulties illustrate some of the issues that have been discussed. The wife began to experience positive changes in her self-concept and in her behavior during the course of therapy, and the marriage subsequently became very conflicted. The Relationship balance model was useful in conceptualizing the impact that the changes in the wife had on the marriage, and in working with the couple in therapy.

When Mary B. first came for individual therapy, she and her husband, Bill, had been married for twelve years. They had two boys, aged nine and eleven. Mary was in the process of completing her PhD in Political Science and had been unable to start work on her dissertation because of feelings of intense anxiety. Her husband had a Master's degree in Business Administration and held a responsible managerial position in a large business firm.

During the time that she was in individual therapy, Mary realized that some of her conflicts involved changing her status from that of a "student" to a "PhD." She was afraid that this change in status would mean that she would feel less feminine. She also found gratification in being financially dependent on her husband, as this made her feel that he cared for her.

As therapy progressed, Mary began to see that her success in a career did not have to affect her sense of herself as a woman. She realized that the gratifications that came from being more independent far outweighed the more child-like gratifications that stemmed from her financial dependence on her husband. After ten months in therapy, Mary was able to start work on her dissertation, and began to feel and act in a more self-confident, capable and self-assertive way.

At about the same time, she reported that her marriage had become increasingly conflicted. Bill had become very critical of Mary at home, particularly in her role of homemaker and mother. He had also started spending longer hours at the office than he had in the past, and would frequently come home after the children were in bed. Mary asked whether she and her husband could come for marital therapy to try and resolve some of their difficulties, and the therapist agreed.

During the marital therapy sessions, it became evident that Bill's self-concept and sense of gender identity was closely tied up with his image of his wife. His masculine identity was partially dependent on his own characteristics, but was also dependent on his wife's characteristics and the nature of the relationship as well. Even though he consciously supported Mary's career, he was threatened by the idea that she would soon be able to contribute to the financial support of the family, and he would be displaced in his role of sole provider. He feared that Mary would see him as a less worthwhile person. He was also threatened by the more active role that Mary was now taking in the family decision-making process, because his image of himself as masculine was also dependent on his ability to exercise greater power than she in making decisions.

Before Mary had started in individual therapy, the marriage had been a traditional one, and had been reasonably satisfying to both partners. Mary had tended to idealize Bill and see him as having more valuable characteristics than she. Bill had felt gratified by Mary's idealization of him. Any problems that had arisen had been worked out through mutual discussion and accommodation. However, Mary had become increasingly aware that she was usually the person who "gave in" whenever there was a difference of opinion. To describe their perception of the marriage in terms of the Relationship balances, both the Positivity and Leadership balances were inequalities. The husband was perceived as having more positive characteristics and playing more of a leadership role than the wife. The Satisfaction balance was an equality.

When Mary began to experience more self-esteem and began to act in a more assertive way as a result of her individual therapy, Bill began to perceive Mary as equal to him in masculine personality traits. Mary shared this perception. Since a wife's masculinity score is involved in all three Relationship balances, these balances then changed in a predictable direction.

Mary now had high levels of both femininity and masculinity, whereas Bill continued to have a high level of masculinity and a relatively low level of femininity. Thus, the Positivity balance had changed so that Mary had more socially desirable traits than her husband. The Satisfaction balance had changed so that the total number of masculine traits within the relationship was greater than the total number of feminine traits. This is because Mary had increased in the level of her masculinity, but there had been no compensatory change in Bill's feminine traits, which would have brought the Satisfaction balance into a state of equality. Thus, the marriage was a more unhappy one, and was characterized by more conflict and dissatisfaction. The Leadership balance had also changed. Although Bill continued to exert somewhat more power than his wife, he was less powerful than he had been before Mary started individual therapy. While Mary was now skillful in asserting herself as well as accommodating, Bill continued to be primarily self-assertive and relatively unwilling to compromise.

The Relationship balance model was useful in conceptualizing some of the attempts which Bill made to restore the stereotypic balance which had previously existed in the marriage. Bill reacted to the threat he felt as a result of Mary's increased masculinity by attempting to increase his own masculine personality attributes, so that he would be higher in masculinity than his wife. He worked longer hours so as to ensure that he would be superior to Mary in his financial achievements. He became critical and aggressive towards her at home in an attempt to show that he was more powerful than she was within the marriage.

On the surface, it might have appeared that Bill's increased aggressiveness towards his wife was primarily negative in character. However, he defined his own gender identity, to a large part, in terms of the power balance between the sexes. One of his overwhelming needs within the relationship was to re-establish a stereotypic power balance in order to shore up his sense of himself as a man, regardless of the cost to the relationship. The only option that he felt he had, given Mary's increased masculinity, was to see himself as higher in masculinity than his wife. This re-established a more stereotypic Leadership balance, and changed the Positivity balance so that he could also see himself as higher in socially desirable traits than Mary. However, one of the unfortunate consequences of his efforts to reassure himself, was that the Satisfaction balance changed so that it reflected much more marital unhappiness than before. This is because both the husband's and the wife's masculine traits had increased to very high levels, but there had been no compensatory increase in the total number of feminine traits in the relationship. This was reflected in the high degree of marital conflict and unhappiness that accompanied Bill's increased aggressiveness towards Mary.

In a marital situation like this one, in which the wife had changed by experiencing increased levels of masculine personality traits, the only option for change that would bring both the Satisfaction balance and the Positivity balance into a more positive state of equilibrium, would be for the husband to increase the level of his feminine traits so that they were equal to the level of his masculine traits, and to the wife's feminine and masculine traits. This would mean that the husband would need to see that the expression of "feminine" feelings, such as concern and empathy for others, did not pose a threat to his sense of masculine identity. This would make the marriage more satisfying for both partners, since the masculine traits in the relationship would be equal to the feminine traits. In addition, the couple would see themselves as equal in socially desirable traits.

However, the Leadership balance would also become an equality, with both wife and husband sharing equally in the decision-making. If the marital partners had previously defined their sense of gender identity by means of a stereotypic Leadership balance, in which the husband was more powerful than the wife, they would need to find new ways of defining themselves. They would need to evolve definitions of their gender identity that were separate from issues of relative power.

The contribution that the Relationship balance model has to make to psychotherapy is to help in conceptualizing the impact that changes in one marital partner will have on the other partner and on the relationship as a whole. This is useful for the individual therapist, who is working with one person, as well as for the marital therapist, who is working with a husband and wife. For even if the therapist is doing individual therapy, it is important to help the client understand the effect that his or her own personal growth may have on the relationship. The model can then help to formulate the other changes that would have to take place within the individual persons and the relationship if the marriage were to survive in a viable way.

REFERENCE NOTE

1. There have been numerous studies that have shown that the masculine sex-role stereotype personality traits are correlated with self-esteem (Whitley, 1983).

REFERENCES

Bem, S. L. (1974). The measurement of psychological androgyny. *Journal of Consulting and Clinical Psychology, 42,* 155–162.

Gerber, G. L. (1977). The effect of competition on stereotypes about sex-role and marital satisfaction. *Journal of Psychology, 97,* 297–308.

Gerber, G. L. (1984). Attribution of feminine and masculine traits to opposite-sex dyads. *Psychological Reports, 55,* 907–918.

Gerber, G. L. (1985). A Relationship balance model for sex-role stereotype traits: Attributions to married couples. Manuscript submitted for publication.

Henley, N. M. (1977). *Body politics: Power, sex and nonverbal communication.* Englewood Cliffs, NJ: Prentice-Hall.

Lewin, M. (1984). Psychology measures femininity and masculinity, 2: From "13 gay men" to the instrumental-expressive distinction. In M. Lewin (Ed.), *In the shadow of the past: Psychology portrays the sexes* (pp. 179–204). New York: Columbia University Press.

Parsons, T., & Bales, R. F. (1955). *Family, socialization and interaction process.* New York: Free Press of Glencoe.

Porter, N., & Geis, F. (1981). Women and nonverbal leadership cues: When seeing is not believing. In N. M. Henley & C. Mayo (Eds.), *Gender and nonverbal behavior* (pp. 39–61). New York: Springer, Verlag.

Rosenkrantz, P., Vogel, S., Bee, H., Broverman, I., & Broverman, D. M. (1968). Sex-role stereotypes and self-concepts in college students. *Journal of Consulting and Clinical Psychology, 32,* 287–295.

Safilios-Rothschild, C. (1976). The dimensions of power distribution in the family. In H. Grunebaum & J. Christ (Eds.), *Contemporary marriage, structure, dynamics, and theory* (pp. 275–292). Boston: Little, Brown.

Spence, J. T., Helmreich, R. L., & Stapp, J. (1975). Ratings of self and peers on sex-role attributes and their relation to self-esteem and conceptions of masculinity and femininity. *Journal of Personality and Social Psychology, 32,* 29–39.

Whitley, B. E., Jr. (1983). Sex role orientation and self-esteem: A critical meta-analytic review. *Journal of Personality and Social Psychology, 44,* 765–778.

Themes in Psychotherapy
With Women
in Male-Dominated Professions

Jeanne Parr Lemkau

For the past ten years I have actively researched the interface between sex roles and occupational choice, specifically focusing on women in male-dominated professions. For five years I have been a faculty member in a medical school, experiencing firsthand the interplay of my personal dynamics and the dynamics of a work environment with few women peers. I have had a clinical practice during this time, and many of my clients have been professional women in male-dominated fields. I would like to share some of what I have learned about the psychological issues faced by women in nontraditional professional careers, with particular emphasis on themes that arise in doing psychotherapy with these women.

I will first summarize briefly what research suggests are common personality and background characteristics of women in male-dominated professions. Then I will characterize some typical interpersonal dynamics of organizations in which women are a clear minority relative to a male majority. I will describe the sample of clients on which my clinical comments are based, outline some of the more frequent themes that emerge in psychotherapy, and offer some suggestions for effectively helping these women.

In an earlier publication (Lemkau, 1979) I reviewed the psychological and sociological literature on personality and background characteristics of women in male-dominated occupations. Such women were typically found to have personalities high on "competency" traits related to the masculine

Jeanne Parr Lemkau is in private practice at 110 North Winter Street, Yellow Springs, OH 45387. She is also on the faculty at the Wright State University School of Medicine, Yellow Springs, OH.

stereotype and ideal. Nontraditional professional women did not appear to differ from other women on the "warmth and expressiveness" traits of the feminine stereotype and ideal. They appeared to share a "tough-minded" realism, good coping skills, and emotional health, although often experiencing situational stress.

In general, the research literature indicates that these nontraditional women experienced strong support from significant men in their current lives. They tended to share background characteristics which fostered achievement and broad sex roles, i.e. parental encouragement of androgynous exploration, high maternal employment, and strong paternal support for both mother and daughter. The data from this review and from subsequent research (Lemkau, 1983) indicate that the nontraditional woman is typically the product of unusual but positive factors.

Hardiness, independence, and resilience are essential for women in male-dominated professions to survive the rigors of their interpersonal environments, both on and off the job. Off the job, their high achievement and competence tends to be perceived as threatening to men, making it more problematic for these women to find male relationships in which they can be unambivalently nurtured and supported. For those who are married, the expectations of wife and mother roles are often superimposed on work roles with very high time and energy demands. If these women weren't tough they wouldn't survive!

The Story of O (Kanter and Stein, 1980) provides a concise overview of what typically happens to women on the job when they are minority members in professions and organizations dominated by men. Clients often find this book, or a chapter on emotional issues faced by working women (Lemkau, 1980), helpful in normalizing their own distress. In a cartoon narration of what happens to an 0 among a group of Xs, Kanter demonstrates the phenomena of visibility, contrast, and assimilation (see also Kanter, 1977).

An 0 among Xs, a woman among men, tends to be spotlighted. Her femaleness makes her highly visible against the sea of maleness. This visibility fosters a constant sense of performance pressure, as onlookers stand by, ready to interpret any shortcomings in terms of her sex. She may know that she is the test case on which the suitability of women for her job will be judged. Even in situations where the woman experiences her male colleagues as wanting her to do well, visibility and performance pressure are likely to take their toll.

The presence of a few women among many men tends to generate a contrast effect, an increased self-consciousness of the norms and culture of the dominant group. The result is a heightened sense of group awareness between the dominant men and the minority women. With a few women in their ranks, the men will tend to form an even tighter network with more masculine norms than they would in the absence of women. The minority women face a dilemma: they tend to be excluded from the male culture on the job, yet if they gravitate toward the women in their work environment they incur further distance from their most relevant professional reference group and and run the risk of being perceived as one of the secretarial pool!

With high visibility and high contrast, the minority members are typically assimilated into the stereotypes held by the dominant members. With little experience of women in nontraditional roles, men resort to familiar generalizations about women and distort their perceptions of these women accordingly. The result is role encapsulation for the women, experienced as a sense of constriction and conflict. (In the midst of teaching rounds, it was my client, the only woman physician in the group that the attending physician sent out for his cup of coffee.)

As a consequence of such interpersonal processes as these and the individual psychodynamics women bring to the job, women in male-dominated occupations face classic double binds in the sex role arena. They are expected to conform to the stereotypes men have of women, and which they themselves have internalized. Perceptions of their performance will be distorted to fit the stereotypes. Yet to competently fill their work roles as lawyers, physicians, engineers, and scientists, they are required to behave in ways that violate these stereotypic expectations. The impossibility of simultaneously fulfilling these conflicting expectations is rarely overtly acknowledged. Little wonder that one client, after reviewing her first three years as an engineer, decided to award herself "the pitbull award for survivability and endurance in the face of insurmountable obstacles."

A woman who daily confronts such sex role double binds and has a traditionally female attributional style of selfblame, is typically demoralized. If this is compounded with an inadequate support system off the job or major marital and family difficulties, depression is a likely result. This frequently observed pattern can be expressed in the formula:

SEX ROLE DOUBLE BINDS + SELF-BLAME − SUPPORT = DEPRESSION

I would like to elaborate on this formula in regard to the women I have seen in psychotherapy. In the past few years I have seen ten professionally nontraditional women in my practice. Seeking relief for depression was the main impetus for treatment. In all cases, depression was either a primary or secondary diagnosis: 6 met DSM-II criteria for depressive neurosis. Of the remainder, 3 were adjustment reactions with depressed mood and the fourth was agoraphobic with an underlying depression. For four of the ten, antidepressant medication was an important adjunct to therapy. My contact with these women has ranged from six months to several years of weekly sessions. Seven of the ten have been in therapy for at least a year, and five of these are still in treatment. All have been white. About half were married or in longterm relationships. One was a lesbian. Ages ranged from 30 to 44. All were employed full time. My clients have included three physicians, an anatomy professor, a toxicologist, a statistician, a genetics researcher, an engineer/firefighter, and two women managers in male-dominated technical fields.

The one background feature that clearly set these women apart from the prototype of the research literature was the prevalence of experiences of parental absence and/or impairment in childhood. Two had fathers who died when their daughters were at puberty. One experienced the father's desertion of the family when she was 8. One had a chronically alcoholic father. Another experienced her parents' divorce and her mother's subsequent alcoholism during her earlier adolescence. Another recalled the repeated absence of her mother from the home during lengthy psychiatric hospitalizations. Major instances of parental absence or impairment characterized 2/3 of my clients. I will discuss the impact of parental unavailability as I see it to be relevant to psychotherapy with these women.

SEX ROLE DOUBLE BINDS

Conflicts between being competent and being feminine are common among women. Such conflicts are heightened for women in environments where their minority status generates the processes of visibility, contrast, and stereotypic assimilation. The demand to perform tasks which require traditionally "masculine" characteristics, such as leadership and decisiveness, makes matters worse. Conflict is inevitable.

The women I have seen in therapy have presented both the conflicts as problems they would like to address, and difficulties which stem from attempts to resolve such conflicts. For example, several clients have shared their distress at finding support from men on the job and at home when they were novices, incompetent, physically ill, or emotionally weak; support which was withdrawn or transformed into hostility when they showed stronger, more expert, and competent behavior.

Terry, an engineer and firefighter, talks of her changing relationship with her male supervisor: "When I came on the job I felt like a kid and my boss took me under his wing. Now I feel at least like an adolescent and he's having trouble with that." Terry's husband was an engineer and firefighter too. Immediately prior to seeking therapy, Terry had been promoted to lieutenant at the fire department. This had generated so much friction with her out-ranked husband that she responded by leaving the fire department altogether. Her already smoldering depression was exacerbated. In speaking of her husband she said, " I can't beat him at anything that's important to him or he devalues the competition . . . I feel like I have to be a chamelion—I have to learn to change colors."

For many clients, such conflicts took them by surprise. Most had fathers who were either unambivalently supportive of their nontraditonal accomplishments or were absent and hence easily idealized: in either case these women were primed to naively expect more support than they found. Their husbands often brought their own expectations to the marriage, naively expecting the nontraditional women they had courted to revert to more stereotypic behavior once married. Kate, a research geneticist, said that her husband has overcome his surprise and disappointment at her desire to continue to work after the marriage and after the arrival of children. The marriage survived in the early years because recurrent health problems required her to adopt a traditionally dependent stance. As the marriage was dissolving, she commented, "He was more comfortable when I was helpless. I don't want to be anymore. I've been playing the doctor's wife but I'm a doctor too!"

Such sex role conflicts need not be generated directly in relationships with men. The internalized stereotypes these women hold give such conflicts a life of their own even in benign circumstances. Suzanne, an anatomy professor found it difficult to think of herself as both scientific and sexual. Her image of a woman scientist was of a desexualized person with horn-rimmed glasses and a lab coat. Whenever she actively pursued her work, she became preoccupied with thoughts of herself as fat, ugly and nonsexual, in spite of being an objectively beautiful woman with an attentive and interested partner.

Individual solutions to sex role conflicts may become problems in themselves. Several women discovered in therapy that their "weight problems" were actually creative attempts to address sex role issues on the job. Betty, a physician, found that her increased weight mitigated unwanted sexual overtures at work. Terry found that when she was plump, it was more acceptable to the wives of her male friends for her to accompany the men on the hunting trips which she loved. Betty, the statistician, believed her weight gave her a more powerful presentation in all male groups which tended to quickly dismiss her opinions. As she worked to develop a verbal and nonverbal style to "give herself more weight," her need for the literal weight diminished. For several women, the book *Fat is a Feminist Issue* (Orbach 1978) has been a helpful adjunct to therapy.

As clients have become more aware of the environmental contributors to their difficulties and have experimented with new ways of confronting sex role conflicts, they have generally needed considerable support. The therapist may be a crucial source of such support at such times when the client cannot easily meet such needs in her day-to-day environment.

The following treatment principles are important to keep in mind to address the sex role component of the formula presented earlier.

1. Conceptualize conflict and stress from both intrapsychic and environmental models.
2. Make conflicts more explicit as a way of enhancing the client's sense of control and awareness of choices.
3. Where conflict is inevitable, normalize stress.
4. Use bibliotherapy as a tool for self-education about environmental and intrapsychic sources of conflict.
5. Anticipate client needs for support after behavioral changes have begun.

ATTRIBUTION STYLE OF SELF-BLAME

Women are taught that human relationships are their responsibility: interpersonal difficulties at work or home tend to quickly trigger soul-searching and self-recrimination. Children who are pushed into parenting roles because of parental absence or infirmity tend to be overly responsible adults. The history of being a "parentified child" tends to compound the attributional style of self-blame that is endemic among women in this culture.

Marie believes that when she was having marital difficulties it was because she was "trying to do too much" by aspiring to carry a full time professional job and be married too. It was a message she had repeatedly heard from her mother who had forgone career opportunities early in her 20s to have a family. Marie identified what she called "doing a Joan of Arc," explaining that she thought that a woman couldn't take on a man's job without becoming a martyr. The dangerous repercussions of her beliefs became apparent as she explored the meaning of a miscarriage she had had several years previously. She interpreted the loss in terms of her mother's belief that no woman could have a career and children too. Losing the baby meant that she had transgressed by "trying to have it all" and she had refrained from further attempts to have children.

Marie illustrates two themes that recur. I have seen the Joan of Arc syndrome in other women. When problems erupt, they assume they must be at fault for "overaspiring" and not accepting the inevitable martyrdom that they see as the price of being in a man's army! And other women too speak of receiving "the curse" from their mothers, ambivalent about seeing their daughters strive for what they themselves had sacrificed.

Difficulties at work may similarly generate negative self-attributions. Terry assumed that if people were not giving her ready positive feedback, it meant she was doing poorly. She felt badly and isolated herself further from her male colleagues. While just recognizing the faulty assumption gave her some relief, she felt much better when she posted a sign conspicuously in her office which said "In the absence of feedback, I assume the worst," a sign which elicited considerable supportive feedback.

Self-attributions of blame block awareness of sexism. Karen came to a session depressed and upset over a recent job interview, ready to get to the bottom of what she had done wrong since she had not been given the position. After we carefully dissected the events of a three day interview it became apparent to both of us that she was never seriously considered but was part of an affirmative action sham. Her depression and self-attribution were quickly converted to anger. At the end of the session she asked poignantly, "So now, what do I do?", beginning to grapple with the political implications of her heightened awareness.

A discussion of self-blame would be incomplete without mentioning the blame women lay on themselves for crimes not committed. The most frequent example is women who feel guilty because their children have a working mother. My approach is typically one of support and education on this issue. I summarize available research on the effects of maternal employment and alternative child care arrangements, and refer them to relevant books, research articles and reviews (Dunlop, 1981; Hoffman, 1979; Scarr, 1984). Consistent with the research, I often reframe satisfying employment as offering benefits to the family as a whole.

Attention to the principles below is helpful in countering negative self-attributions.

1. Explicitly address sex differences in attribution styles.
2. Support the client in generating attributions that encompass environmental realities.
3. Provide a model of simultaneously considering both environmental and intrapsychic factors as these may contribute to emotional distress.
4. Where self-blame is based on lack of knowledge use education and bibliotherapy to enhance woman's information base.
5. Anticipate undermining by men at home and on the job as woman's attributional style changes.

SUPPORT

For a woman in a male-dominated profession, needed support may be in the form of emotionally "being there," modeling an androgynous approach to life and offering tips to facilitate performance on the job.

Initially I have seen in my clients a strong tendency to deny needs for support. As parentified children, these women have often become more comfortable giving than receiving support. Sometimes this theme gets played out in therapy when the woman either goes to great lengths to take care of me or becomes frightened and pulls back when feelings of vulnerability or dependency are experienced. Dealing with transference and underlying family relationships has been fruitful in freeing up such women to be more assertive in their own behalf.

One must often deal with the woman's immediate social environment as well. Rosanne explained the rules that governed her primary relationship;

> If I do something for myself, he says I'm treating him as a second class citizen or that I'm selfish. I can only do something for myself if I'm on the verge of a nervous collapse. It's as if we're in competition with each other in order to be taken care of.

On the verge of going back to school, she characterized her husband's response, "I'm not getting any support for the way I want to live my life."

For Betty, holding back from anticipating every need of her

spouse was a critical first step toward garnering more support for herself, but it was a scary one.

> I've been an emotional filling station and I'm not getting much back, but it's scary to put myself out there in a way other than taking care of someone . . . listening has always been my way of holding onto a relationship. What will happen if I ask him to listen to me?

In my experience, women have readily talked about conflicts with men both on and off the job. It has taken more probing on my part to elicit information on their relationships with women. To integrate into their male-dominated environs, many have "identified with the aggressor," distancing themselves from other women and from the women's movement. With little contact with other nontraditional women it becomes easier still to view themselves as exceptions and to stereotype women along the lines of their male colleagues. Since their integration into male support networks is often marginal, loneliness is common.

A major therapeutic task is to assist women in reconnecting to a female community that will support them in their "deviance." I have sent women to local feminist support groups, and to local chapters of American Women in Science and the Society for Women Engineers. I also urged a depressed firefighter to search for other women firefighters. She returned jubilant the next week, with a stack of newsletters entitled *Women in Fire Suppression,* having found the editor in Dayton Ohio!

To address the support component of the formula, the following guidelines can be helpful.

1. Directly give support for self-acceptance, risk-taking, sex-role deviance, idiosyncratic solutions to difficult problems, and for skills development.
2. Address woman's denial of her needs for support. This may entail making explicit the caretaking role some women adopted in response to an infirm or absent parent.
3. Help the woman evaluate how well her support needs are being met, and brainstorm means of increasing support from both male and female reference groups.

4. Facilitate linkages with potential sources of support, be they formal professional organizations or informal contacts with women in similar positions.

Supportive psychotherapy with a strong component of education can be immensely helpful to women in male-dominated professions who seek help for depression. I would like to close with some comments of Ann, a physician who had accommodated to her male-dominated environment by denying her own needs and taking care of everyone else's. Her words suggest both the potential and the challenge involved in doing psychotherapy with women in male-dominated professions: "I feel vulnerable putting myself out in a way other than taking care of people. I feel both scared and powerful—I could come on strong!"

REFERENCES

Dunlop, K.H. (1981). Maternal employment and child care. *Professional Psychology, 12,* 67–75.

Hoffman, L. (1979). Maternal employment. *American Psychologist, 34,* 859–865.

Kanter, R.M. (1977). *Men and women in the corporation.* New York: Basic Books.

Kanter, R.M., and Stein, B.A. (1980). *A tale of "0": On being different in an organization.* New York: Harper and Row.

Lemkau, J.P. (1979). Personality and background characteristics of women in male-dominated occupations: A review. *Psychology of Woman Quarterly, 4,* 221–240.

Lemkau, J.P. (1980). Women and employment: Some emotional hazards. In C.L. Heckerman (Ed.), *The evolving female: Women in psychosocial context.* New York: Human Sciences Press, 107–137.

Lemkau, J.P. (1983). Women in male-dominated professions: Distinguishing personality and background characteristics. *Psychology of Women Quarterly, 8,* 144–165.

Orbach, S. (1978). *Fat is a feminist issue.* New York: Berkeley Publishing Corporation.

Scarr, S. (1984). *Mother care/other care.* New York: Basic Books.

When the Therapist is White and the Patient is Black: Considerations for Psychotherapy in the Feminist Heterosexual and Lesbian Communities

Beverly A. Greene

The process of psychotherapy is a complex interaction between two people. It is further complicated when the patient and the therapist differ from one another on some major dimension. Psychotherapy presumably helps patients to overcome stereotypic views of themselves and to understand their own individuality, worth, and ability to utilize inner strengths in the service of growing and coping. Therapists, however, will be unable to assist patients in this manner if they are unable or unwilling to recognize and relinquish a need to see a patient in a particular way.

The assessments that we form of our patients are filtered through reflective mechanisms of our own experiences and attitudes. Terry Kupers (1981), defines transference as the unconscious distortion a patient introduces into therapy by displacing onto the therapist the feelings, ideas and memories that derive from or were directed toward previous important figures in the patient's life. Ralph Greenson (1964), defined this phenomenon as an individual's reacting to a person in the present in a manner similar to the way that individual reacted to someone in their past. It may also be seen as a repetition, a new edition of an old relationship (Vontress, 1971). Countertransference represents the same process on the part of the

Beverly A. Greene is a clinical psychologist in private practice. She is also Director of Inpatient Child and Adolescent Psychological Services, Kings County Hospital, Brooklyn, NY and Clinical Assistant Professor, Department of Psychiatry, SUNY-Downstate Medical Center, Brooklyn, NY.

41

therapist and can refer to feelings elicited by the patient in the therapist. These feelings on the part of the therapist can be used constructively in the treatment process to enhance an understanding of what the patient is attempting to make of the therapist. However, if therapists are unaware or refuse to understand and acknowledge those feelings, they may be inadvertently used in the service of maintaining their comfort with their own beliefs and values. This will obscure the therapist's view of who the patient is and can be destructive in treatment.

This article will examine the ways in which white therapists may be influenced by racial differences when their patients are black and the form those issues may take in therapy. These issues may appear in spite of the patient's or therapist's gender or sexual preference. The racial and cultural context within which therapy occurs and its influence on the perceptions therapists hold of their patients will be examined. Finally we will look to some of the implications of these differences, in the context of the United States, in the treatment of black female patients by white female therapists within and without the feminist and Lesbian communities.

I have chosen to focus on the issue of race because it is my contention that any commitment that the feminist and Lesbian feminist communities have to feminist principles should include an understanding of racism.

Many groups in America face discrimination because of the stereotypes associated with their sex, sexual preference, race, religion, age, physical appearance, socioeconomic status and level of education. By stereotypes we refer to the interpretations of a group or individual's behavior or beliefs when based on a distortion of the characteristics found in that group or individual. The distortion may assume several forms. It may consist of the attribution of negative characteristics, overgeneralized to a specific group in spite of the fact that other groups may also possess that characteristic. It may appear as an assumed lack of positive attributes found in others groups, as well as the group in question. It may also appear as the failure to acknowledge or the tendency to minimize the impact of some salient characteristic or experience that bears directly upon how a person is seen, treated or behaves.

Evaluating the meaning of behavior is a complicated task

when a patient and therapist do not share cultural values or experiences. These differences, however, are not often acknowledged as salient factors in therapy. The patient's health is usually understood in terms of his or her conforming to the cultural values of the dominant group.

It may be necessary for stigmatized groups to pool their resources politically, economically and socially to protect themselves from discriminatory practices. However, the combining of these groups into masses referred to as "the oppressed," "minorities," "women," or "Lesbians" may not be helpful in developing a clinical understanding of the impact of those differences in psychotherapy. The factor of racial difference has been isolated here with the assumption that white therapists who are members of the feminist or Lesbian communities do not necessarily view black people any less stereotypically than white therapists who are not.

This by no means implies that there are no racial issues present when black therapists treat black or white patients, or that they are less important. Nor does it imply that only black therapists are suitable for black patients. Furthermore, it is not assumed here that there are no significant ethnic or cultural differences between white therapists and white patients. There are, however, more white mental health professionals than black, and the white therapist-black patient dyad is most common, particularly in public mental health clinics and hospitals (Kupers, 1981). While the majority of black patients are seen by white therapists, the corollary of this is not so for white patients. Black people are forced, if they are to survive, to have some understanding of the workings of the mainstream. White people are rarely in a similar position vis-à-vis the culture of black persons. Furthermore, most white and black therapists have little or no formal training in the treatment of non-white patients (Hersen, Kazdin & Bellak, 1983).

Essential to an understanding of the phenomenon we will examine is an understanding of the context within which it occurs. The treatment process between white therapists and black patients is complicated by two interrelated and specific factors. One is the factor of cultural differences between black and white Americans. The second is the history and existence of racism in our society.

CULTURAL DIFFERENCE

The observation of differences between racial and ethnic groups is often confused with being racist in and of itself. People may be of equal worth, however, without having to share the same characteristics and experiences. Equality need not be equated with sameness. Myers & King (1983) discuss the importance of making a distinction between "existential" and "functional equality." Existential equality may be seen as the ideological principal which affirms the equal worth of all human beings. Functional equality, however, represents the result of an interaction between one's native abilities and potential, and the society's structuring of options, opportunities, barriers and constraints to developing those abilities. The latter contains obvious variables which may not be within an individual's control, and may on this level render people "unequal."

An acknowledgement of differences between individuals and groups does not imply that those differences must be based on deficits, although there is a pervasive trend in behavioral and social science literature to do exactly that. A need to appear "color blind" may have some of its origins in a fear of either recapitulating this phenomenon or finding racism within the self. Members of oppressed groups may be so fearful of divisiveness that they tend to obscure the differences between themselves and other victims of oppression. For therapists, this may result in an avoidance of confronting their own values and, most importantly, acknowledging the meaning of the differences between themselves and their patients. Differences evoke anxiety as a result we may see a need to actively deny the difference. Perhaps another explanation for "color blindness" may be the belief that "the impact of racism or race on personality is superficial and subordinate to psychodynamic forces that are presumed to be universal" (Thomas & Sillen, 1972).

Steven Moffie (1983), however, suggests an alternative to this view of "universal psychodynamic forces," and introduces the concept of a transconscious. He defines the transconscious as that "which is derived from the interaction of all aspects of the personality with the surrounding social groups, the regulation of drives, emphasis on particular perceptual modes, superego values and the internal representation of the culture in the self."

In therapy this need to be color blind may only result in further obscuring the therapist's view of who the patient is. The issue of color blindness will be examined again, specifically, the outcomes it may elicit in psychotherapy.

Hilliard (Hersen et al., 1983) defines culture as the shared creativities of a group of people, including language, values, experiences, symbols, tools, cognitive styles in learning and problem solving, rules, etc. Therapists' cultural identifications can influence how they perceive and respond to the cultural symbols of their patients. Therefore, therapists of all cultures must examine their own backgrounds and must confront their own biases when dealing with any culturally diverse group. What is maladaptive in one situation may be quite adaptive in another.

In the context of interracial psychotherapy dyads, white therapists must be sensitive to the context in which black people have lived and continue to live. While time does not permit a lengthy elaboration of "cultural specifics" of black Americans, it is fair to suggest that "a set of core values and behavior which in its gestalt remains distinctively characteristic of and understood by a majority of black people" (Boyd-Franklin & Hines, 1982) does exist in a form which is comprehensible to therapists of other cultures. While this complicates treatment, it is not unresolvable. Some of these differences as they exist between black and white women will be reviewed later. It must be clear that among black people or any other group there remains a wide range of individual differences in coping strategies and responses. Still, many black Americans lead lives that may be very different from mainstream America. Color can be seen as a salient and usually obvious physical characteristic of a black person and a variable which can often predict where that person will work, live, socialize, attend school, receive health care and how much money they may earn. In interracial therapy dyads, skin color is a real difference which may elicit transference and countertransference issues earlier and in a more pronounced form (Owens, 1984). Black people live in a culture which frequently reminds them of their skin color and the label of inferiority that accompanies it.

To over- or underestimate the impact of skin color on a person's life does them a disservice by failing to acknowledge the individual's complete experience. To ignore or minimize this experience risks overlooking the many strengths in black individuals and families that can be mobilized to help them overcome present difficulty.

RACISM

We live in a predominantly white American culture which is permeated by racism. Charles Pinderhughes (Willie, Kramer and Brown, 1973), defines the essence of racism as "a relatively constant pattern of prejudice and discrimination between one party who is idealized and favored, and another who is devalued and exploited in a common relationship." This is particularly evident when one examines the different views of and privileges accorded to white as opposed to black persons. More than a matter of historical fact, it is a present, and sad reality. Black people in America have been systematically discriminated against for hundreds of years, by whites. A pattern of institutional discrimination has been embedded in the fabric of our political, social, economic, and educational systems, based on the belief in white supremacy. What follows from that belief is the assertion that black people and all that characterizes them renders them inferior to white people. When these assumptions are acted on, the result is that black people do not have access to the same level of privileges and treatment as white people, rather they receive inferior treatment. Because racism has been so embedded in our institutions, racist practices may be routinely acted out by people who may not consciously accept racist views or be pathological. Avoidance of this acting out may require conscious effort.

In psychotherapy, when a member of a dominant or idealized group treats a member of a dominated or devalued group, it is reasonable to assume that many of the social tensions, fears, angers and resentments attached to this situation may have an effect on the treatment process. Michelle Owens (1984) sees the normative power relationship between blacks and whites in our society as one which can be easily recapitulated in therapy when the therapist is white and the patient is black.

Racism and Clinical Training

The mental health professions have not been apart from but are a part of this culture. Most therapists have been exposed to the mainstream's value system. The practices and theoretical assumptions of mental health professionals often reflect the values of the dominant group, most often the white middle class.

An abundance of the research literature on black people is blatantly stigmatizing. It has often been used to lend "scientific" support to the belief that black people are inferior or pathologically deviant when compared to white people along many dimensions. Those dimensions include intelligence, family cohesion and stability, aggression, sexuality, and impulse control among others. The failure of many white social scientists to point out the false premises and methodological errors present in many of these studies as well as their practice of using this material in major policy decisions constitutes little more than scientific racism or the "scholarly dozens." Haskins and Butts (1973) define the "dozens" as a "word game (often played by black urban children) in which close members of a person's family are degraded." Usually, the verbal denigration of a person's mother is the ultimate insult ("your mama"). Scholarly dozens then represents a racist form of blaming the victim for his or her own misfortunes.

According to Robert Guthrie (1976) in *Even the Rat Was White,* psychology as a discipline saw its emergence at a time in history when Western culture was permeated by overt racism and Social Darwinism. Research in psychology was greatly influenced by the Nativists' argument that social differences between individuals and groups were based on biological, inborn differences, not significantly influenced by the environment.

The attempts of black slaves to escape from bondage were often interpreted as an expression of their pathology. Likewise, a psychiatric argument in favor of slavery suggested that black people were more likely to experience mental disturbances if they were set free (Thomas & Sillen, 1972). Black people were often described in the literature as "childlike," "a primitive race," and "in need of domination" (Thomas & Sillen, 1972).

The work of Sigmund Freud does not generally contain formulations of psychopathology based on racial bias. However, American psychoanalytic writings from the inception of the *Psychoanalytic Review* and the *American Journal of Psychiatry* were riddled with racist views in a most pernicious form (Thomas & Sillen, 1972).

In 1887, G. Stanley Hall, the first president of the American Psychological Association, referred to black people as a "primitive race in a state of immature development." In the *Psychoanalytic Review* (the first psychoanalytic periodical in English, founded in 1913 by William Alanson White), black people were depicted as a "race at a relatively low cultural level, who during its years of savagery has learned no lessons in emotional control" (Thomas & Sillen, 1972). Carl Jung, in an address to the Second Psychoanalytic Congress in 1910 reported,

> the causes for repression can be found in the specific American Complex, namely, to the living together with lower races, especially with Negroes. Living together with barbaric races exerts a suggestive effect on the laboriously tamed instinct of the white race and tends to pull it down. (Thomas & Sillen, 1972)

Lauretta Bender, regarded as a pioneer in American child psychiatry, wrote in 1939,

> There has appeared to be a special pattern in behavior disorders of Negro children that displays itself in several ways. This is related to the question of motility and impulse. Two features which almost anyone will concede as characteristic of the race are (1) the capacity for so called laziness and (2) the special ability to dance. The capacity for laziness is the ability to go to sleep or to simply do nothing for long periods, when it fits the needs of the situation. The dancing represents special motility patterns and tendencies. These two features present themselves in the behavior problems that come to us and may be an expression of specific brain impulse tendencies.

Erik Erikson wrote in 1950,

Negro babies often received sensual satisfactions which provide them with enough oral sensory surplus for a lifetime as clearly betrayed in the way they move, laugh, talk and sing. This sensory treasure helped to build a slave identity, mild, submissive, dependent, somewhat querulous, but always ready to serve with occasional empathy and childlike wisdom.

Erikson's hypotheses are at ironic odds with other writers who saw black people as "nonverbal" and dangerously prone to violence.

Kardiner and Ovesey (1962) suggested that the personality traits of black people are all derived from their experience as members of an oppressed group. From this hypothesis they concluded that black people could not benefit from therapy, rather that an increase in their self esteem was wholly dependent upon the complete removal of racism and discrimination. Since psychotherapists cannot do this they might easily view the plight of black patients as hopeless. This seemingly benign assumption can become a dangerous self-fulfilling prophecy. They also noted that frigidity was "quite frequent" in black women and that sex seemed "relatively unimportant" to the black man (Thomas & Sillen, 1972). In direct contradiction to their hypothesis, other research maintains pervasive assumptions of hypersexual potency, sexual abandon and large genitalia as characteristic of black men and women. Thomas and Sillen (1972), report numerous citations which asserted that black women were seen as "promiscuously yielding to white men" and that black men were "uniformly hungry" for white women. The latter was often presented as justification for lynchings and the literal castration of black men.

The research on locus of control presents black people as "passive, motivated only by external events and deficient in the internal drive needed to control their own destiny" (Chunn, Dunston and Ross-Sherif, 1983).

Black patients have been reported to be more resentful and suspicious (Gardner, 1971), difficult to establish rapport with, untreatable, incapable of insight, nonverbal and concrete (Seagull & Jones, 1977) and because of their history to suffer inescapably from low self esteem (Thomas & Sillen, 1972) and submissiveness (Sattler, 1970). Other than pejorative explanations were rarely sought.

Hollingshead and Redlich (1958), observed the tendency of white middle class therapists to discriminate against the poor and members of minority groups. They found that the most severe diagnoses and the least amount of therapy were offered to patients who were poor and black.

Yamamoto, James, Bloombaum and Hatten (1967) found that in a clinic staffed by white therapists, black patients were less likely to receive dynamic individual or group psychotherapy and were seen for fewer sessions with higher attrition rates than were white patients.

The sensitivity of many black people to potential exploitation or maltreatment by whites has been termed "cultural paranoia" (Grier and Cobbs, 1968). Although it was intended to describe an adaptive mechanism, this appears to be a somewhat pejorative explanation for such behavior. The term "paranoia" implies a pathological, maladaptive, hypersensitivity to or fear of something which if it exists at all, does so in a mild, non-threatening form. As might be expected, black and white people may have markedly different views as to how prevalent or threatening racism may be. As black people may experience the effects of racism more often and more directly than white people, this phenomenon might be better understood as a physiological or psychological predisposition or ability to perceive a wider range of environmental stimuli as stressful and to react to them accordingly (Myers & King, 1983).

Aside from its effect on public policy, the impact of this body of research on the training of mental health professionals is an important one. It is not simply the specific course content which may support and transmit racist ideas, but the philosophy, assumptions, theories, goals, methods and expected outcomes underlying many of those courses (Chunn et al., 1983).

There has been comparatively little research, much of it quite recent, which examines the phenomenon of racism as a maladaptive condition. A few attempts to explain this phenomenon of racism will be examined.

James Comer (Thomas & Sillen, 1972), defines racism as,

a low level defense and adjustment mechanism utilized by groups to deal with psychological and social insecurities similar to the manner in which individuals utilize psychic defenses and adjustment mechanisms to deal with anxiety. A given society may promote and reward racism to enable members of the group in control to obtain a sense of personal adequacy and security at the expense of the group with less control.

Ackerman (Bloch & Simon, 1982), in an attempt to discern the dynamic basis of anti-Semitism, isolated several common characteristics of Jewish and non-Jewish anti-Semitic patients. They were seen as pervasively anxious, with the anxiety manifested in social discomfort; as possessing a confused self image; exhibiting partial failure at reality adaptation; and disturbances of conscience. Central to these patients was a strong need to affiliate with a dominant group, perhaps as a consequence of their confused self images, and to renounce emphatically any of their differences from the dominant group. Hence, having renounced parts of their own uniqueness to gain acceptance by the dominant group they may be quite resentful of anyone who can or will not do the same. A parallel may be drawn here between the psychodynamics of anti-Semitism, racism, and homophobia. A person who experiences ego dystonic feelings may need to renounce those feelings in order to be or feel accepted by the dominant group. These persons may then experience the presence of persons who openly or otherwise express these feelings comfortably as an eternal source of irritation. Ackerman also noted among anti-Semites a predisposition to "blame" the outside world for their misfortunes.

Frances Cress Welsing (1974), suggests that the belief in white supremacy as it is manifested in racist practices in America is the derivative of a deep sense of inadequacy and inferiority on the part of white people, which occurred when European white people, "without color and in fewer numbers," were confronted with large numbers of people of color in the world. Psychoanalytic theory supports the view that any neurotic drive for superiority represents a compensatory mechanism for a deep internal sense of inadequacy and inferiority. She asserts that the response constituted a reaction-formation defense mechanism. This defense represents the tendency to unconsciously convert something that was experienced as desirable but unattainable into something to be discredited and despised. Welsing suggests that the unconscious desire for color is reflected in the fact that the American cosmetics industry earns millions of dollars manufacturing, promoting and selling products whose chief purpose is to add color to the face and body. She notes further that a large population of Americans appear willing to risk the dangers of skin cancer to obtain a "good" tan. This is conspicuously juxtaposed against a society which devalues people of color. Another part of her thesis is the dominant genetic factor of color production, to which the state of color absence acts as a genetic recessive factor. It is noteworthy that the concept of biological race is governed by social fiction in America. In many states, the offspring of one black and one white parent remain legally and socially considered black in spite of the obvious fact that one half of that child's "genetic equipment" came from a white parent.

Another explanation for racist attitudes is that they represent the projection of unwanted or unacceptable drives, desires, and impulses onto another group who is then defined as completely different in its humanness from the dominant group. The assumption of many whites that they must be vigilant or openly aggress against blacks, "because blacks hate whites," may also represent a projection of whites used to mitigate their guilt or fears of retribution.

Racial Issues in Therapy

Whatever the explanation for racism may be, its effects may not be left "outside the door" when patient and therapist come together. Terry Kupers (1981) articulates four problematic stances which a white therapist may adopt when confronted with a black patient. They are discussed here, with other problematic issues.

The most obvious problematic stance a white therapist may take is Bigotry. This is represented by the therapist's conscious or unconscious belief in white supremacy, and as a consequence, the feeling that the black patient's problems are an outgrowth of the patient's racial inferiority. The patient's pathology or problems may be stressed or exaggerated at the exclusion of strengths and adaptive mechanisms. The bigoted therapist may use scientific racism or the "scholarly dozens" to justify making racist decisions.

Another less obvious but nevertheless racist stance is that of Color Blindness. As noted earlier in this discussion, if we concede the existence of pervasive racism, we may conclude that the black patient's experience and awareness of it may differ from that of the white therapist. If therapists fail to recognize, at the very least, the potential for pervasive and insidious effects of racism on a person's life, they may interpret some communication from the patient as a distortion before clearly establishing that the distortion exists. If white therapists need to deny the effects of racism, they may collude with the patient's need to deny its effects as well. The patient may sense the therapist's reluctance to confront the issue and respond with a fear that expressing his or her pain and resentment of racism will alienate the therapist. Therapists cannot help a patient confront and develop strategies for dealing with reality if they engage in the defensive flight and avoidance of an anxiety provoking issue. Hence color blindness may be seen as a form of resistance.

A third stance is Paternalism. Alvin Poussaint (Kupers, 1981) once referred to this as the "Moses syndrome." It involves the attribution of all of a patient's problems to society and the effects of racism. To do this will fail to help patients understand any role they may have in their own dilemma. There may also be a tendency on the therapist's part to overlook or minimize severe psychopathology and conceal personality difficulties in the patient. Patients may be viewed simplistically as culturally disadvantaged or deprived. Clemmont Vontress (1971), refers to paternalism as the "Great White Father Syndrome." Here, the patient is encouraged to put herself unquestionably in the hands of the omnipotent, all knowing, white therapist. This demand may have its origins in the therapist's defensiveness and need to feel powerful. It may, however, serve only to foster a dependency which can interfere with a patient's ability to grow and become independent. This stance may undermine the expression of the patient's anger if the therapist appears "too good and understanding of the effects of oppression." Generally, both the patient and therapist can use this stance in the service of avoiding a personal involvement in therapy by substituting social problems for personal ones (Gardner, 1971).

A fourth possible stance, often a result of the therapist's racial guilt, is unquestioning compliance with the rhetoric of Black Power. The term "Black Power" is used here to refer to belief that one's discriminated status justifies a failure to take into account the feelings or needs of others. There is some overlap here with the stance of paternalism. Here the therapist may fear a realistic confrontation with the patient. Therapists in this example may have conscious or unconscious concerns about their own racism leaking out into the treatment situation. This can result in a failure or reluctance to set appropriate limits or to interpret acting out. The therapist may also fear that if the black patient's anger is triggered or unleashed it will become uncontrollable, violent and irrational. When therapists harbor this belief they may be predisposed to "putting a lid" on the patient's overt expressions of anger, forgetting their usual convictions about the importance of expressing such feelings (Gochros, 1966). If the therapist's anxiety is communicated to the patient, the patient may respond by strengthening defenses and avoiding certain material. Therapists in this example may need to prove that they are "not like other white people" perhaps before even determining what the patient thinks white people are like. Therapists may feel that as members of the white community they must assume some guilt for society's wrongs but be unclear as to how much guilt to assume (Gochros, 1966).

It can be generally stated that when a white therapist confronts a black patient, he or she may have beliefs of questionable validity, gathered from the professional literature, the attitudes of training supervisors, the majority of whom are white, and his or her own conscious and unconscious feelings and attitudes about black people. The black patient may also harbor feelings about the white therapist. Ralph Greenson (1964), warns that there may be mutual anxiety and some distrust on the part of the patient resulting in a delay in establishing a working alliance. There may be attempts to determine racial attitudes as each adjusts their behavior in such a way as to minimize vulnerability. In addition, each may act out culturally conditioned patterns of interaction with whites or blacks

(Gardner, 1971). Again, the normative power relationship between blacks and whites may be re-enacted (Owens, 1984).

In the initial stages of treatment, the black patient may consciously or unconsciously put the white therapist to a series of "tests" to determine if the therapist will accept him or her as an individual. This may assume the form of suspicion, verbal constriction, playing dumb, ingratiating behavior or open resentment (Gardner, 1971). It remains, however, the therapist's responsibility to be familiar with the black patient's culture to some extent, and with his or her own personal feelings and motivations for and about working with black patients.

WOMEN, RACIAL DIFFERENCES, AND PSYCHOTHERAPY

The final section of this article attempts to address issues relevant to the treatment of black female patients, Lesbian and heterosexual, when the therapist is a white female.

Black women experience the combined effects of racism, sexism and, for black Lesbians, homophobia. The interrelationship between these three characteristics must be appreciated for its complexity when compared to the experiences of white feminists and/or Lesbians. It is important that therapists who work with black women understand this complexity. Major problems in psychotherapy may occur if the therapist assumes that shared gender and/or sexual preference renders racial and/or cultural differences of minimal importance. It has been suggested that black feminists and Lesbians have much in common with their white counterparts. This has raised questions about the perceived reluctance of black women to enthusiastically embrace the "women's movement."

In the American hierarchy of social status, black women find themselves at the bottom of the proverbial heap, with black Lesbians finding themselves under the heap. As a slave, the black woman was little more than a laborer and breeder. She was defined legally as a piece of property. Her children, often the result of forced sexual relationships, were frequently taken from her and sold, as they were considered pieces of property as well. Lacking any status or legal rights, she became prey to black and white men as well as the whims of her mistress. If a black woman found herself in the midst of a forced liaison with her master, she could well expect his wife's resentment. Her vulnerability to the sexual urges of white men further complicated her relationship with a black man, who may also have seen her as his "property."

Slaves who worked in their mistress's household were often convenient targets for white women. Many white women of that era may have identified with the black woman's narrowly defined role in that white males defined the roles for both of them. However, many white women identified with their oppressors and used their limited authority to terrorize the black women toiling in their homes, perhaps clinging to the notion that there was still someone to whom they were superior.

Perhaps the magnitude of forced sexual liaisons with white and black men contributed to a prevailing view of black women as "morally loose and sexually promiscuous" (Smythe, 1976). Although all women were regarded as the originators of sexual sin, white women were elevated to a pedestal of sexual purity and virtue, while black women became the embodiment of evil and sexual lust. This phenomenon raises specific questions as to how it affects the current view of black Lesbians. If one examines the myths surrounding the sexuality of black women with the myths related to Lesbian sexuality, no doubt the reality of who the black Lesbian is remains obscure. The fact that black women were often accused of leading white men away from sexual purity and into sin suggests a tendency to see these women as having choices that were never really available.

Another form of discrimination directed at black women from fellow blacks and whites was color prejudice. Noting that in slavery light skinned blacks often received better treatment than darker skinned blacks, many blacks and whites developed preferences and resentments toward lighter skinned women. Just as a favored sibling will be envied for the trait which gains her preferential treatment, she will also be the target of resentment from other siblings for being given "special treatment." Women, both black and white, were expected to conform to certain standards of appearance. While many white women may not or choose not to aspire to this standard, it remains a standard based on Caucasian features. To be considered beautiful was to have as many Caucasian features as possible. Hence black women came to be seen as less publicly desirable.

We must note, however, that public desirability or in this case the lack of it, did not always govern private conduct. One may raise the question as to whether or not this issue carries over even into the Lesbian community. Data pertinent to this issue will be presented later.

The issue of preferential treatment deserves some additional attention here. Many black women continue to work in the homes of white women. Often black women were employed in menial jobs not considered worthy of white men and women. Perhaps because she may have been perceived as less threatening, the black woman was often chosen for work instead of the black man. Given our sexist society's view of "manhood" this caused further difficulties between black men and women. A black man who had no job or who could not support his family was regarded as less of a man. It became easy for black men to focus their rage on black women as opposed to white males who in fact held the power of decision over who worked, who did not and where. The scholarly dozens were used to attribute the problems of black people to the "matriarchal" nature of black families. This sexist notion assumes that families headed by women castrate men and cause psychopathology in children.

Despite myths that the recent plight of all American women was essentially the same, research and census data suggest this is not so. The data suggests that black women have always worked outside the home in greater numbers than white women. Furthermore, black women continue to outnumber white women in lower paid occupations (Smythe, 1976).

Freudiger and Almquist (1983) suggest that women who occupy many statuses and who are forced to enact many roles are particularly vulnerable to role conflict and strain. This may be seen as particularly true for black women for whom female sex role expectations tend to be perceived as less reachable and less clear than for white women. This may be compounded in some areas for black Lesbians. This study compared life satisfaction scores on a number of dimensions between black and white women. Bell and Weinberg (1978) conducted an extensive study of the characteristics and preferences of homosexual men and women. The findings in these two studies revealed interesting differences in the experiences and preferences between black and white women. Their pertinent aspects will be reviewed here.

Religious involvement emerged as the single most important influence on the life satisfaction scores of black women, and the second most important variable in predicting white women's life satisfaction scores. This was consistent with Bell and Weinberg's data in which significantly more black Lesbians described themselves as religious in the conventional sense than white Lesbians. The black church has traditionally been the main source of creative and social outlet for black people, as well as a vehicle for the talents and leadership abilities not permitted expression in the larger society. This may account for some of the church's importance to black women, in spite of its often negative view of homosexuality.

In the area of psychological and physical health, significant differences were revealed. Black women perceived themselves as significantly less healthy than white women. Similarly, black Lesbians perceived themselves to feel lonely more often, to be in poorer health, to demonstrate a greater number of somatic symptoms, and to display more tension than did their white counterparts. White women, however, were more likely to have considered suicide than black women. This particular finding should not be comforting. The rate of suicide for black American females between the ages of 20 and 24 in 1970 was 30.2% per 100,00 compared to a rate of 13.6% for white females of the same age group (Allen, 1973). Kiev and Anumonye (1976) report that suicide represents the most common form of death in young black women aged 15-19. The definition of suicide is expanded here to include deaths directly related to drug overdoses, victim precipitated homicide and drunk driving. Suicide among young black women is 14th highest in the world and rose 80% between 1949 and 1969 (Marvis, 1969). It is difficult to say definitively that race is the causal variable, there are probably others as well. It remains, however, hard to believe that it is not a major contributing factor.

Financial satisfaction represented the most important variable for white women. Freudiger and Almquist (1983) explain this finding as something which occurs as a consequence of the differing expectations which white as opposed to black women have about the possibility of obtaining financial rewards. It was suggested that white women are socialized to expect financial rewards either from their own efforts or the efforts of their fathers or male partners. Black women may not believe, because of job discrimination against black men and women, that financial success is obtainable. Black Lesbians generally reported less satisfaction with their jobs than white Lesbians.

With respect to marriage and children, marriage had a slight negative effect on the life satisfaction scores of black women. The same authors suggest that many of the material gains that many white women may derive from marriage to white men are not available to black men and therefore not to black women. This was attributed to the assumption that the pressure of racism in our society brings other pressures to bear on black couples. Tensions and frustrations between black men, who are not allowed to participate fully and equally in a society which emasculates them, and black women, who feel cheated as well by the betrayal of the American dream, are often directed within the marriage as opposed to the external society. It is unclear how these tensions are manifested in Lesbian couples where both partners are black. It is likely that pressures of a different sort are inherent in these relationships given the racist and homophobic nature of our society, thus compounding the issue of race. It may be hypothesized that black Lesbians may not have the same expectations of a black Lesbian partner as a black heterosexual woman might have of a black man. This may diminish the tension in this area.

Freudiger and Almquist (1983) report that while children are a source of "pride and satisfaction" for black women and that the "mother role" is one that is highly prized, the actual presence of young children "detracts slightly" from the life satisfaction scores of black women, and white women as well. Black women (both Lesbian and heterosexual) tend to have significantly more children than white women. This is explained in part by the fact that a larger number of black women that white women go directly into the job market after high school rather than college. White women generally begin having children between the ages of 25-29; black women begin somewhat earlier, between the ages of 20-24. What becomes clear is that a substantial number of black children are born to mothers who are younger, less well trained and educated, and less economically secure than white women. These women are left with the difficult demand of raising a child when they are least well equipped to do so (Myers & King, 1983).

Age represented a variable which revealed significant differences between black and white women. After the age of 65, white women show a drop in life satisfaction scores not observed to a similar degree in black women. This difference was attributed to the different roles which these women play in their respective communities at this age. Black women are often treated with the respect of "elder stateswomen" of their communities or families. In fact, therapists who work with black patients and/or their families often find that a grandmother or aunt or great aunt in fact raised a child, not necessarily the child's natural mother. In some cases, the person raising the child may not necessarily be blood related (Boyd-Franklin & Hines, 1982). In this manner, black women maintain active positions within their families. They are consulted for advice on a variety of matters, not exclusively but often around issues of childrearing, placing them and their accumulated wisdom in a highly valued role. The corollary of this has not been observed to the same degree in elder white women. These findings may also be related to the standards of beauty which women in our society are held. These youthful and essentially caucasian features are always somewhat unattainable for black women. One may raise the question as to whether or not black women "give up" on attempting to approximate them at an earlier age (out of a belief that they are unattainable) than white women. With a perceived loss of attractiveness and perhaps a diminished role in their families, white women may face greater social "losses" with age than black women, both Lesbian and heterosexual.

With respect to politics and education, white women reported significantly more satisfaction from voting and from educational status than did black women. Interestingly, white Lesbians had the perception that their sexual preference made them less liberal politically while black Lesbians felt their political stance was liberalized as a result of their sexual preference.

Finally, race, social status and frequency of sexual contact was compared for black and white Lesbians (Bell & Weinberg, 1978). Three quarters of the white Lesbians interviewed reported that all of their partners had been white, while less than one quarter of the black Lesbians reported that their partners were black. It is unclear what causal connections are involved here. Does this reflect the existence of fewer black Lesbians than white or does it reflect a preference for or adherence to a particular beauty standard? Similarly, two thirds of the white Lesbians interviewed reported having partners of similar social position, while only one third of the black Lesbians interviewed revealed similar findings. On measures of frequency of sexual contact, less educated black Lesbians reported themselves to be significantly more sexually active than their better educated black counterparts. Black Lesbians generally reported greater frequency of sexual contact than white Lesbians. It was noted, however, that the sample of black Lesbians interviewed were significantly younger than their white counterparts which suggests some degree of sample bias.

Still finding themselves at the bottom of the social heap, many black women view the feminist movement as a "family fight" between white men and women, regardless of their sexual preference. While the author does not support this view entirely, it must be taken into account. Regardless of their sexual preference, white women continue to have access to privileges in our society denied black women on the basis of color. White women have and continue to receive "vicarious" power and privilege (as mothers, daughters, wives and lovers) as a result of their relationships with white men. It must be clear that white women pay a price for this, and the white Lesbian may have less access to these vicarious privileges than the white heterosexual woman. While it is better than being the "slave of a slave," vicarious power is not to be confused with true power in the form of self actualization and freedom of choice.

In spite of the dehumanizing and limiting experiences that black women have been exposed to, they continue to work, survive, hold families together and build in their communities. Robinson (1983) sees black women as the essence of "psychological androgyny." Traits of self-reliance, independence, assertiveness and strength, to so-called masculine traits which feminists strive to adopt, have been reflected in the achievements of black women throughout history. This has not protected her, however, from having these traits turned into negative attributes. There have been and continue to be double standards for the same phenomena when comparing black and white women. The "supermom" with an "alternative lifestyle" is juxtaposed against the "emasculating matriarch" or "unwed mother" who presides over an "illegitimate" or "broken family." These characteristics were blamed, within a clearly sexist and racist frame of reference, for undermining the role and status of black men. This, coupled with the mythical black matriarchy, makes black Lesbians even more threatening. In addition to their strengths as black women, they clearly choose not to "partner" with men. The rejection of sexual partnership with black men is often seen as a failure to support and empathize with their oppression. As black Lesbians share the concerns of the black community for the survival of black people, this may contribute to the difficulty of integrating all of her "selves" in a community. The sexual preference of the black Lesbian is assumed to undermine the black family and possibly the struggles of black people. The result for some black Lesbians is to feel outcast from a community of great importance to them.

The concessions offered white women on the basis of their "femininity" even with obvious hidden agendas were not offered to black women at all. She was expected to work as hard in the fields as a man, care for her mistress's household, and then care for her own family. The "femininity" of the black woman was largely ignored.

It may be said that isolation, self-hate and the psychological stress that attends them are traits shared by racial minorities as well as Lesbians. There is a need for secrecy and discretion (Anthony, 1982), a pressure to find partners too quickly (Sang, 1977), and a difficulty in establishing a sense of self within Lesbian relationships (McCandlish, 1982) in a racist, sexist and homophobic society which complicates therapy issues for black Lesbians. Because of their isolation from the mainstream, both black people and Lesbians form distinct cultural communities of their own. Black Lesbians then exist within a subgroup of two subgroups, where elements of each group may be rejecting of the other group in what has been termed an invisible minority. Within this invisible minority the possibility for further social isolation may be even higher than that for either group alone.

Displaying an enormous reservoir of strength and surviving over great odds make it difficult to avoid the temptation of romanticizing the plight of black women (Hooks, 1981). While black women are not riddled with deficits, their position is certainly not to be envied. We must not confuse endurance or survival with overcoming the combined and complex effects of oppression. Endurance and survival come at a price which often includes adapting to ongoing, high levels of stress and not infrequently moving from crisis to crisis with little respite. That adaptation may involve the development of strategies designed to maintain survival which do not then allow for truly creative development and growth to the limits of one's potential.

White women and Lesbians who practice therapy with black women must be sensitive to the fact that their membership in an oppressed group does not prevent them from being oppressive. Furthermore, even though the philosophy of feminism is theoretically opposed to racism, that philosophy does not shield black women from the day to day exploitation by white men and women, some of whom may be homosexual. Henley & Pincus (1978), in a study of the interrelationship between sexist, racist, and antihomosexual attitudes, found that white women's attitudes were significantly less sexist than white males' attitudes, but they were not significantly less racist. The social tensions inherent in relationships between black and white women will not necessarily be left "outside the door" when a black woman enters therapy with a white women, whether the therapist is feminist, Lesbian, or both.

The therapist then has a difficult task. This task involves maintaining awareness of the stressful consequences of our culture's racism and its interrelationship with homophobia and sexism. It seems clear that our society fosters a double burden on black women and a triple burden on black Lesbians' ability to cope, and that this may have a role in contributing to psychopathology. We cannot, however, as therapists view all the problems of an individual as a direct and simple result of "oppression" without maintaining an awareness of how an individual may contribute consciously or unconsciously to her own dilemma. The therapist must be able to separate realistic racial-cultural issues from intrapsychic issues.

The meaning of the differences observed between black and white women, heterosexual and Lesbian, are not always clear. The relationships between the observed differences and race may not always be linear, many are probably multiply-determined. What emerges, however, is that psychotherapists must be aware of these differences and the ways in which their sequelae may be manifested in and complicate psychotherapy. Many of the concepts discussed here may be useful toward that end.

REFERENCES

Allen, N.H. (1973). *Suicide in California*: 1960–1970. Monograph, State of California, Department of Public Health.

Anthony, B.D. (1982). Lesbian client, Lesbian therapist: Opportunities and challenges in working together. In Paul, W., Weinrich, J.D., Gonsiorek, J.C. & Hotvedt, M.E. (Eds.), *Homosexuality: Social, psychological and biological issues. Beverly Hills, CA: Sage Publications.*

Bell, A.P. & Weinberg, M.S. (1978). *Homosexualities: A study of diversity among men and women.* New York: Simon and Schuster.

Bender, L. (1939). The behavior problems of Negro children. *Psychiatry, 2,* 213–228.

Bloch, D. & Simon, R. (1982). *The strength of family therapy: Selected papers of Nathan Ackerman.* New York: Brunner Mazel.

Boyd-Franklin, N. & Hines, P.M. (1982). Black families. In McGoldrick, A., Pearce, B. & Giordano, C. (Eds.), *Ethnicity and family therapy.* New York: Guilford Press.

Chunn, J.C., Dunston, P. & Ross-Sheriff, F. (Eds.). (1983) *Mental health and people of color.* Washington, DC: Howard University Press.

Erikson, E. (1950). *Childhood and society.* New York: W.W. Norton and Company, Inc.

Freudiger, P. & Almquist, E.M. (1983, April). *Sources of life satisfaction: The different worlds of black women and white women.* Revised version of a paper presented at the annual meeting of the Southwestern Sociological Association: Houston, TX.

Gardner, L.K. (1971). The therapeutic relationship under varying conditions of race. *Psychotherapy, Theory, Research & Practice, 8,* 76–86.

Gochros, J.S. (1966). Recognition and use of anger in Negro clients. *Social Work,* January, 23–34.

Greenson, R. (1964). *The technique and practice of psychoanalysis.* New York: International Universities Press.

Grier, W. & Cobbs, P. (1968). *Black rage.* New York: Basic Books.

Guthrie, R.V. (1976). *Even the rat was white: A historical view of psychology.* New York: Harper and Row.

Haskins, J. & Butts, H.F. (1973). *The psychology of Black language.* New York: Harper and Row.

Henley, K.M. & Pincus, F. (1978). Interrelationship of sexist, racist and antihomosexual attitudes. *Psychological Reports, 42,* 83–90.

Hersen, M., Kazdin, A.E. & Bellak, A.S. (1983). *The clinical psychology handbook.* New York: Pergamon Press.

Hollingshead, A.B. & Redlich, P.C. (1958). *Social class and mental illness: A community study.* New York: Wiley and Sons.

Hooks, B. (1981). *Black women and feminism.* Boston, MA: South End Press.

Kardiner, A. & Ovesey, L. (1962). *The mark of oppression: A psychosocial study of the American Negro.* New York: World Publications.

Kiev, A. & Anumonye, A. (1976). Suicidal behavior in a black ghetto: A comparative study. *International Journal of Mental Health, 5,* 50–59.

Kupers, T. (1981). *Public therapy: The practice of psychotherapy in the public mental health clinic.* New York: The MacMillan Company.

Marvis, R.W. (1969). *Social forces in urban suicide.* Hornewood, IL: The Dorsey Press.

McCandlish, B. (1982). Therapeutic issues with Lesbian couples. In Gonsiorek, J. (Ed.), *Homosexuality and psychotherapy.* New York: Haworth Press.

Myers, H.F. & King, L.M. (1983). Mental health issues in the development of the Black American child. In Powell, G. (Ed.), *The psychosocial development of minority group children.* New York: Brunner Mazel.

Moffie, H.S. (1983). Sociocultural guidelines for clinicians in multicultural settings. *Psychiatric Quarterly, 55,* 47–54.

Owens, M. (1984). Racial issues in interracial supervision triads: When the supervisor is Black, the therapist is white and the patient is Black. Unpublished manuscript.

Robinson, C.R. (1983). Black women: A tradition of self-reliant strength. *Women and Therapy, 2,* 135–143.

Sang, B. (1977). Psycotherapy with Lesbians: Some observations and tentative generalizations. In Carter, D.K. & Rawlings, E. (Eds.), *Psychotherapy for women: Treatment toward equality.* Springfield, IL: Charles C Thomas.

Sattler, J.M. (1970), Racial "experimenter effects" in experimentation, testing, interviewing and psychotherapy. *Psychological Bulletin, 73,* 137–160.

Seagull, A. & Jones, A. (1977). Dimensions of the relationship between the Black client and the White therapist. *American Psychologist, 32,* 850–855.

Smythe, M. (Ed.) (1976). *The Black American Reference Book.* Englewood Cliffs, NJ: Prentice-Hall.

Thomas, A. & Sillen, S. (1972). *Racism and psychiatry.* New York: Brunner Mazel.

Vontress, C.E. (1971). Racial differences: Impediments to rapport. *Journal of Counseling Psychology, 18,* 7–13.

Welsing, F.C. (1974). The Cress theory of color confrontation. *Black Scholar Magazine,* May.

Willie, C., Kramer, B. & Brown, B. (Eds.) (1974). *Racism and mental health.* Pittsburgh, PA: University of Pittsburgh Press.

Yamamoto, J., James, Q.C., Bloombaum, W. & Hatten, J. (1967). Racial factors in patient selection. *American Journal of Psychiatry, 124,* 630–636.

The Application of an Individual/Collective Model to the Psychology of Black Women

Harriet G. McCombs

This paper is concerned with the psychological construction of African-American women; the implications of that construction and a proposed reconstruction. The purpose of this paper is to urge the adoption of black women's interpretations of their experience as the starting point for research and therapy. The adoption of a phenomenological approach to women's psychology is not new. The inclusion of a social phenomenological approach which explicitly incorporates ethnic and gender identity as a unity is new.

It makes intuitive sense that the objective world experience of the object of psychological inquiry and the recipient of psychological services should be centrally positioned in the practice of psychology. Despite its intuitive sense, the idea is not adhered to in practice. Much of the psychological inquiry and therapeutic solutions to black women's lives are based on the experiences of others outside the culture of black women and inappropriately applied.

The awareness of this situation should lead us to the critical analysis of the tenets of psychology and to the development of a more accurate psychology. Awareness alone does not begin to unravel the webs of myths, misconceptions, and ill-conceived intervention strategies which surround the lives of black women. Without a structured approach to the search for avenues which serve as better research and therapeutic models we will be left with only a heightened awareness of our inability to come to

Harriet G. McCombs of Yale University is currently a visiting faculty member at the University of South Carolina, 2322 Washington Street, Columbia, SC 29204.

grips with our profession as it operates in the real world vis-à-vis black women. In the search for new avenues, an alternative approach to the practice of psychology seems to be in order.

Rather than focusing on problems and pathology, our focus will be on adjustment to changing social environments. Further, the modes of adjustment will need to be evaluated in terms of the full range of possible responses to them. From this starting point, adjustment can be positive, negative, or neutral. Implicit in this point is the fact that black women can develop into psychologically healthy individuals (cf. Gardner, 1980; Lorion, 1974). It is crucial that we understand the importance of a psychologically healthy African-American woman. Its importance lies not only in the characteristics of a healthy individual, but in the introduction of the concept itself (i.e., black women make healthy adjustments to environments and persons manifesting neurotic if not psychotic expressions of prejudice, racism, sexism, and discrimination directed toward them) in mainstream psychology.

THE INDIVIDUAL/COLLECTIVE SELF

The approach to research and the practice of psychology provided in this paper relates to Third World women in general and African-American women in particular. In its elemental form, the theoretical approach suggests that individuals perform three psychological tasks: they interpret experience, evaluate experience, and react to that evaluation. Individuals experience the objective world in a variety of ways and are motivated to interpret those experiences through their personal history, knowledge, and values. Through their individual interpretations they formulate a personal world-view. Further, they evaluate and validate the accuracy of their personal view in terms of their adjustment or mastery of the environment (Kelly, 1955). Finally, from this evaluation, feelings of personal self-worth and competence are generated (McCombs, 1985).

Similarly, the social or collective groups to which individuals belong carry out the same functions. Social groups interpret experience, evaluate experience, and react to those evaluations. It is important to note that the individual is inextricably connected to the social group. Neither she nor the collective can revoke membership. The collective relationship is not chosen but ascribed (Allport, 1954) by virtue of birth. Thus, the individual is provided with a cultural world-view which operates simultaneously with the personal world-view which constitutes an individual/collective world-view.

The use of the term "individual/collective" recognizes and emphasizes the fact that black women's identity is determined by both a personal (individual) history consisting of the unique developmental dynamics of that individual and a social (collective) history consisting of the developmental experiences of black women as a group.

"The individual/collective identity is an 'I/We' identity; I am what I experience as an individual *and* what we experience as a people" (McCombs, 1985, p. 10). The changing social roles of black women interact with and influence the changing events in the mainstream culture of which they are a part. Conversely, the changing events in the mainstream culture are influencing the changing roles of black women. With continual growth, new situations arise and new avenues are made available to and explored by black women. Due to their enormous complexity, the full implications and ramifications of the directions black women are now taking are not fully understood by all involved, including black women.

THE AFRICAN-AMERICAN WOMAN AS A PSYCHOLOGICAL OBJECT

Within a research and therapeutic context, black women have, within the last decade, emerged as a group having a social psychological uniqueness—apart from black men and white women. The recognition of this psychological uniqueness emerged from women's studies and other disciplines such as English and History, where black women's writings and historical past could be clearly distinguished from the larger body of American literature or history and from African-American literature and history.

The use of the ethnocultural identification of African-American is important here because it allows a cultural basis, a naturally occurring context within which to view black women. Much has been written about ill-chosen starting points of ana-

lyses of the experiences of black women. Following the suggestions of scholars such as Nobles (1972) and Jackson (1979),
more psychologists are now reformulating the starting point for
the analysis of African-American psychological experiences. In
that the black woman is a recent arrival as a unique object of
psychological study, other academic disciplines are helpful in
engineering the psychosocial contextual lens through which to
view the African-American woman.

Incorporating the Social Context

It is of fundamental importance that the experiences of African-American women be examined from the point of assessing
societal limitations of black women's experiences and expressions in each period of social history (Stetson, 1983). Moreover, there is the need for a fundamental reconstruction of the
psychosocial activities of American society that takes into account the range of black women's experiences within changing
psychosocial environments in which they have lived. Clearly,
this points to the fact that the proposed theoretical framework
is an interim interpretation. It is amenable to change with major changes in the psycho-cultural environment. It does, however, provide an approach for the study and interpretation of
black women through social psychological concepts.

From a psychosocial perspective, the contemporary African-
American woman exists in the context of a desegregating racial
and sex-role society. The importance of these social phenomena
illustrate the unique position the contemporary African-American woman currently occupies. Many experiences that are available to contemporary black women (both in a positive and negative sense) were unavailable to the previous generation of black
women. This social reality raises issues related to the dynamics
of adjustment. More specifically, it suggests that the type of
psychological adjustment required by contemporary black
women is quite different from the type of adjustment required
by the previous generation. Further, it suggests that modes of
adjustment undoubtedly will be different for future generations. (Common elements can be identified across all periods for
successful adaptation to the changing social environment.) The
present social period requires the black women to literally create the map as she travels.

This paper is particularly concerned with the African-American woman who has a high degree of contact with others outside of her historically traditional segregated environment. It is thought this would be the woman who is more likely to seek psychological services than the woman with low contact with those outside the traditional segregated community. It is less likely that the woman who has low contact with mainstream culture will seek help from the psychological profession.

It is suggested that many of the adjustment difficulties experienced by the African-American woman currently in therapy are critically linked with changes in traditional societal and familial structures, and further, that these difficulties are strongly associated with the increasing range of life-style possibilities. The increasing range of life-style possibilities, in turn has been accompanied by increasing responsibilities. Both the opportunities and responsibilities are sources of individual and collective psychological tensions.

FUNCTIONAL ANALYSIS OF ADJUSTMENT IN MAINSTREAM CULTURE

From the perspective of this paper, the mainstream culture appears as an organized system of cultural rules which seeks to transform black women into being "mainstream culture persons" by negating who they are and suggesting most strongly that they adopt a new identity tied to a new collective rather than their original collective. That suggestion is made through the promise of accruing mainstream social rewards. This perceived functional aspect of mainstream culture affects black women's perception of and adjustment to it. Within this transformation process, African-American women are asked to leave their collective identity outside of their interactions with mainstream culture and adopt another collective's perspectives as their own.

To take on the mainstream culture identity is to take on a white, male-oriented identity resulting in the total negation of self for black women. It is not the mainstream culture as a tool for obtaining educational or employment opportunities that poses adjustment difficulties. It is the functional nature of the mainstream culture, however, in its total context (eth-

nicity × sex × class interactions) that poses adjustment difficulties for black women.

In the cases where psychological adjustment has not been
successful the unified individual/collective self has usually been
disassociated into the component selves (cf. Mead, 1934).
There are personal as well as collective examples of the disas-
sociation of the total self of black women in mainstream culture. One example is the situation wherein black women are
asked to identify themselves and respond to social situations
only as required by the mainstream role (e.g., lawyer) or as
either black *or* female; at other times black women are asked
to combine two elements (e.g., black lawyer or female lawyer)
and omit one (e.g., black or lawyer). This neurotic demand
upon black women seeks to separate and abstract objective
equalities of their identity, thereby abstracting qualities which
are the source of many unique experiences. The question
raised here is, who or what is the source of the demand to
affirm selected aspects of one's total self.

High Contact With Mainstream Culture

The challenge for African-American and other Third World
women to maintain their identities within the mainstream cultural context arises from the fact that the mainstream culture's
identity is different from their own. Moreover, mainstream
culture has not anticipated, expected, or planned for their inclusion. Reacting to the African-American woman occupying a
new social role, the mainstream culture seeks to impose an
invalid world-view upon them. Black women enter the new
areas with a knowledge of their identity and the identity of the
mainstream culture (this may be seen as being bicultural).
Therefore, black women who decide to enter the non-traditional areas do so with the understanding that it will be a new
collective experience, but will also be a challenge to their tradi-
tions. In order to maintain themselves they must perform their
mainstream duties without loss of their identity or integrity.

The affirmation of black women's total individual/collective
self by the mainstream environment is then a process of selective affirmation. This process occurs not only in the mainstream culture, but also outside of it—where interpersonal
relationships are established. For black women who have high

contact with the mainstream culture, the process can be destructive in a figurative and literal sense. The actual mainstream training and education they receive reflect a mind/body dualism that can only result in the African-American woman denying her own ethnicity and womanhood if her identity is not firmly integrated.

It is suggested that the experience in mainstream culture not only substantiates the existence of an "ideal type," which is used as basis of comparison among individuals and between groups; but, it also attempts to produce the "ideal type." The ideal type is no longer characterized by whiteness or maleness, but rather by the willingness and ability to protect and sustain the status quo. (This should not be interpreted as meaning that racism and sexism are dead.)

It is the adaptation of the idealized style of functioning which actually masks the adjustment difficulties of black women with high contact with mainstream culture. From all outside appearances she is functioning quite, if not exceptionally well (given her collective and personal history), except for the minor presenting problem on which the therapist cannot get a handle or gain closure.

For black women, it is a denial of their essence, past history, and ultimately future history. Elements of the mainstream culture plead ignorance of these implications. The community, however, does not. The selective affirmation process occurring within non-traditional areas causes some black women to disassociate and affirm themselves as individuals devoid of an African cultural heritage or representing an entire collective rather than as unique persons with whole intact individual/collective identities.

THE PROCESS OF DISASSOCIATION

The questioning that takes place among black women with high contact with mainstream culture is not necessarily negative and can be taken as a signal of alert. In fact, questioning is a vital part of being an African-American woman in the mainstream cultural setting at this point in social history. The questioning allows black women to be conscious of their individual/collective goals and aspirations vis-à-vis the purpose and functions of the roles or niches they occupy. The questioning forces a re-examination of the values of black women. Exposure to the mainstream culture does not leave one devoid of its influence. Black women realize this and combat those influences daily. If the questioning regarding the value and purpose of the new role is prolonged it may produce a general sense of alienation, inactivity, and confusion. In a clinical sense, it may produce psychosomatic illness, insomnia, depression, stress, and anxiety reactions.

Black women begin the questioning process by attempting to adapt to a neurotic environment which does not in any real way validate their existence as unified individual/collective selves. The questioning may begin by asking themselves how they are perceived by the collective as well as how they perceive their collective identity. Black women with a high degree of contact with the mainstream culture often suspect that the collective community views them as existing outside of it. This suspicion may be an accurate one considering that a high degree of contact with mainstream culture lies outside of the immediate experience of the majority of Black America. Further, it may be accurate considering that becoming highly involved in the mainstream culture is often accompanied by perceived social amnesia—wherein many "mainstreamed" black women not only move out of the black community but also attempt to deny that they were ever a part of it. As a result, they may conclude that the community does not understand their total identity, and also they may feel that their mainstream status is a wedge between themselves and the collective community. They are not affirmed in the mainstream nor their communities. This may result in black women feeling that they have no kinship to important elements in their lives.

CASE DESCRIPTION

The person described for the illustration of the individual/collective theory became a national figure because of the tragedy of her life.

Lenita McClain, 32, black woman, professional journalist, winner of the Peter Lisagor Award from the Headline Club (The Chicago Chapter of Sigma Delta Chi, the national journalism honorary fraternity); the 1983 Kizzy Award for outstanding black women role models; and the top honors from the Chicago Association of Black Journalists for commentary. First black to become member of the *Chicago Tribune's* editorial board with a salary of approximately $50,000. Individually and collectively she was part of the first generation of recognizable numbers of corporate African-American women. Last year in March 1984 she was selected by *Glamour* as one of the ten most outstanding working women in America. Two months later she committed suicide.

Presented are several statements written by McClain in *Newsweek's* (October 1980) column, "My Turn."

It is impossible for me to forget where I came from as long as I am prey to the jive hustler who does not hesitate to exploit my childhood friendship. I am reminded, too, when I go back to the old neighborhood in fear— and have my purse snatched—and when I sit down to a business lunch and have an old classmate wait on my table.

I wait at the bus stop with attaché case, I meet my aunt getting off the bus with other cleaning ladies on their way to do my neighbor's floors.

I am burdened daily with showing whites that blacks are people. I am, in the old vernacular, a credit to my race. I am my brother's keeper, and my sisters', though many of them have abandoned me because they think I have abandoned them.

Some of my "liberal" white acquaintances pat me on the head, hinting that I am a freak, that my success is less a matter of talent than of luck and affirmative action. I may live among them, but it is difficult to live with them. How can they be sincere about respecting me, yet hold my fellows in contempt? And, if I am silent when they attempt to sever me from my own how can I live with myself?

I have worked for these amenities and deserve them, though I can never enjoy them without feeling guilty. These comforts do not make me less black, nor oblivious to the woe in which many of my people are drowning. As long as we are denigrated as a group, no one of us has made it. Inasmuch as we all suffer from every one left behind, we all gain for everyone who conquers the hurdle. (p. 21)

THERAPEUTIC IMPLICATIONS

During this social period the movement of black women has the potential of becoming a powerful force in changing mainstream culture. In this respect, many black women occupy roles previously unavailable to them as a social group and are attempting to draw from them those things which are useful to them as individuals and as a collective. They recognize the new areas are a threat to their individual/collective identities, yet, they also understand the tremendous potential of such opportunities.

The potential lies in black women's ability to create an alternative and perhaps an enhanced life-style. No one can deny the impact of black liberation and feminist theories upon the overall consciousness (and in some cases, behavior) of society. If black women are able to carve out a space consistent with the reality of their experiences it will have a rippling effect throughout society. The process is both empowering and exhausting as it means they must develop their own potential and change society too.

It may be essential for the alternative mainstream life-style to develop within the confines of previously all-white and all-male structures of American society. Furthermore, because of black women's personal and social historical position, the development of an alternative life-style may be impossible without them. For black women who are involved in such a development, the struggle that ensues between mainstream culture and themselves is one of necessity and not of choice. The challenge for black women is to remain who they are in the previously unavailable areas and maintain their cultural integrity, as well as to be instrumental in the development of viable approaches that make their reality the fundamental basis for psychological adjustment.

African-American women who maintain a strong collective identity (i.e., identify themselves as part of the collective and recognize the similarities between the community experience and their experiences in the mainstream culturally) are affirmed by the collective community in their totality. Black women who recognize that their experience in the mainstream culture is an individual as well as a collective one find the African-American community also recognizes their mainstream experience as being an important aspect of their collective experience. In this regard, black women in the mainstream often find that the collective community has collective pride in the knowledge that one from the community has taken advantage of the opportunities which exist in the mainstream environment.

SUMMARY

As the numbers of black women who enter mainstream culture and therapy continue to grow, these issues will have to be addressed. In conjunction with these issues, others will have to be readdressed. On a global level the politics and ideology of psychological research involving African-Americans will need to be thoroughly examined. For example, if one considers psychology's approach to the study of African-Americans and women, one sees that it attempts to study the relationships in the world devoid of context, particularly ethnic and gender contexts. This approach denies the material reality of existence—the objective world. This is not only a denial of the world and of the people as they exist in it, but it is also a distortion of the world.

In a survey of the psychological literature on black women during the period between 1960 and 1980, one finds the term matriarch to have been quite popular in the psychological literature. It was applied most often to black women but was applied to other Third World women. The literature implicitly and explicitly stated that the matriarchal family pattern was deviant and pathological. Black women who headed households were identified as causing developmental problems for their children, especially their male children. One study (Rosen, 1969) suggested that the factor of matriarchy may be one of the "original causes" which "push" a lower class black male into delinquency. The single parent family was a "social and sociological problem" (Burgess, 1970).

While it is not necessary to point out that since 1970 the number of women who had households has increased dramatically and that since 1980 women constitute the majority of the work force, it is necessary to contrast this information with the fact that the number of matriarchs has increased and the once popular term (label, if you will) has not been applied. In addition, the number of working women has increased dramatically. The literature does not view the new working woman as it did the woman who worked during the 1960s and 1970s.

Within a real world context, we see the tremendous impact of changing social and economic conditions on family structure. Yet, as a result of the ideological aspect of psychology, "single parenting" is not viewed pathologically; the "career/working" woman is the norm. It is such distortion which is built into the psychological methods and perspectives that is responsible for the illusory aspects of the ideology.

The complexities of the psychologically based ideology and changing social phenomenon are apparent. For black women, the establishment and maintenance of themselves in terms of the reality of their individual/collective life experiences is crucial for their psychological and emotional wellness. The psychological health and emotional wellness of black women in mainstream culture is contingent upon the development and substance of their total being. The total identity of black women must be expressed and exhibited vis-à-vis individual/collective responsibilities within the mainstream environment.

From a research and therapeutic perspective, the abstraction of the African-American woman from the social context divorces her from her history. In this respect, the individualized approach is anti-historical and smacks of the selective affirmation process. It is necessary for black women to use their life experiences in their mainstream cultural interactions. For black women, the imitation of a white, male oriented life-style is absurd. Black women must bring to bear their unique perspective into psychological adjustment.

In this sense, black women must be partially detached as well as attached to the mainstream culture. The detachment allows for a critical analysis of the mainstream culture's responsibilities and their own individual/collective responsibilities as well as an understanding of the long-range effects of their presence and behavior in mainstream culture. It would be futile for black women to adopt a total stance of detachment from mainstream culture. They must attach themselves in such a manner that allows for clarity of direction. Black women in their attachment to mainstream culture must acquire a sensitive understanding of the particular problems with which their personhood and culture are being confronted.

Black women in the latter half of the 20th century are a new and different group within the social fabric of mainstream culture. The needs of black women are different. The situation calls for a radically different praxis that recognizes their isolation and alienation. Socially there is a need for the creation of an environment where there exists the ability to generate a critical analysis leading to the expression and development of individual/collective abilities within the mainstream culture.

Neither the mainstream culture nor black women will be the same as a result of the current social interaction. For black women, an affirmation of total identity is necessary. There must be affirmation of themselves as AFRICAN-AMERICAN WOMEN and challenge others to respond to them in their totality. The affirmation of the realities of black women, particularly within psychology, will be especially difficult given the history of ethnocentric and gender biases found within the discipline. Despite the difficulty, it is the task that is before us.

REFERENCES

Allport, G. W. (1954). *The nature of prejudice.* Reading, MA: Addison Wesley.

Burgess, J. K. (1970). The single-parent family: A social and sociological problem. *Family Coordinator, 19,* 137–144.

Gardner, L. H. (1980). Racial, ethnic, and social class considerations in psychotherapy supervision. In A. Hess (Ed.), *Psychotherapy supervision: Theory, research, and practice.* New York: John Wiley & Sons.

Jackson, G. G. (1979). The origin and development of black psychology: Implications for black studies and human behavior. *Studia Africana, 3,* 270–293.

Kelly, G. A. (1955). *A theory of personality.* New York: Norton.

Lorion, R. P. (1974). Patient and therapist variables in the treatment of low-income patients. *Psychological Bulletin, 81,* 344–354.

McClain, L. (1980, October). The middle-class black's burden. *Newsweek,* p. 21.

McCombs, H. G. (1985). Black self-concept: An individual/collective analysis. *International Journal of Intercultural Relations, 9,* 1–18.

Mead, G. H. (1934). *Mind, self, and society.* Chicago, IL: University of Chicago Press.

Nobles, W. W. (1972). African philosophy: Foundations for black psychology. In R. L. Jones (Ed.), *Black psychology.* New York: Harper and Row.

Rosen, L. (1969). Matriarchy and lower class Negro male delinquency. *Social Problems, 17,* 175–189.

Stetson, E. (1983). Black feminism in Indiana, 1893–1933. *Phylon, 44,* 292–298.

The Feminist Therapist and the Male Client

Zoya S. Slive

Television commercials now show men cooking gourmet dishes and changing babies' diapers. Does this mean that men have invaded the world of women, the way women have made inroads into men's work places? Does this mean men have become equal to women? Have stereotypical roles finally broken down?

Not quite. Upon further observation of the popular media, it seems that men still have the power to choose. It seems they have taken the goodies for themselves, leaving the women to do the dirty work. They are creative in the kitchen and have fun with the kids—after all, diapers are disposable today.

Do you ever see on TV a man sniff the foul odors in the bathroom or hold a discourse over the advantages of one wax product over another to make your kitchen floor shine? And what about the window washing commercials? The women are always on the inside looking out, while the men are outside, either suspended on ropes from the top of a high building or washing windows on the outside of a dreamy little house with an idyllic garden in the background.

It seems nothing has changed. Men are still out there enjoying the great outdoors, while women do the dirty work inside. Even when men do dangerous work, such as washing the windows of a skyscraper, they are rewarded by a peek inside the office of an attractive woman executive.

Or have things changed?

Turning to the real world, in the privacy of my office, I see other faces and hear different voices. I hear male voices that are not so happy. They are the voices of men who have suf-

---

Zoya Slive is affiliated with the Boston Psychological Center for Women, Inc. and is also in private practice at 1 Wallace Place, Cambridge, MA 02138.

fered and who are trying to break out of their traditional roles and stereotypical behavior. I see and hear men who want to live their lives according to new rules. I hear men searching for new self-definitions.

I do not know how representative these men are. Many of them are in therapy because they are depressed, because they are dissatisfied with their jobs and their relationships. Even if they are extreme cases, even if they possess an unusual amount of stress or even some pathology, they are probably not atypical.

If the women's movement has been good for the mental health of women, as Barnett, Baruch and Rivers (1983) have amply demonstrated, why should not the same feminist principles be good for the mental health of men as well? Perhaps men are finally realizing that patriarchy might give them power, but it does not give them happiness. In fact, patriarchy may be just as bad for their health as it is for the women's.

Take the case of a fifty-four year old man, divorced from a wife who subsequently died from a combination of alcohol and cancer, who is alienated and estranged from his children, who presents himself in therapy extremely depressed and self-castigating, barely able to function at work. He blames himself for his wife's demise, as well as the break-up of his family. His story reveals that as a young man, he was so busy making a living and forging ahead in his career, he never noticed the beginnings of his wife's decline.

His story further reveals that given the kind of background and upbringing he experienced, combined with a rigid division of labor in his marriage (which was typical for his time), it is unlikely that he could have noticed or have been aware of the genesis and early development of his wife's and his family's disintegration.

Now, at the age of fifty-four, he is very much aware of his tragedy and his attitude toward himself and toward women has changed drastically. He is desperately trying to survive, desperately trying to reconnect with his children and to salvage whatever relationship is possible with them. As with a rehabilitated individual, he would like to make a fresh start toward leading a very different life than the kind he led as a young man and in his maturity. It is a challenging undertaking and I would like to help him to achieve his goal.

Or take the case of a much younger man, in his middle

thirties, who is also depressed, who struggles with anger and frustration and occasional violent outbursts against his wife, who, in conjoint therapy, made an enormous effort to understand his violence and learn to control it. He understood that his problems derive from his predictable low self-esteem and low sense of self-worth as a child of an alcoholic parent. Additionally, he is beginning to understand his conflict and ambivalence toward his wife's career. On the one hand, he respects his wife, supports her and rejoices at her success and fulfillment. On the other, he deeply resents it, for the more successful and fulfilled she becomes, the more he feels himself to be locked into his present position, locked into a career which he chose at an early age "for all the wrong reasons," as he describes it now.

It was the American Dream which propelled him toward a professional career, one which allowed him to escape a dreary, oppressive family background, to become an unreproachable citizen, an outstanding provider, and, in his words, "to associate with nice people." In spite of his having achieved his initial goals, he is not happy. He does not like himself. Approaching mid-life, he is confused and depressed. He talks about wanting to quit his job and find a livelihood that would interest him more and be more meaningful to him and be more consistent with his values, even if it would pay him less. He does not know what that job could be, or how to achieve it.

But the crucial question is whether he will permit himself to make any significant changes. Will he permit himself to entertain the notion that he, like his wife, could also have an occupation which provides him with enjoyment, satisfaction and self-fulfillment? Thus, before he is able to make any effective changes, he must resolve many internalized social, cultural and class conflicts.

I would like to help him do that.

Or take the case of yet another man, a young doctor, who upon the birth of a second child, becomes terrified to touch his children, who is convinced that if he does, he will harm them in some way.

In therapy, he begins to see how his crisis has laid open some unresolved issues and trauma from his own childhood and adolescence, which in turn leads to a close and painful reexamination of his relationship to his own parents and his childhood. In therapy he can become a child again and deal with his infantile rages, his need for love and acceptance, and when satisfied can become a stronger and healthier adult. I am happy to serve in his re-mothering process and happy to help guide his growth and development.

Or take the case of a single father, who à la Kramer obtained custody of his child. In his case, however, it is a daughter. Against all odds, the demands of his jobs, and the intrusiveness of well-meaning grandparents, he is determined to raise his daughter himself. Not an easy task. Where can he go for support, understanding and guidance?

In therapy he talks a lot about what he would like for his daughter and his vision of the woman he would like her to be. Sometimes he gets discouraged at the enormity of his task.

I would like to help lighten his load.

There are other pertinent cases I could cite, but because of time constraints, these cases must suffice to support the following conclusions.

First, in spite of the fact that at first glance these cases of male clients may seem disparate because of the differences in presenting problems and issues dealt with in therapy, they have a common denominator.

Second, there is no doubt that these men have been influenced by the women's movement in terms of recognizing their own problems and in terms of wanting to be supportive of the women in their lives. The women's movement has helped give them a new awareness of relationships and a new desire for greater equality.

Third, they look at their careers from a new perspective, with new priorities and new expectations. Simply bringing home a paycheck is not sufficient for them. Their jobs must be more meaningful and more fulfilling.

These are not new criteria or aspirations for women, nor are they completely new for men, but today more men seem to apply them more freely, less apologetically. In my opinion, the women's movement has helped more men in our society—and I should add that they are mostly middle class men—to understand and seek self-fulfillment. Today more men are willing to make material sacrifices to attain it. More men are prepared to measure achievement and success at work against other needs. Trade-offs are made.

It is no longer a foregone conclusion that a man wi
success at work as a sine qua non. In my practice I
creasingly seen men who view their fathers as negat
models. They are eager to avoid making their fathe.., mistakes. These men want to spend more time with their children.
As one man said to me, "I don't want to wake up one morning
when I am fifty and realize, as with my own father, that I don't
know my children at all." He added that he would readily give
up a promotion if his efforts at setting limits and refusing to put
in overtime in order to spend more time with his children were
to be viewed critically by managers of his company.

Another man expressed the need to be closer to his own
father and made that a priority in his therapy. He believes
that by overcoming his anger and by better understanding his
father, he would relate better to his own children. He would
feel more loving toward them.

The nature of the father role and fathering is beginning to
be taken more seriously. It is no longer unusual to learn of
fathers fighting for the custody of their children and of judges
inclined to consider the father as a viable parent.

The Association for Psychoanalytic Medicine and the American Academy of Psychoanalysis recently held seminars on the
psychology of men and issues of male identity and relationships.
It is safe to predict that educators, psychologists and researchers
will look increasingly at the degree and quality of involvement
of fathers in the psychological development of their young children. This will lead to reexaminations and debates, sometimes
heated, over the process of attachment and separation, identification and identity formation, oedipal issues and issues of ri-
valry and competition between father and son.

An important factor that unites the men in the cases I have
cited is courage. These men have the courage to come to therapy. They have the courage to acknowledge that they need to
make important changes in their lives. These changes involve
relationships, attitudes toward work, values and priorities. But
above all, these changes involve new self-definitions and new
images of masculinity.

When we consider that in the course of their transformation
these men must ask themselves very painful questions which
entail painful comparisons and conclusions, their courage to
continue their quest becomes more notable. They may no

longer subscribe to aspects of what society considers masculine and macho. Yet they may not be certain if they can reject all of these traditional attributes outright. For example what can they offer women if women are able to acquire status, prestige, security and protection on their own? What is the glue that is going to hold their relationships with women together?

Jung once characterized American men as emotionally lazy, with their libidos totally directed toward their work. Today characterization needs modification, but admittedly not a radical one. The number of men becoming more comfortable with their emotions and new self-definitions remains small, and sadly we can expect further setbacks, particularly in the present political and social climate. Without a movement such as the women's movement, and with little support from other men, it will be a long while before men in great numbers will find and trust their new selves.

Perhaps their predicament helps explain why some men seek out women therapists and particularly feminist therapists who are principally concerned with the process of self-exploration and the choices that new gender images may present.

Moreover, many men are more comfortable with a woman therapist than a male therapist. They expect women therapists to be more accepting, less judgmental. They find them less threatening. They need not compete with them, or pretend to be strong, when they feel weak and vulnerable.

And what do I as a feminist therapist feel when I work with a male client? Surprisingly, much less of a difference than I would have anticipated a decade ago.

Yes, I am aware that my male clients, by virtue of gender, have more power by and large, more opportunities, and are likely to have been less victimized than my female clients.

Yet, they too are dealing with change, growth, transformation and new self-definitions. They are making decisions, choices, and trade-offs. Although they are likely to be in more privileged positions, their self-examinations are no less painful than those of my female clients.

They prefer not to take the traditional safer road offered by society or their social class, but instead take a lonelier, more risky and untried path. The path is hazardous and the equipment they carry can become a heavy burden.

Sometimes we recognize very familiar patterns. Unquestioned values rear their heads. The habit of blaming others or the habits of denial, passivity and avoidance present themselves as seemingly insurmountable obstacles.

In brief, for a feminist therapist, working with a male client is not unlike working with a female client. When working with women, the challenge is often to channel their anger in constructive ways and to help them discard their roles as victims in order to achieve their goals.

Similarly, the challenge with men is to help them reframe or reformulate their problems by encouraging them to use their new values and new criteria for the sake of their new objectives.

Why would a feminist therapist be willing to take on the burdens of men? Don't we have enough problems of our own? Of course we do.

Many women and most feminist therapists chose a separatist path. I did too, to some extent. I chose to affiliate myself with an organization that treats women primarily, the Boston Psychological Center for Women. It was a political decision, made about ten years ago, in order to help narrow the gap between the number of women seeking therapy and the number of women providing therapy.

It was also made with the belief, which I still hold, that in our time, not only do women better understand women's problems, they also deal with them better. I also believe that the time has come for women and men to work together to shape a vision of our future. We can join forces with men who realize that the women's movement has been a healthy, reinvigorating cultural movement, with a far-reaching impact in private and public life; and with men who are engaged in self-exploration and the examination of their images of masculinity and the choices these images pose.

Much is at stake. The courageous choices made today by women and men will have far-reaching impact on future generations of heroines and heroes.

REFERENCES

Barnett, R., Baruch., G. and Rivers, C. (1983) *Lifeprints: New patterns of love and work for today's woman.* New York: McGraw-Hill Book Company.

Psychoanalytic Resources
for the Activist Feminist Therapist

Mary Hayden

> We must constantly encourage ourselves and each other
> to attempt the heretical actions that our dreams imply.
>
> *Audre Lorde*

As feminists we have a commitment to the liberation of
human beings from the oppressive patriarchal structures into
which we have been socialized. If we believe that the personal
is profoundly political, it is our obligation to understand and
evaluate every method for releasing the human psyche from
bondage and allowing it to emerge free and whole. For many
feminists, psychoanalysis seems an unlikely resource to draw
on for this task; they have written it off as a hopelessly phallocentric theory put into practice by a medical establishment
intent on pacifying a predominantly female patient population. While there is much truth in this characterization of
psychoanalysis as it has evolved historically, I hope in this
paper to reclaim the radical social critique and revolutionary
agenda which has always been inherent in the psychoanalytic
method even when unacknowledged or actively suppressed by
Freud and his patriarchal successors. I hope to show also that
the central method of psychoanalysis, free association and
exploration of the unconscious in a relationship of trust and
dedication to truth, is a model of human growth with great
potential social impact.

In order to appreciate the power tapped by the psychoanalytic method before it was burdened by patriarchal assumptions, we return to the early case of Anna O., whose real name
was Bertha Pappenheim, and who was treated by Freud's older
colleague, Josef Breuer. Breuer, who regularly used hypnosis,

Mary Hayden is in private practice at 16 S. Oakland, #212, Pasadena, CA 91101.

found that in her case of hysteria it was not very helpful. What did seem to be curative, as Akhter Ahsen points out in a reinterpretation of the case (1974), was the patient's own catharsis of her terrifying feelings through what she called "the talking cure," or jokingly, "chimney-sweeping." This cure proceeded on her own timetable as she relived the painful events surrounding her father's death until her disabling symptoms disappeared. While the nurturing ministrations and consistent interest of Breuer were apparently important to the unfolding of the patient's story, she herself was able to face the fear and pain of her repressed feelings without interpretation or manipulation by her doctor.

Having confronted her fears and found her strength, Bertha Pappenheim was free to express herself fully. In her subsequent career as a social activist and writer she founded agencies which served the needs of victimized women and children and campaigned for an end to sexism in Jewish civil law. She proclaimed, "To know of wrong and remain quiet makes one partly guilty." She did not remain silent; she crusaded for women's rights through her prolific writing, which included a German translation of Mary Wollstonecraft's "A Vindication of the Rights of Women." She had found her voice and she used it.

What is interesting from a feminist point of view is that Freud had difficulty accepting that Anna O. was really cured (Breuer & Freud, 1957). Furthermore, he failed to make much of her achievements as a social activist, feminist writer, and educator. The fact that he could not acknowledge female power when he saw it emerging, first in the unconscious, and then in the life of a talented and creative woman, leads me to believe that from the beginning Freud was threatened by the outcome of the very process he discovered.

This view is substantiated by the facts (Masson, 1984) surrounding Freud's suppression of the truth about incest which occurred in his female patients' families. Freud originally reported this information to his colleagues, but later retracted it in order to protect the image of his dead father and to insure his own professional advancement (Freud, 1977). Freud had to betray the truth his own method had revealed because it threatened the basic patriarchal myth of the benevolent father.

Freud's subsequent formulations of infantile sexuality and

the Oedipus complex focus on the desires of the child and completely exclude a consideration of the dynamics of power in the patriarchal family. From the female vantage point it is clear that Freud's theory selectively distorts the data that Freud's method yielded. This is shown dramatically by French feminist Marie Balmary. She argues in her book *Psychoanalyzing Psychoanalysis* (1979) that one can use psychoanalytic method on Freud's writings to reveal the conflicts that caused him to avoid bringing "the hidden fault of the father" to light.

Balmary looks in Freud's narratives for significant omissions and symptoms with unexplained causes; these, when analyzed, show how he used his theories to repress the insights his clinical method produced. Her work is an exciting demonstration that psychoanalytic method can be used to unseat Freudian theory. It also suggests interesting avenues for feminist theorists who want to explore the ways in which male intrapsychic conflicts blind them, like Oedipus, to the defects of patriarchal authority.

Freud, in his early work with women, stumbled upon what modern revolutionaries know: that when oppressed people begin to talk they discover their power. When oppressed people probe their deepest fears and pains in an atmosphere of trust, they tap a rich repository of power which has been driven into the unconscious because it is forbidden expression in daily life.

Freud was unable to acknowledge the most revolutionary aspects of his work with the unconscious, but some of his successors, whose contributions have been obscured by history, were dedicated to a political psychoanalysis. In an interesting book called *The Repression of Psychoanalysis* (1983) Russell Jacoby describes a brief period in the late 1920s and early 30s when a circle of analysts, many of whom were women, exchanged secret letters in which they discussed the radical potential of psychoanalysis. They included Otto Fenichel, Annie and Wilhelm Reich, Edith Jacobson, and Kate Friedlander. This group did not share Freud's victim-blaming interpretation of the childhood origin of neurosis. Both Reich and Fenichel agreed that Freud was avoiding a critique of the social order by attributing the cause of human suffering to internal drives rather than to external oppression.

The political Freudians hoped to keep their ideas and their community alive even in exile from Nazism. However, this was not to be. In the United States, where most of them sought asylum and a new life, analysis was taken over by the medical establishment and women were pushed out. An individualistic, pathology-oriented, biological model replaced the broader historical and political scope of European psychoanalysis. This left the development of radical political ideas to male Marxists.

I think that remembering the political Freudians is useful because they shared some of the same quarrels with Marxists that contemporary feminists have. Jacoby remarks that they were always fighting on the one hand against analysts who had no appreciation of social reality and on the other hand against Marxists who had no appreciation of individual reality. Feminists, both in America and Europe, who have looked to Marxism for its social vision, have been disappointed by its inattention to the personal dimensions of collective experience (MacKinnon, 1982). Furthermore, when feminists such as Chodorow (1978) and Dinnerstein (1976) have tried to combine psychoanalytic theory with sociological theory, they have tended to see the direction of causation as one way—from social to individual (Elshtain, 1982). Although their analyses are incisive commentaries on the way patriarchal gender arrangements shape the human psyche, they fail to include a consideration of how individuals affect society. This dimension is much needed if we are to create a dynamic account of how the personal is political.

In the last decade feminists have begun to appropriate the method and language of psychoanalysis in order to create a new vision of humanity in community. Jacoby's (1983) characterization of the political Freudians could only apply equally well to them: "(They) sought to remain loyal both to the depth dimensions of psychoanalysis—its unconscious and erotic levels—and its humanist implications" (p. 23). Intriguing ideas for such a feminist psychoanalysis are proposed by political scientist Jean Bethke Elshtain in an essay for the *Signs* issue on feminst theory (1982). There she calls for a return to the Freud who celebrated the inexhaustible and infinitely expressive aspects of the human psyche, which we glimpse through slips of the tongue, humor, and dreams. This is, of course, the Freud who was open to the unconscious. She writes, "If psychoanalytic feminism begins to move in these directions, it will make contact with speech, identity, and action along the whole range of public and private possibilities" (p. 142).

Because psychoanalytic theory posits a storehouse of energy at the core of the individual it allows for the development of a fully interactive model of human beings in community. Informed by feminist ideas, this emergent psychoanalysis is non-dualistic, that is, holistic. Rigid dichotomies between mind and body, spirit and sensuality, inner and outer reality are replaced by more dynamic and relational descriptions of experience in this kind of theory. This new psychoanalysis fully welcomes the power for personal and social transformation which lies in the unconscious.

In individual psychotherapy as well as still-to-be created collective efforts, consciousness-deepening can occur alongside consciousness-raising. Feminist therapists and educators can demystify psychoanalytic concepts relating to power—identification with the aggressor, the self-hate of victims, and the projection of disowned feelings onto the less powerful—and make them widely understood. Even in traditional treatment settings therapists can affirm their work as a radical social project whenever they probe their clients' deepest terrors, rages, dreams, and desires. Feminists can acknowledge that a surface psychology of survival skills and coping methods is not enough; we are as women attempting to create a new psychosocial identity.

In order to accomplish this task we need a depth psychology which allows us to tunnel down through layers of oppression and pain to reclaim the self submerged there. Underneath self-hate, fear of punishment, and terror of one's own power, women who look inward discover two potent resources: anger and the erotic. In the course of psychotherapy, anger about injustice in the world often supercedes private agony over personal legacies of pain. Feminist therapists do not seek to defuse such rage or find a quiet solution for it. Action to create a more humane world is a logical response to experiencing dehumanization and should be supported. Similarly, the erotic, once fraught with shame and fear, becomes a capacity for enjoyment in ways that truly satisfy. In poet Audre Lorde's words:

> When we begin to live from within outward, in touch with the power of the erotic within ourselves, and allowing that

power to inform our actions upon the world around us, then we begin to be responsible to ourselves in the deepest sense. . . . Our acts against oppression become integral with self, motivated and empowered from within. (1984, p. 58)

As we feminists face what looks like the formidable power of patriarchal structures surrounding us we need to remember that the transformation of society that we must have if we are to survive will not come by mimicking the power strategies of our oppressors. It is by redefining power in terms of self-determination and cooperation among equals that we will ultimately create the world that our humanity demands. Meanwhile we must draw strength for the struggle from the deepest recesses of our minds and hearts and learn to share with each other the riches we find there.

REFERENCES

Ahsen, A. (1974). Anna O.—Patient or therapist? An eidetic view. In V. Franks & V. Burtle. *Women in therapy: New psychotherapies for a changing society.* New York: Brunner/Mazel.

Balmary, M. (1979). *Psychoanalyzing psychoanalysis: Freud and the hidden fault of the father.* Baltimore, MD: Johns Hopkins University Press.

Breuer, J. & Freud, S. (1957). *Studies on Hysteria.* New York: Basic Books.

Chodorow, N. (1978). *The reproduction of mothering: Psychoanalysis and the sociology of gender.* Berkeley, CA: University of California Press.

Dinnerstein, D. (1976). *The mermaid and the minotaur: Sexual arrangements and human malaise.* New York: Harper & Row.

Elshtain, J. B. (1982). Feminist discourse and its discontents: Language, power and meaning. In N. O. Keohane, M. Z. Rosaldo, & B. C. Gelpi (Eds.), *Feminist theory: A critique of ideology.* Chicago: University of Chicago Press.

Freud, S. (1977). *The origins of psychoanalysis: Letters to Wilhelm Fliess* (M. Bonaparte, A. Freud, & E. Kris, Eds.; E. Mosbacher & J. Strachey, Trans.). New York: Basic Books.

Jacoby, R. (1983). *The repression of psychoanalysis.* New York: Basic Books.

Lorde, A. (1984). *Sister outsider.* Trumansburg, NY: The Crossing Press.

Masson, J. (1984). *The assault on truth: Freud's suppression of the seduction theory.* New York: Farrar, Straus & Giroux.

MacKinnon, C. (1982). Feminism, Marxism, Method, and the State: An Agenda for Theory. In N. O. Keohane, M. Z. Rosaldo & B. C. Gelpi (Eds.), *Feminist theory: A critique of ideology.* Chicago: University of Chicago Press.

A Feminist Examination of Family Therapy: What Is Women's Place?

Michele Bograd

As a feminist and as a psychologist, I experience a professional and personal tension in my clinical work. I am well aware that psychotherapy is potentially a sexist social institution, and that as a psychotherapist I can unwittingly contribute to women's oppression by using psychological models biased against women, employing male-defined standards of mental health that devalue or render deficient women's psychological strengths, or utilizing techniques that perpetuate traditional and restrictive gender-defined behaviors. For several years, I found a balance between my feminist and clinical ideologies in my work as a family therapist.

There is little overt evidence in family systems theory of the blatant sexist biases evident in earlier psychoanalytic models of female development. Compatible with a feminist perspective, most family therapists do not use traditional psychiatric labels. They also examine the social context for determinants of behavior and value concrete behavioral change. Women are emerging as leaders in the family therapy field and, as therapists, can experiment with active directive techniques that expand our interactional repertoire beyond more traditional female styles of empathy and nurturance. While family therapists have historically ignored the issue of gender in systems theory and interventions, there has been a growing interest in the last several years in women's place in family therapy.

In general, however, a feminist examination of family therapy has tended to suggest modifications of family systems the-

Michele Bograd is in private practice at 50 Chauncey Street, Watertown, MA 02172.

ory, as if sensitivity to women's issues can simply be assimilated into current systemic models. In contrast, I'd like to suggest that such simple modifications may not adequately create a place for women in family systems theory. The construction of such a place may rely on a more radical critique of family systems theory that necessitates a restructuring of the basic theoretical axioms of family systems theory and requires a critical reassessment of our roles as family therapists.

Although there are important theoretical and technical differences between major schools of family therapy, I will use general and non-technical terms to highlight feminist concerns common to the field as a whole. After suggesting possible sexist biases reflected in everyday family therapy interventions, I will examine facets of family systems theory that shape these practices and that make it difficult to pose certain questions about the place of women in families and in family systems theory.

What is women's place in family therapy? In general, the family systems literature does not address the role of women in the family nor the position of women as a class. Since family therapists seek information on the organization of the system, on how parts reciprocally interact with each other, it is not within the function of family systems theory to identify any family position as of particular concern or interest (Goldner, 1985; James & McIntyre, 1983). Furthermore, family therapists attempt to understand the integrity and rules of a system as it is based on the assumption that many forms of family systems can accomplish functions necessary to our society. Because of this, family therapists tend to avoid prescribing a particular family structure or type of male/female relationship as appropriate, normal or healthy. The ostensible neutrality of family therapists on issues of women and their appropriate roles contributes to rendering these issues invisible (Jacobson, 1983).

But invisible does not mean non-existent. Profeminist family therapists have recently suggested that most family therapists tacitly hold to an ideal of traditional family structure characterized by the gender-based allocation of instrumental and expressive roles, which is viewed as normative and necessary to mental health (Goldner, 1985; Hare-Mustin, 1978, 1980; Margolin, 1983; Nichols, 1984; Women's Project in Family therapy, a,b). This ideal of working father, housewife mother and children ignores the fact that 60% of all women ages 18–64 are in the workforce, and that one out of seven families are headed by women. Furthermore, this ideal shapes many family systems theoretical models and interventions and may lead to sexist biases, in theory and in practice.

A radical feminist analysis of psychology and culture reveals that reality as we understand it is male-defined, rendering the experiences of women invisible and unrecorded. Family systems theory utilizes language based on cybernetic models, which is ostensibly scientific and value-free. But closer examination of family therapy language suggests that it may contain sexist biases. First, key terms in family systems theory reflect prototypically male ideas as standards of mental health. Family therapists focus on dimensions such as hierarchy, differentiation and boundaries. The most clearcut example of this is Murray Bowen's Differentiation of Self scale that defines the well-adjusted individuals as one who is characterized by rational objectivity, the ability to separate thought and emotion, and the capacity to free him- or herself from a relationship context (Hare-Mustin, 1978). From such a point of view, women are often described as enmeshed, undifferentiated or overinvolved. The issue here is not to deny the value of all family therapy concepts, but to question the utility of one-dimensional concepts where the prototypically male pole is valued and the prototypically female pole is defined as unhealthy (Women's Project in Family Therapy, b). A feminist perspective redefines female qualities as sources of strength, rather than as evidence of the deficiency of women. Instead of enmeshment, a feminist family therapist substitutes such terms as interdependence, intimacy, capacity for communion. Such women-defined standards of relationships are sadly lacking in the family systems literature. Their inclusion might necessitate a fundamental restructuring of basic family therapy concepts.

A second way that family systems language is male-defined is the way in which sequences of behaviors are punctuated. The building blocks of family systems theory and interventions are the description of transactional sequences. While family therapists acknowledge that how behavioral sequences are described depends on the viewpoint of the observer, they present systemic formulations as if they are neutral descriptions of a system. Closer examination from a feminist perspective, however, suggests that such descriptions reflect a male-oriented view of the system, and often contain common sexist stereotypes biased against women. For example, let us examine how family systems therapists sometimes construct a systemic formulation of incest.

First, there is the behavioral description. The father is sexually involved with his daughter. The mother/daughter relationship is estranged. The daughter has a parentified role. The mother takes little or no action against the father. Second, there is the systematic formulation of these behaviors, which is an *interpretive* statement that writes in the presumed motivation of individual family members. This often reads: the mother abdicates her sexual role, forcing the daughter to take her place. The father, filled with sexual tension, uses his daughter for nurturance and gratification. The mother colludes with the tryst to alleviate her own feelings of inadequacy. Note how prevalent sexual cultural assumptions about wifehood, male prerogative, and sexuality inform this formulation. They include: (1) a wife owes her husband sexual fulfillment; (2) men are driven by sexual tensions tht demand immediate release; (3) when a wife refuses her husband sex, it is his prerogative to seek other outlets; (4) the wife's inability to protect her daughter is evidence that she has failed as a mother.

A feminist systemic formulation of incest explicitly seeks to illuminate the woman's perspective. It is the father who has failed as parent and husband. He has not simply discharged sexual tension in deviant ways, but has abused his power. The mother takes no action, not because she supports the incest, but because she is immobilized and lacks power in and out of the family. The daughter complies with father because she has little choice by virtue of being a female child. The feminist systemic reformulation, which identifies, validates and renders visible the experiences of women, is not simply a question of semantics. Such a formulation challenges family therapists to evaluate the biases they bring to their examination of family process and structure.

When family therapists employ systemic formulations that are biased against women, they may unwittingly use these formulations to guide clinical interventions and treatment goals, which in turn may perpetuate culturally dominant notions of the proper place of men and women. Take the prototypic family structure that family therapists commonly describe as composed of peripheral disengaged father and overinvolved mother enmeshed with symptomatic child. The treatment plan normally entails efforts to engage the father with the child and to reduce the mother's involvement. It has been suggested that potent meta-messages about the roles of men and women are communicated with this intervention (Women's Project in Family Therapy, b). The mother's involvement is labeled problematic as the power attributed to the father by virtue of his distance and place in the public sphere is reinforced. Bringing back father is seen as the key to solving the problem. "Restoring" him to power (as if he does not already yield considerable control over the family) is often at the cost of the mother's own limited role in the family.

Even when family therapists are sensitive to such issues, we can relate to our female clients in ways that require them to be "good" conventional women. Because women are often more attuned to emotional nuances and relationship issues, we often rely on wives to be compliant clients. We can enlist their aid in engaging their husbands in treatment, even as our systemic formulations indict the wife for undermining her husband or for keeping him out of the family. It is evident how family therapists take for granted the wife's commitment to therapy when we see how much attention is paid in the family therapy literature to the issue of how to engage the husband in treatment. In this way, family therapists place more emphasis on male participation (Robbins, 1983). This reinforces the idea that wives should accommodate themselves to their relationships, and simultaneously acknowledges the wife's skills in feelings and interpersonal relationships, while devaluing their importance.

These examples are only the tip of the iceberg. As I began to examine my own practice as a family therapist, I became aware of how often I unconsciously suggest tasks that are gender-specific; how I will ask the wife about the child's developmental history and the husband about finances; how I will request that couples negotiate behavioral contracts that reinforce that the wife should be willing to compromise and to bargain for her rights (Jacobson, 1983; Margolin, 1983); how impatient I sometimes feel with emotional and angry women who won't rationally dialogue with their detached and distant husbands, while I turn to these same women for support in facilitating the expression of feelings. Because I consider myself to be a family therapist sensitive to women's issues and sexism, I began to wonder why I had been so blind to these previously subtle and now glaringly blatant biases. I realized that there are facets of family systems theory that had limited my vision. I will address these through discussion of the role of the social context in family therapy and of the concept of power in family systems theory.

From its inception, family therapy has emphasized that the family as a system is embedded in and reciprocally interrelated to the larger social context. But in practice, family therapists tend to focus on the nuclear family as a relatively closed system. In this way, family therapists are not systemic enough because they minimize the impact of culture and the ways in which family structure and society form a circular self-perpetuating cycle. Currently, family therapists approach transactional patterns between men, women and children as if they are a function of each individual family system. This focus on the internal functioning of the family leads to the family being viewed as an interpersonal event, detached from the socio-historical context, which privitizes the family and ascribes responsibility to individual family members for their transactional patterns (Goldner, 1985; James & McIntyre, 1983; Lerner, 1983; Margolin et al., 1983).

Take again the common clinical formulation of peripheral father, overinvolved mother and symptomatic child. A family therapist might suggest that the child detours conflict away from the marital system, or that the husband's disengagement is a result of the wife's enmeshment with her mother, or that the child's acting out protects the mother from her own depression. This intrafamilial focus ignores that this family structure is a feature of most families in our society. When family therapists do not take into account how families are structured by extrafamilial forces and constraints, they may erroneously label certain processes as pathogenic, while ignoring the presence of other crucial transactional patterns. A focus on the internal functioning of the family also suggests that it is due to the idiosyncratic personal histories of the individual husband

and wife, rather than to the rules characterizing male/female relationships in society-at-large (Goldner, 1985; Hare-Mustin, 1980; Lerner, 1983).

If the social context were included in family systems theory, this would increase the explanatory power of systemic formulations through description of extrafamilial factors that constrain change and would broaden the range of available interventions. For example, the beginning of a more comprehensive systemic formulation of the infamous triangle might read: mother is intensely engaged with the child because she is isolated as a housewife and because women are designated as primary caretakers of children. In a position of limited power in the domestic sphere, she allies with even more powerless child against her husband who is richly joined to the public domain and who has material and symbolic resources available to him through his culturally defined role as a man and as a husband. Rather than focusing on the woman's role simply as wife or as mother, a therapeutic intervention might be to facilitate the woman's entrance into extrafamilial life with recognition of the familial and social forces that would oppose this move.

This example suggests that family systems theory is comprised of constructs that have the potential and flexibility to describe the reciprocal relationship between family processes and structures and the larger society in ways that could ameliorate current biases against women in family therapy. Although the social context is commonly excluded in systemic formulations, this could be remedied without a radical revision of family systems theory. But there is another element of a feminist critique that family therapists cannot address because of the limitations of family systems theory. This is the dimension of power and the context of inequality that exists between men and women, husbands and wives.

Power and inequality, as defined by feminists, do not have a place in family therapy. More precisely stated, the theoretical framework of family systems theory precludes examination of the unequal distribution of power. This occurs in two ways. First, an axiom of family systems theory is that men and women constitute a system characterized by circular causality and reflexive relationships in which their behaviors mutually influence and constrain the other. In discussion of these interrelated parts, the issue of gender is virtually ignored in family therapy. While some family therapists appear to address the issue of power as they examine the structural dimensions of hierarchy in families, they focus almost solely on the appropriate generational boundaries between parents and children. Family therapists rarely address the social reality of the hierarchical relationship between husbands and wives and ignore the question of inequality, because there is no emphasis on one member of the family having unidirectional or greater influence than any other member (Hoffman, 1981). Instead, male/female relationships are approached as complementary mutually regulated interactions of oppressor and oppressed where each part plays an equivalent functional role in maintaining the system (Libow et al., 1982). From this perspective, inequality disappears since the powerless are defined as playing as significant a part in their oppression as are the powerful.

In the second popular family systems approach to power, power does not simply disappear, it is defined as theoretically irrelevant. A leading family systems theorist states that power is simply a metaphor, a way of looking at the world that is outside the circular epistemology of self-correcting systems because it reflects the erroneous application of a linear epistemology that is not part of the theoretical base of family systems theory. He states that the epistemological habit of punctuating the world in terms of power leads to interventions and conceptual distinctions that are neither ecologically pure nor pragmatically effective (Keeney, 1983). With this statement, political issues are collapsed into questions of metatheory.

In contrast, feminists believe that symptoms in women are often a result of a clear and unambiguous unequal hierarchical relationship between husband and wife. While acknowledging that there are transactional components to dominant/subordinate dynamics that help maintain the unequal power relationship, feminists do not underestimate the reality of domination. From this perspective, the current no-fault view of family dynamics or the view that power is not a clinically useful construct victimizes the member of the family who is least powerful, almost always the woman. Feminists challenge systemic notions of power and inequality by suggesting that part of the system, the man, exerts unilateral influence and control over the other family members. Out of an analysis of gender and power in families, feminists view the traditional family structure as anything but ideal for it is the basic unit of male power through which men have institutionalized physical and coercive access to women.

I believe that were family therapists to take seriously the concept of power and to accept it as a pragmatically and conceptually important distinction, his would necessitate a radical restructuring of family systems theory, a questioning of the ideal of the traditional nuclear family, and a redefinition of the goals of family therapy. We would need to expand our notions of the functional equivalence of parts of a system. For example, an early systems theorist suggests that models of mutual interactionism fail to allow some variables in the system to have primacy or priority over others (Buckley, 1967). If we take as a given that men as a class have unilateral control over women, then we must revise the basic systemic assumption which makes impossible the discussion of this reality.

When inequality is recognized as a notion that has conceptual, clinical and real world consequences, then as family therapists we will need to grapple with questions that are at the heart of our clinical practices—and which are rarely addressed in the family systems literature. The first question is: As family therapists, are our primary loyalties to the family as a system or to its individual members? Many family therapists are advocates for the system as a whole because we assume that restructuring the system will ultimately benefit each of its members. But a feminist perspective suggests that the requirements of a conventional family system may entail the subordination of the personal needs of individuals, most typically the wife and mother. But if as feminists we choose to take an active role as advocates for the women in the family, this may destabilize the family as a unit. As a feminist family therapist, must I choose to advocate either for the woman or for the family—or is a compromise possible?

The second question is: Should family therapists promote certain kinds of family structures and processes as standards of appropriate family functioning? As I suggested earlier, most family therapists approach families with implicit values about the ideal family system, which generally reflect normative and traditional definitions of family life in contemporary culture. This is most evident in structural family therapy. Other models of family therapy take a more radical therapeutic position by stating that the therapist should remain studiously neutral regarding the final structure of the family. For example, many strategic therapists are interested primarily in symptom removal alone and not in restructuring the family. The newer systemic models of family therapy attempt to induce a crisis in the family in order to stimulate the system at a metalevel to change its typical way of changing. In this model, the therapist makes no value judgment about how the family reorganizes itself following a clinical intervention. Given social and cultural constraints, it is likely that most families will reorganize themselves along more or less conventional lines.

Since family therapists rarely examine the family as a social institution that is historically situated and maintained by the cultural context that the family reciprocally perpetuates, family therapists cannot and do not comment on what type of family structure is either desirable or viable, particularly regarding women's roles (James & McIntyre, 1983). By accepting the current family form as it is, or remaining silent on its effects on individual family members, family therapists can by default serve a conservative function by contributing to the maintenance of a traditional family structure. This is of particular concern to feminist family therapists since there is a substantial body of literature suggesting tht the roles of wife and mother as currently socially defined are not conducive to women's mental health.

The third question is: If family therapists believe the context of inequality in families may limit the development of both men and women, how do we define our role as therapeutic agents of change? Most commonly, family therapists define their primary task as that of treating the presenting problem of the family. But most families do not identify their presenting problem as that of inequality (Hare-Mustin, 1978; Margolin et al., 1983). Many families want symptom removal and do not seek a radical restructuring of family roles. If I follow the family's lead, I may help remove the symptom without addressing the social and familial context that created it (Klein, 1976). I can help people change their behaviors without significantly challenging the family status quo. Although I can focus on obvious family dysfunction, I may ignore the woman's willing conformity to traditional scripts that may not be in her long-range self-interest (Lerner, 1982). But is it my role as a family therapist to impose my values about the roles of women and the structure of male/female relationships on a family that may not desire these changes? If I respect the family's definition of what they want to change, do I contribute to maintaining a crucial and primary interpersonal context that perpetuates inequality between husbands and wives, if not that of women as a class?

I began this paper with the question: What is the place of women in family therapy? As a feminist, I explored the ways in which common family therapy approaches can be biased against women, either because systemic descriptions are based on stereotypic cultural images of male/female interactions or because systemic interventions reflect traditional ideals of the conventional family that perpetuate restrictive roles for women as wives and mothers. This led me to examine some theoretical assumptions of family systems theory and to question whether the theory that guides our work speaks adequately to the oppression of women in the social and familial context of inequality.

I believe that a feminist critique may lead to conceptual and technical changes that might reduce the amount of sexism that is woven in very subtle ways into family systems theory and practice. But from a more radical perspective, my belief is that feminism poses a challenge to the basic theoretical assumptions of family systems theory. I believe that were family therapists to integrate the notion of inequality into their theoretical frameworks, to approach the family as a system that limits the personal development of women as well as of men, and to view our roles as advocates for a non-sexist social form, then we would need to radically reconceptualize our systems theory, redefine our treatment goals, and question our roles as agents of change.

To put it in systemic terms, without an analysis of the inequality intrinsic to the family, of the reciprocal relationship between family and society, and of the oppressed condition of women in families and in society, family therapists can only achieve first order change, which occurs within a family system but leaves the system unchanged in fundamental ways. We will not be able to accomplish the greater goal of second order change—one that changes the system itself to promote equality for women inside and outside the family.

REFERENCES

Buckley, W. (1967). *Sociology and modern systems theory.* Englewood Cliffs: Prentice-Hall Inc.

Goldner, V. (1985). Feminism and family therapy. *Family Process, 24,* 31–47.

Hare-Mustin, R. (1978) A feminist approach to family therapy. *Family Process, 17,* 181–194.

Hare-Mustin, R. (1980). Family therapy may be dangerous for your health. *Professional Psychology, 11,* 935–938.

Hoffman, L. (1981). *Foundations of family therapy.* New York: Basic Books Inc.

Jacobson, N. (1983). Beyond empiricism: The politics of marital therapy. *American Journal of Family Therapy, 11,* 11–24.

James, K., & McIntyre, O. (1983). The reproduction of families: The social role of family therapy? *Journal of Marital and Family Therapy, 9,* 119–129.

Keeney, B. (1983). *Aesthetics of change.* New York: Guilford Press.

Klein, M. (1976). Feminist concepts of therapy outcome. *Psychotherapy: Theory, Research and Practice, 13,* 89–95.

Lerner, H. (1982). Special issues for women in psychotherapy. In M. Notman and C. Nadelson (eds.), *The woman patient: Aggression, adaptation and psychotherapy.* New York: Plenum Press.

Lerner, H. (1983). Female dependency in context: Some theoretical and technical considerations. *American Journal of Orthopsychiatry, 53,* 697–705.

Libow, J., Raskin, P., & Caust, B. (1982). Feminist and family systems therapy: Are they irreconcilable? *American Journal of Family Therapy, 3,* 3–12.

Margolin, G., Fernandez, V., Talovic, S., & Onorato, R. (1983). Sex role considerations and behavioral marital therapy: Equal does not mean identical. *Journal of Marital and Family Therapy, 9,* 131–145.

Nichols, M. (1984). *Family therapy: Concepts and methods.* New York: Gardner Press Inc.

Robbins, J. (1983). Complex triangles: Uncovering sexist bias in relationship counseling. In J. Robbins & R. Siegel (eds.), *Women changing therapy.* New York: Haworth Press.

Women's Project in Family Therapy. (a). *Mothers and sons, fathers and daughters.* Monograph series, Vol. 2., No. 1., Washington, D.C.

Women's Project in Family Therapy. (b). *Mothers and daughters.* Monograph series, Vol. 1, No. 1., Washington, D.C.

Elderly Women
in Family Therapy

Martha E. Banks
Rosalie J. Ackerman
Elisabeth O. Clark

The need for a focus on family therapy with geriatric patients is demonstrated in the literature which includes alarming numbers of references to abuse of the elderly. Most of the victims of such abuse are women, and the abusers are frequently members of the victims' families (O'Malley, O'Malley, Everitt, & Sarson, 1984). There are a variety of stresses experienced by families engaged in the care of an elderly person, such as illness of a caregiver (Satariano, Minkler, & Langhauser, 1984) conflicting and/or competing roles (Brody, 1981), changes in family status (Cicirelli, 1983) placement of a frail elderly family member in an institution (Beland, 1984) and the distance between identified patients, primary caregivers, and other family members (Hays, 1984). Family therapy can be used to assist caregivers of elderly patients in the management of the stress which can lead to abuse (Ratna & Davis, 1984).

This paper presents three aspects of elderly women in family therapy. The first issue is the treatment of female patients in an inpatient geriatric-psychiatric state facility. Second, female primary caretakers of male geriatric medical inpatients in a government facility will be examined. The final perspective will be of the moral, ethical, and legal issues which impact on the treatment of elderly women.

Martha E. Banks is at the Brecksville Veterans Administration Medical Center, Brecksville, OH. Rosalie J. Ackerman is at the University of North Carolina at Chapel Hill, NC. Elisabeth O. Clark, is at the University of California at Los Angeles, CA.

107

FAMILY THERAPY IN THE INPATIENT
GEROPSYCHIATRIC SETTING

Older women as psychogeriatric patients are in triple jeopardy for stigmatization (Trager, 1984). Agism, sexism, and negative conceptions of mental illness combine to present unique issues for those women. Members of social minority groups face an additional source of discrimination. Chronic and acute, serious and multiple medical problems plague older women. A variety of social losses including spouse, friends, siblings, home, familiar roles, health, and financial security contribute to depression. Lack of power, depersonalization, benign or deliberate neglect, and dependency are psychological factors of concern. Negative community images, poverty status, and sparse treatment opportunities contribute to a pessimistic quality of life for psychogeriatric patients.

One treatment strategy that is infrequently used is family psychotherapy with extended family members of the psychogeriatric woman patient. Some of the family issues that need to be addressed include: minimal contact between the patient and her family; decreased family commitment to the inpatient; negative prejudices of the family toward the institution; feelings about the actual hospitalization of an ill family member; and long-standing family conflicts (Barnes, Raskin, Scott, & Murphy, 1981). Each of these issues will be described in detail. These descriptions illustrate clinical impressions of one of the authors, working in a state mental hospital facility caring for the psychogeriatric population.

There is often a limited number of family members who contact the patient. Frequently, only one person is designated, consciously or unconsciously, by the extended family as the "caregiver" to the patient, and is the face-to-face contact person. Hence, roles of the family system become more rigidly redefined with hospitalization. Relationships continue, although the family members might seldom see each other.

The family support network reallocates its efforts in terms of physical, emotional, and financial resources (Weeks & Cuellar, 1981). From the therapeutic treatment perspective, family therapy sessions most often are oriented toward crisis intervention at the time of hospitalization for the patient or immediately before community placement of the patient. Very few families maintain an ongoing therapy relationship while their relatives are psychogeriatric inpatients. A fragmented family is available for psychotherapy. Elderly inpatients often have visiting family members who are older than themselves. Others have younger siblings coming to visit. Some have adult children who visit without bringing their spouses or their children.

Family members have negative prejudices against the state mental hospital. There are also prejudices against certain diagnoses (Knapp, 1984). This contributes to the social isolation of the inpatient and to her increased reliance upon the institution to provide emotional and environmental support.

Contact with the family members is either regularly scheduled for weekly or biweekly sessions, or is unscheduled and occurs just after admission or prior to discharge. Scheduled family therapy deals with a broad variety of issues including prior conflicts, the capacity of the inpatient to adjust to a return to the community, emotional factors of depression, paranoia, delusions, anxiety, suffering, anger, and physical problems of the inpatient and other family members. Unscheduled family therapy contacts deal with issues of hospitalization and long-standing conflicts (e.g., resentment, guilt, anger) that precipitated and/or were exacerbated by the hospitalization. Support of the inpatient is most evident in families maintaining ongoing therapeutic relationships, with the strains and obligations of the family members in caregiving roles being a focus of the psychotherapeutic interventions. Other issues include education about the aging process as it influences mental status, and affective responses to the behaviors labelled as "problems" by the family.

FAMILY THERAPY IN THE INPATIENT MEDICAL SETTING

Family therapy with the elderly is difficult in an inpatient medical setting for a variety of reasons. First, the physically ill elderly are frequently reluctant to be involved in psychotherapy, which is seen as an indication that they are not only ill, but also "crazy." Once so labelled in the family context, there is danger of stigmatization unless the psychologist *quickly* intervenes with an educational approach about the purposes and goals of psychotherapy. Unless this is handled carefully, there is an increased risk of depression on the part of the patient, which can lead to negative medical consequences. It should be noted that similar misinterpretations are made by primary caregivers, especially when they are seen individually.

Secondly, the elderly are treated, with few exceptions, by professional staff members who are young enough to be their children or *grandchildren*. This brings into play a number of transference and countertransference issues which should be dealt with openly. The greatest facilitation frequently comes from increased personal sharing on the part of the psychologist—more of such sharing than might be appropriate for work with younger families. An important focus must be on maintaining respect for *all* of the family members, regardless of age or *apparent* degree of impairment. One way to provide an atmosphere of respect is to use titles and last names, rather than following the trend in many geriatric settings, where people are inappropriately addressed by their first names or impolite euphemisms (e.g., "Gramps") without regard to the feelings of the patients. Although other staff members might continue to address the patients and their family members on a first-name basis, the psychologist, who uses titles both in direct conversation and in reference to the patients, can increase the respect for those patients with the provision of the respectful address.

Assessment is a third issue which presents problems for the psychologist who does family therapy. Psychological assessment of the elderly medically ill patient is difficult at best, as it is frequently impossible to sort out the effects and side-effects of (multiple) physical illness(es), medication(s), true dementia, pseudodementia, and anxiety. Many of the standard psychological tests do not have norms for the aged (Price, Fein, & Feinberg, 1980) or assume that everyone over the age of 65 years belongs to the same cohort, and/or the medically ill populations. Furthermore, there exist few family assessment instruments, and *none* of those address the multifaceted issues of the geriatric family. Therefore, while it is difficult to assess the status of the inpatient, it is virtually impossible to use standardized measures to assess the family situation, in order to develop appropriate psychological treatment goals or recommendations for the family. This creates a dilemma for the psychologist who has been trained to do a thorough standard assessment as a prelude to treatment; assessment must be customized with respect to the immediate and long-term needs of the families with whom one is working.

A fourth issue involves understanding the meaning of a diagnosis by the patient and family. It is important to recognize that the elderly population being treated today grew up in eras during which medical treatment was unsophisticated as compared to current medical practice. Therefore, many of the diseases to which this population is susceptible (e.g., bronchial pneumonia) are treatable at the present time, but meant certain death in years past. Families often have myths about the ability of an elderly patient to be successfully treated or rehabilitated, believing that normal aging is a disease process, and/or that progressive dementia is part of normal aging. This is an important issue in family therapy, as decisions about aggressive treatment, or the withholding thereof, are based on the family's understanding of the disease process. Myths regarding contagion often lead to isolation of the inpatient from the rest of the family. An important facet, therefore, of family psychotherapy is an educational one, in which the psychologist must encourage increased communication among the physician, the patient, and the family and/or aggressively pursue accurate information of a medical nature.

Inpatient facilities are primarily concerned with the treatment of individuals, who are identified as "patients" or "residents." As a result, there is frequently a focus *away* from families, beyond consideration of "cooperation" with staff in the provision of care. Unfortunately, this results in ignoring other potentially ill family members (Satariano et al., 1984). In settings where the patients are primarily males, the "hidden patients" are most frequently women, who have been identified as primary caregivers. Those women are often still involved in caregiving activities after their male relatives have been institutionalized. Issues which are addressed in family therapy with those caregivers include loss of role, resolution of old conflicts, lack of preparedness for the responsibilities which were previously handled by the ill relative, conflicts due to multiple roles, loss of old support systems, guilt, and negative criticism from less involved relatives. Many of the families are faced with financial disaster, such that the caregiver, usually the wife of the inpatient, is unwilling to spend money for the management of her own medical needs.

Family intervention is *slowly* becoming a focus of the inpatient treatment, in the medical setting in which one of the authors works. A forum for discussion of general caregiving issues is provided through monthly multiple family group sessions, which are open to all relatives and interested friends of the residents (Teusink & Mahler, 1984). There is a didactic portion of the sessions which is designed to provide some structure for discussion. The group members are encouraged to raise issues which are of immediate importance to them. It has been noted by therapists that certain disease entities or syndromes have high social status in the minds of families, as reflected by behavior in multiple family support groups. For example, spouses of patients diagnosed as having senile dementia of the Alzheimer's type frequently believe that the difficulties they had in management of the patient in the home were greater than those faced by families of patients with other diagnoses. This hierarchical perspective can be destructive in the group setting; it must be recognized and dealt with openly as a treatment issue.

Upon admission, the family is invited to attend a meeting of the multidisciplinary team which is responsible for the care of their relative. This provides an opportunity for the family to meet the professional staff and to ask questions about the specific care of the patient. The staff uses this forum to encourage continued family involvement, so that the patient is not isolated (Rubin & Shuttlesworth, 1983). Psychotherapeutic intervention at the family level occurs when there is apparent conflict, as manifested by infrequent visits, overt arguments and/or physical fights during visits, lack of cooperation between family members and staff (e.g., bringing in contraindicated foods and/or medications, refusal to provide appropriate clothing) frequent unsubstantiated complaints from family members, and/or obvious psychological withdrawal from the patient. In such instances, the family is scheduled to be seen on a regular basis, with the understanding that the sessions are for the primary benefit of the patient.

Frequently, in family therapy sessions, there is a revelation of longstanding conflict which has been exacerbated by the illness of the identified patient. In some instances, the "patient" has been hospitalized due to the inability of a caregiving spouse to continue to manage the patient at home.

A major focus of family therapy is on discharge planning. Families are given the opportunity to discuss placement options, including adjustments which would need to be made for a successful return of the inpatient to the family home (Panella, Lilliston, Brush, & McDowell, 1984). In such instances, a strong emphasis is placed on the assessment of the ability of the patient and the caregiver to function together under the restrictions imposed by the identified patient's illness. The possibility of abuse is addressed openly, with encouragement to arrange for respite and other supports which would facilitate a successful return to the home; abuse of the identified patient is considered as well as abuse of the caregiver by the identified patient. Past methods of resolving conflict are examined, with consideration of the changing abilities of the family to adjust to their new situation. Exploration of alternative placements takes into account the patient's need for continued care, as well as the needs of other family members. Family decision-making is supported using a forum for asking questions, coordinating services, and expressing feelings of guilt, anger, helplessness, and hopelessness.

Although the focus of the family psychotherapy sessions is on benefits for the inpatient, there are frequently individual sessions provided for the primary caregiver, under the guise of information gathering. Those sessions are designed to provide a forum for the expression of frustrations which might otherwise go unspoken. Issues which have emanated from such sessions include revelation of past abuse, historically conflicted marriages and other family relationships, blaming of the inpatient for creating the severity of the illness which led to institutionalization by ignoring medical advice, desires to be rid of the difficult tasks of caring for an ill relative, difficulty taking on responsibilities, conflicting pressures due to multiple roles, and the inability to assertively deal with negative criticism from other family members or associates.

MORAL, ETHICAL, AND LEGAL ISSUES

Psychologists who routinely assess the progressive deterioration of dementia patients, as well as those who counsel their family caregivers, either formally in support groups, or informally in the context of patient visits, face a number of difficult issues over the course of the patient's decline. These issues can loosely be divided into ethical, moral, or legal subdivisions, but, in reality, the ramifications of any particular problem or decision can straddle all three categories. From the perspectives of both the patient and the family, the rights of each party and the position or the support that the psychologist might lend will be explored.

Some of the issues to be considered include reporting the diagnosis and prognosis, genetic issues, changing status of the patient, and the final stages. Each of these will be discussed in detail.

Although a physician is usually the one to give the diagnosis, the family and patient might need more concrete information, such as the results of neuropsychological testing. The psychological evaluation and report provide the patient and family with a structured environment in which to gain emotion-laden information. The issues here concern the patient's right to confidentiality and the family's right to knowledge that might drastically alter their lifestyle and long-range plans (Gwyther & Blazer, 1984).

An additional issue is the problem of reporting the diagnosis only to the patient, knowing that she or he might be unable to assimilate the information fully or to report it to the family (Hermann, 1984). It is important to understand what the patient does with the information presented and what it means to the person.

Most families are very concerned about the issue of heredity; parents for their children and children for themselves and their own children. Available genetic data are not often clear, and risks seem to vary among families. The uncertainty of the literature makes it more difficult for the psychologist to realistically address those family concerns. Yet, there is an obligation to share the estimates from those studies that are available. The family has the right of support in interpreting and assimilating those data. This requires a high degree of patience, willingness to repeat information, and, above all, the ability to ask family members what they have understood to maximize their making the best use of the information.

For patients with marked deterioration, or with those who progress downhill over time, the clinician might need to explore issues·of money management and driving of motor vehicles. The perceived right of a person to manage his/her own affairs or to drive must be weighed against the family's rights as well as those of the society at large. Incompetence on the road is another area in which society expects restriction of privileges with the declining health of an adult. Another management issue involves institutionalization and, again, the patient's right to a certain quality or freedom of life versus the family's right to relinquish the burden of fulltime care; this is a potent conflict area. Especially in question are research designs and some clinics' position that a measure of success in family intervention is the length of time that the patient remains at home (Dyck, 1984). There is a need to acknowledge that both the identified patient and the hidden patient, or overburdened caregiver, have a right to a reasonable lifestyle and quality of life.

Dementia of the Alzheimer's type follows an inexorable downhill course with no cure or halt to the progression currently available. The final outcome is death, often ten to fifteen years after the onset of symptoms. The patient's wishes regarding maintenance of life and extraordinary measures are seldom known (Gibson, 1984). Families are often conflicted over the best course of medical and psychological management. The psychologist who has an ongoing relationship with any given family might be pulled into the final decisions over the right of the patient to live or die, the right of the institution to employ heroic life-saving measures, and the rights of the family.

REFERENCES

Barnes, R. F. , Raskind, M. A., Scott, M., & Murphy, C. (1981). Problems of families caring for Alzheimer patients: Use of a support group. *Journal of the American Geriatrics Society, 29,* 80–85.

Beland, F. (1984). The decision of elderly persons to leave their homes. *The Gerontologist, 24,* 179–185.

Brody, E. M. (1981). "Women in the middle" and family help to older people. *The Gerontologist, 21,* 471–479.

Cicirelli, V. G. (1983). A comparison of helping behavior to elderly parents of adult children with intact and disrupted marriages. *The Gerontologist, 23,* 619–625.

Dyck, A. J. (1984). Ethical aspects of care for the dying incompetent. *Journal of the American Geriatrics Society, 32,* 661–664.

Gibson, D. E. (1984). Hospice: Morality and economics. *The Gerontologist, 24,* 4–7.

Gwyther, L. P. & Blazer, D. G. (1984). Family therapy and the dementia patient. *American Family Physician, 29,* 149–156.

Hays, J. A. (1984). Aging and family resources: Availability and proximity of kin. *The Gerontologist, 24,* 149–153.

Hermann, H. T. (1984). Ethical dilemmas intrinsic to the care of the elderly demented patient. *Journal of the American Geriatrics Society, 32,* 655–656.

Knapp, N. (1984). Institutionalized women: Some classic types, some common problems, and some partial solutions. In Lesnoff-Caravagelia (Ed.), *The world of older women.* New York: Human Science Press.

O'Malley, T.A., O'Malley, H.C., Everitt, D. E., & Sarson, D. (1984). Categories of family-mediated abuse and neglect of elderly persons. *Journal of the American Geriatrics Society, 32,* 362–369.

Panella, J. J., Lilliston, B. A., Brush, D., & McDowell, F. H. (1984). Day care for dementia patients: An analysis of a four-year program. *Journal of the American Geriatrics Society, 32,* 883–886.

Price, L. J., Fein, G., & Feinberg, I. (1980). Neuropsychological assessment of cognitive function in the elderly. In Poon, L. W. (Ed.), *Aging in the 1980s: Psychological Issues.* Washington, D.C.: American Psychological Association.

Ratna, L. & Davis, J. (1984). Family therapy with the elderly mentally ill: Some strategies and techniques. *British Journal of Psychiatry, 145,* 311–315.

Rubin, A. & Shuttlesworth, G. E. (1983). Engaging families as support resources in nursing home care: Ambiguity in the subdivision of tasks. *The Gerontologist, 23,* 632–636.

Satariano, W. A., Minkler, M. A., & Langhauser, C. (1984). The significance of an ill spouse for assessing health differences in an elderly population. *Journal of the American Geriatrics Society, 32,* 187–190.

Teusink, J. P. & Mahler, S. (1984). Helping families cope with Alzheimer's disease. *Hospital and Community Psychiatry, 35,* 152–156.

Trager, N. (1984). Social class and the older family member. In Lesnoff-Caravagelia (Ed.), *The world of older women.* New York: Human Sciences Press.

Weeks, J. R. & Cuellar, J. B. (1981). The role of family members in the helping networks of older people. *The Gerontologist, 21,* 388–394.

II. SPECIAL POPULATIONS OF WOMEN

Women are profiting from equal opportunities and from the breakdown of traditional sex roles. Yet women continue to predominate as victims of violence and in certain mental health disorders. The focus of this section is on women who constitute "special populations." These women may be experiencing problems in living that affect women more than men, but therapists may not have the training or experience for their special needs. Thus, the articles in this section provide recommendations for treatment and services needed by particular subgroups of women.

The first article in this section examines the issues and recovery process facing adult incest survivors. *Kathy Swink* and *Antoinette Leveille* describe the experience of incest as the abuse of power within the framework of patriarchal society. Victim reactions to incest are described in detail as they impact on multiple levels of victims' lives. The authors provide recommendations for the recovery process from victim to survivor, from powerless to empowered.

In an attempt to conform to societal standards of thinness, women are using radical means to control their weight. Self-starvation, gastric stapling, and jaw-wiring are all used to shed pounds, often at the risk of death. A recent survey of women's greatest fears determined that a large percentage of women feared becoming fat more than any other disaster. We can only imagine how different our world would be if women reoriented their energy into politics or art! *Melanie Katzman, Lillie Weiss*, and *Sharlene Wolchik* examine bulimia as an eating disorder that is associated with low self-esteem, poor body image, need for approval, and depression. Their treatment program for bulimia focuses on examining the cultural expectations for thinness and the socialization for women to suppress anger and assertion with food.

Although women are socialized since childhood that marriage will result in a state of "happily ever after," the reality is that most married women will divorce, separate with, or outlive their spouse. Even women who plan not to marry have often not been seriously encouraged to pursue a career. Consequently, many women are seeking "reentry" employment. *Kathryn Towns* and *Rie Gentzler* describe their reentry program for women in business and education careers. Relying on feminist principles and non-directive counseling, the program relies heavily on already placed women in the community as role models and sources of social support. Even more important, the program has begun to facilitate prevention strategies by educating young girls in non-traditional careers.

Since biblical times, laws have permitted and often encouraged men to batter their wives. Even today, the media condones violence (even in cartoons for children) and the police are often reluctant to intervene in cases of violence where the perpetrator is married to the victim. *Rosemarie Ieda* provides a political and historical analysis of the battered woman in the context of the family. She describes the implications of the role of "wife" in industrialized society and how violence in the family begins and maintains itself. Finally, strategies for intervention and prevention are provided.

Men predominate as the perpetrators of nearly all types of illegal behavior. Consequently, there has been little focus on issues confronting female prisoners. *SeEtta Moss* describes the prevalence of neglect faced by women in prison, including child care, educational, health, and mental health needs. She presents some data on physical and sexual abuse experienced by female prisoners prior to incarceration, and presents recommendations for change.

From Victim to Survivor: A New Look at the Issues and Recovery Process for Adult Incest Survivors

Kathy K. Swink
Antoinette E. Leveille

INTRODUCTION

Sexual abuse is an issue with which therapists are increasingly faced as public attention is focused on the problem and victims are coming forward. Estimates of occurrence indicate that from 10% to 40% of all children experience some form of sexual abuse, with girls generally believed to be victimized 2 to 10 times as frequently as boys. Abusers of children are almost always related to, or well known and trusted by their victims. Sexual abuse has been occurring in epidemic proportions with little or no treatment for the victims until the past decade. These past victims are now revealing themselves as they realize that they may be able to grow to become survivors of their ordeal rather than continuing in their victim roles.

How do we, as feminist therapists, empower these victims to become survivors? In the seven years that we have been working with sexual assault victims, we have found that we cannot rely on traditional theories or approaches. Rather, we have gradually formulated our own understanding of the process of both victimization and the recovery process on the path towards survival.

Kathy K. Swink is a sexual abuse counselor and is also in private practice at 222 Atlantic Avenue, Providence, RI 02907. Antoinette Leveille is in private practice at 762 Pontiac Avenue, Cranston, RI 02910.

© 1986 by The Haworth Press, Inc. All rights reserved.

119

INCEST DYNAMICS

A therapist working with victims of incest must first have a clear understanding of the issues, dynamics, and effects of incest. We define incest as sexual experience (including comments, exposure, fondling, or sexual penetration) between people in a family or caretaking relationship which implies that one person (the abuser) has authority and power over another (the victim), and takes advantage of that position to use and/or degrade the victim sexually. This would exclude sexual experimentation between two equal and willing siblings close in age. However, siblings with a significant difference in age and/or power so that one can coerce, force or otherwise manipulate the other would definitely be included as incestuous. Likewise, family friends or extended family members of greater size and power would be considered incestuous abusers if they engaged in any sexual activity with the youngsters.

Incest is the extreme expression of a patriarchal society. It trains the young victims from the start that their place/purpose/function in society is for the needs of others, especially of males. Brothers of incest victims often assualt their own children because they have learned that this is how men treat their children. Male victims also may identify with their assailants and become abusers. Females generally tend to adopt the victim role and maintain it since it is supported and accepted by our patriarchal culture.

The paramount dynamics in incest are the abuse of power and the abusers' disregard for the needs of the victims. The distinguishing characteristics are confusion of boundaries, roles and appropriate behaviors.

Incest occurs in troubled families. It is not the original cause of the problems, but it certainly intensifies them. In an incestuous family, the abuser (most often the father or father figure in the home and therefore often referred to as father in this paper) has needs to feel powerful and loved and also to release pent-up anger, hostility and frustrations for which he has not found appropriate outlets. He is not looking for sexual satisfaction, which he would most appropriately seek with his wife, or another consenting adult. Rather, he responds to the admiration and ego boost he receives from his child and has insufficient impulse control or consideration of her needs to stop himself from engaging in sexual behavior with her. The dynamics and effects are very much the same regardless of the relationship between the abuser and the victim. Since father-daughter incest is most common, we usually refer to those roles for simplicity's sake.

Generally, the incest perpetrator will build up the relationship and abuse very gradually to suit his needs and thereby train his victim. In general, he tends not to take responsibility for his feelings and behavior, but rather places inappropriate expectations and responsibilities on the daughter. Thus there exist role reversal and muddled boundaries within the relationship so that the daughter is taking care of father's needs rather than the other way around.

As part of his power and control, he will make impossible double-bind demands, impose strict authoritarian rules, or else, manipulatively play a "Poor Me" role to maintain his central, controlling position within the family. There are also incestuous rapists who will forcefully, brutally, and sadistically rape their children, but they are in the minority. A father generally doesn't need extreme force to get his daughter to do what he wants since he's already in the position of authority. After all, she was taught to obey her parents. So she goes along with it even though she feels that it's not right, because she needs to please her father, win his attention and affection, and he usually has some rationalizations or enticements to keep it their "little secret." The mother and other family members are generally victims of the same dynamics and so don't feel capable of recognizing the abuse or standing up to the abuser.

The young victim learns to disregard herself, to distrust her perceptions, to allow her body and sexuality to be used for another's pleasure, to learn to get affection through seductive, sexual, manipulative behavior. She feels betrayed—for if she can't be safe at home in her own bed, where can she be safe? If she can't trust her own family, whom can she trust? She feels hopeless that anyone will recognize the incest as a problem, will believe her, won't blame her, or can do anything to protect her. She feels guilty and responsible because she wants love and attention from her father, has been trained into a role of responsibility, and often learns to manipulate her father as he has manipulated her even though she doesn't want or enjoy the sexual abuse. Because of her feelings of guilt, her fear of breaking up the family, hurting the other family members or other repercussions, and her fear of not being believed, she is not likely to disclose the secret. And so it continues until she can move out of the house, or it is discovered, or a younger sibling takes her place. She also feels betrayed by her other family members who do not protect her or believe her when she tries to tell them what's going on.

Issues of Incest Therapy

Incest affects every aspect of the victim's life. In working with adults who were abused as children, we have seen a wide range of reactions to the abuse, and the victims frequently tend to react in extremes rather than moderate ways. We will list the issues which we have found to be the most frequently affected.

1. First, the client must *accept that the abuse really happened.* Most abused children have no mechanism for dealing with the abuse other than denying or minimizing it. At least half of our clients partially or totally blocked their abuse experiences for self-protection. Others said, "Well, it wasn't so bad." One woman came into therapy after she had told her fiancé about her repeated sexual assaults and saw the look of horror on his face—she had never considered it anything out of the ordinary plight of women before. Thus, they must break through the denial which had previously protected them.

2. Once faced, the *myths and facts* of incest must be clarified. Since abusers put the responsibility for the incest on them, victims believe that they must have seduced them somehow. They must learn that the perpetrators were in control and therefore responsible for the abuse. Other myths that must be debunked include: that incest is to satisfy sexual needs, that mothers set their daughters up knowingly, that incest is all fantasy and doesn't really happen, that children enjoy sex with adult family members, that children can learn about sex best by experience within the family, that incest victims can never be fully functioning human beings, that incest makes people "turn gay," that incest is a very rare occurrence, or that incest only occurs in lower class rural families. As soon as a woman walks into her first incest therapy group,

many of these myths are dispelled and the others quickly follow.

3. Children growing up in incestuous families tend to be *isolated* from other people both within and without the family. The families are not close; and in order to hide their secrets from the outside world, children are not encouraged or allowed to make friends, to go visiting or to have friends visit them. Thus, many are trained to withdraw. One of my clients recalls twenty different hiding places that she had within the house. Some rebel and become very outgoing, jovial, involved in many extracurricular activities in order to have lots of people and distractions to cover up the reality of the abuse. Both reactions are ways of avoiding the abuse, and continue as patterns after leaving the abusive family situation. Both leave the victim feeling alone and isolated.

4. When they are ready to begin facing the abuse, most victims will have *dreams, nightmares and/or flashbacks* of the abuse. If these had been totally blocked previously, they can be very frightening and confusing as they seem to be coming out of nowhere. It feels as if she is being further victimized as she relives these experiences, but this time from within her own mind rather than from someone outside. It is most helpful to understand that these flashbacks come as a sign or a push from within to face the memories, that she is now ready to deal with this material, and that she can work with this part of herself rather than fight against it. These pushes come for good reasons and we can learn to trust this natural process.

5. Most victims have some left-over *fears and phobias*. Most cannot sleep without a light on, or they are overprotective of themselves and their children, or they cannot have sexual activity that reminds them of the abuse. Some also have specific phobias stemming from the incest, such as buttons, closets, attics, basements, belts, screwdrivers, etc. Sometimes they will overcompensate for their fears and only have sex with a man who resembles the abuser, or request spanking along with intercourse as ways of replicating the abuse in an attempt to finally master it.

6. The *family dynamics* in incestuous families are very confusing to an outsider. The male dominance is extreme although sometimes subtle, boundaries are muddled and inconsistent, rules change or arbitrarily apply to some children but not to

others or to adults, communications are minimal, children are not respected, children must carry out most of the chores and responsibilities but none of the authority. Naturally, a child growing up in a chaotic family assumes that this is how all families and groups of people interact, and expects to always play the roles of the scapegoat, lost child, or abuser. Thus equal, healthy, nurturing relationships are very difficult to learn without help.

7. *Role reversals* are central in the incest family structure. No one learns to be responsible for her/himself, but rather for everyone else. Therapists will notice incest victims frequently saying, "So-and-so makes me feel. . ." or "I couldn't do that because I'd make so-and-so feel. . ." They have been trained to consider everyone else's needs before their own and feel terribly guilty and afraid if they dare to care for themselves in any way. Frequently, incest will be revealed when an older sibling finds out that a younger sibling is being abused as well—she wouldn't complain on her own behalf, but will for the sibling.

8. One of the primary feelings with which the victims of incest are plagued is *guilt.* Because their abusers foisted the responsibility for the abuse on the victims, they feel guilty and tend to continue taking on guilt and inappropriate responsibilities until they realize that they can forgive themselves and place the guilt back where it belongs—on the abuser. Likewise, they must learn to take appropriate responsibility in order to gain a sense of having some power and control in the world.

9. All victims tend to suffer from *depression.* They have been trained to be helpless and the natural response to a helpless situation is to give up. There is no hope, no motivation for change—just existence. They have also learned to suppress their emotions, which also causes depression. Many have lived at this level for so many years that they don't recognize it as depression, but just the way life is. Then a glimmer of hope shines through that life might be different. Depression has been a means of survival throughout the ordeal and it is not given up easily.

10. A child who is sexually abused grows up hating her body. Her *body image* is ugly, dirty, disgusting, "damaged goods," yet overpoweringly seductive to men. If the victims

responded sexually to the abuse, then they feel especially ashamed and betrayed by their own bodies. In response to these body images, they tend to go to extremes: they make themselves as unattractive as possible (to avoid sexual attention), they may dress and act very primly (to counteract their image), or they may dress and act seductively (to play the role they have been trained for). Sometimes the discrepancy between body image and appearance is quite large: anorexics believe they are fat, strikingly beautiful women how ugly they are, or unattractive, unkempt women will boast of being beautiful and sexy.

11. The effects of incest often emerge in *physical manifestations,* such as migraines, backaches, gastrointestinal and genitourinary problems, lethargy, unexplained muscle failure (especially weakness in the legs), and ringing in the ears. Some of these symptoms are a direct result of the abuse, such as hemorrhoids from anal rape, or yeast infections from intercourse, backaches from torturous positions and tension. Others result from the anxiety and stress of maintaining the secret and repressing all the feelings associated with it.

12. Many incest victims also manifest *self-destructive behaviors* which take many forms ranging from smoking to suicide. Since they have been trained in the role of the scapegoat, they have learned to blame themselves for everything and to feel worthless and hopeless. We will discuss some of the specific forms of self-destructive behaviors which we have found to be most common.

12.A. Residential treatment programs for *substance abuse* are finding that as many as 90% of the women and 60% of the men in treatment were sexually abused as children. There is a common tendency among incest victims to use alcohol or other drugs to suppress feelings. This tendency seems to grow out of the child's position of maintaining the family secrets and sacrificing the self. Often there is some substance abuse in the family of origin which the victim imitates. Any substance abuse problem must be cleared up before treatment can be effective in the other areas. The Alcoholics Anonymous program has been extremely helpful in facilitating sobriety. However, their philosophy is patriarchal and causes a few problems for incest victims in that AA insists that each member take responsibility for all that has happened to him/her, and that they must forgive everyone so as to be free of resentment and anger. Incest victims tend to take too much responsibility, especially for the abuse, are too quick to forgive everyone but themselves, and suppress anger rather than releasing it. Nevertheless a 12-step program can be extremely helpful in counteracting many other self-destructive tendencies.

12.B. Frequently incest victims continue in their victim roles and find themselves in *abusive relationships*. The women frequently marry men who eventually physically and/or sexually abuse them and/or their children. Having known only abuse, these women often do not recognize this behavior as out of the ordinary, or as preventable. Women in these situations generally need a great deal of support and encouragement to escape from present abuse before they can begin to resolve the issues of past abuse. They often come into treatment to work on the past abuse which is being recalled by present abuse. They begin working on it for some initial understanding, but as they begin to see the parallels in their present situation, they are faced with the realization that they are still being victimized. Then they must make a decision to either stay and try to improve the current relationship or to leave it and begin anew. After this decision is made and they feel stronger within themselves, then the incest issues will emerge again and the situation will be conducive to therapeutic resolution. In other words, they cannot work through past abuse while they are still being abused.

12.C. Another common self-destructive behavior is an *eating-disorder*. Incest victims may be bulimic, anorexic, or compulsive over-eaters. This stems from the body image problem—they want to deny or cover their sexual attributes. A colleague who specializes in eating disorders has found that at least 60% of her clients have been sexually abused and that eating disorder groups help to foster the dissolution of amnesia. If the eating problem is severe, health must be stabilized before other issues can be resolved. However, compulsive over-eaters, for example, can frequently benefit from incest therapy alone or in conjunction with Overeaters Anonymous. As they find a way to express their feelings, they no longer have a great need to swallow them with food. They learn to nurture themselves in other, more satisfying ways.

13. A major difficulty for incest victims is *trust*. They have

learned to distrust people in order to avoid further betrayal. Therefore, they are generally slow to trust people in their lives, yet surprisingly eager to trust a therapist who listens, understands, and supports them as incest survivors. We see their distrust and fear as a healthy sign since they are demonstrating that they care enough about themselves to protect themselves. Because we believe our clients, the trust issue does not tend to be a problem in the therapeutic relationship with adult clients.

14. The area in which trust presents difficulties is within other *relationships*—with lovers or husbands, with friends, with co-workers. Incest victims often use the incest secret to test for trustworthiness—if a person can hear about the incest without being disgusted, judgmental, or rejecting, then they must be all right. Another difficulty with relationships is the lack of appropriate models and experience with healthy ones— they do not know how to have healthy relationships. Thus therapy includes teaching and modeling healthy interactions.

15. Most women who were incest victims tend to *overvalue men*. They may distrust and even hate men, yet they firmly believe that they cannot succeed in this world without a man. Thus they may choose to remain in an abusive relationship rather than separate and live without a man. This is an area where a feminist philosophy is essential.

16. *Sexuality* creates numerous problems for these women. They tend to avoid sex altogether, or they are promiscuous or vacillate between periods of celibacy and sexual activity. Sex is extremely important here since it is central to their self-image. However, flashbacks are very common during sexual activity which is reminiscent of the abuse, so sex can become fearful and frustrating. Generally, the former victim needs to be in control of the sexual activities to the point of being free to stop or change positions at any time so she won't feel as though she is being victimized again. When both partners have been victims, they must reach a delicate balance of control and find positions/activities comfortable for both. Sex has been associated with the abuse of power so most of these victims have great difficulty enjoying an equal, loving encounter. Frequently, they trained themselves to deny any sexually pleasurable feelings during the abuse so it is difficult now to let go and enjoy these feelings and allow themselves to reach orgasm.

Gay clients have an added dilemma in that they resent and yet fear the myth that the sexual abuse made them gay.

17. *Intimacy* is frightening because of the vulnerability involved. Whether a woman is avoiding sex or having frequent sexual encounters, she is avoiding intimacy. The fear of intimacy comes from the betrayal of trust as well as the burden of keeping the incest secret. As a result, many will keep up appearances of normality so as to avoid intimacy and possible further betrayal and/or rejection.

18. Having been in the helpless position of a victim with no *control,* these women tend to have difficulty moderating their control in situations. Either they relinquish all control (usually to men) and remain victims, or they try to maintain control of everyone and everything around them. They demonstrate extreme self-restraint, yet are always in fear of losing self-control. Suicide is the ultimate expression of self-control to avoid self-expression.

19. The greater fear of losing control is with the expression of *anger/rage.* There has been so much rage building up over the years during and since the abuse that it seems overwhelming. They are afraid that if they acknowledge and begin to express some anger, they will go berserk and begin killing and destroying everyone and everything within reach. Suppressing or abusing are the only models they have had for dealing with anger. They don't want to become abusive so they try to hold it all inside, but they keep snapping at people or overreacting to minor irritations. This is a sign that the anger is ready to come out—they must first acknowledge their right to be angry, realize that they cannot hold it any longer, and then find healthy outlets for its expression. Venting the rage is an enormous relief.

20. Once the rage is released, they regain their *power.* While they are suppressing their anger, their energy is so bound up in that effort that they feel powerless. Powerlessness is very familiar, whereas power and strength are feared as the instruments of abuse. Once they come into their own power and realize they can use it appropriately, they are free to be survivors and no longer victims.

21. The *self-concept* gradually blossoms through therapy. They enter feeling worthless and weak and evil, then graduate feeling proud and strong and good.

22. Frequently after a Gestalt psychodrama *confrontation of the abuser* and non-protecting family members, the client feels ready to confront them in person. Naturally, if the abuser is dead, or very violent and vindictive, or completely uncaring, then there would be nothing to gain and too much to risk to confront him. However, once the victim has regained her power she can sometimes solidify that gain by confronting her abuser and/or family members. Generally they still fear that the non-protecting parent will fall apart and so must be protected, yet we have found that most of the time these parents are able to either listen and be supportive or maintain their defenses to protect themselves. Abusers rarely accept any responsibility when confronted, but they usually understand that this person is no longer willing or available to be a victim and that they must behave themselves (e.g. with grandchildren) or they will be turned over to the authorities. The purpose of confrontation is not to bring about any change in the confronted person, but rather for the former victim to publicly and formally relinquish the victim role and to assert her new-found survivor status. In cases where they fear that the abuser is still abusing children, the confrontation generally includes a threat to report him if he is ever found to be abusing the children. A few of our clients are suing their fathers in civil suits to force them to pay for psychotherapy, to expose them as child molesters and potentially to force them into therapy to stop their abusive behaviors. In cases of the abusers being unavailable physically or emotionally, confrontation can be done in psychodrama with a very powerful impact.

Besides the emotional issues, we have found a number of basic skills which most incest victims are lacking and need to learn and develop.

23. Decision making—part of independence and trusting oneself.

24. Parenting skills—we learn most about parenting from how we were parented. Since they want to abandon their parents' model, they need new ways to substitute. If a client has identified with her abuser and is an abusive parent to her own children, then she must be treated as a perpetrator first to stop the behavior and accept responsibility for this abuse, before she can resolve her own victimization.

25. Communications skills—communications are confused in

incestuous families. Everyone assumes that the others will know what they need/want/feel, so it is important that these people learn to speak for themselves, especially in "I Statements."

26. Assertiveness—this has been squelched by the incest dynamic and so must be learned and practiced.

27. Relaxation training—many have no idea how to relax without chemicals.

28. Self-defense—it is helpful to learn some basic strategies of self-defense so they don't feel helpless and vulnerable. They can learn to present themselves as strong, confident, capable women, not victims.

RECOVERY PROCESS

We have found that group therapy is the most effective form of treatment for those clients who have enough strength to be ready for it, usually after and in conjunction with individual therapy. There is no better way to break through the isolation, the feeling that no one else can possibly understand, the feeling of being a freak, the ideas that all incest victims are crazy, or nymphomaniacs, or ugly, or poor, or stupid, or bad.

During the first session of group therapy we go over business details·such as ground rules and voting for topics for the 18-week agenda. Then we start sharing our stories. Each person tells at least who the abuser was, and how old she was when her abuse started and ended. We encourage them to share more information if they can, such as how it happened, what type of abuse(s) occurred, and the lasting effects which they are still experiencing. As leaders, we also share our own experiences of sexual assualt and its effects. Each person is listened to, maybe asked a few clarifying questions, and supported and thanked. We notice that even at this first session the bonding begins strongly. Sometimes these women have never dared to be close with other women before, but very few of our clients hesitate to bond with the others. Those who are hestitant are those who are still hiding a secret from the group (e.g. that they are lesbian, or that they have abused their own children). When the secrets are out, heard, believed, and accepted, the closeness which results is very powerful and awe-inspiring. These women are embarking on new ways of relating to others from the first night of group. We encourage the bonding by having everyone share phone numbers so that they can talk and meet outside of group time.

We offer an egalitarian environment with an atmosphere of trust, acceptance, respect so that each person can be responsible for herself rather than the others. We organize the group so that there are clear boundaries and structure, and then within that framework allow the clients to have considerable control. We share our own experiences and feelings and agendas so that we are not in a position of controlling authority. Thus we form the opposite atmosphere from the incestuous family which was very isolated with muddled boundaries, secrecy and unclear roles. Traditionally-run groups operate similarly to the incestuous family: the leaders are clearly in the controlling authoritarian position, they make judgements and decisions about the clients ostensibly for the clients' benefit, give the clients all the responsibility for their own growth but very little control over it. They discourage communications and interactions among members except through the leaders so that secrets and unresolved, unexpressed feelings abound. Traditional therapy groups perpetuate patriarchal values and authoritarian structures and thus are dangerous to the incest victims.

As leaders, we offer ourselves as sources of information, as fellow human beings with similar experiences, and yet with a different perspective. We present ourselves as people who may have worked out more of our issues than the clients, but not as perfectly evolved human beings. We do not utilize group time to work on our own issues, but sometimes work on them together during our processing time afterwards. We are intimately involved with our clients (not sexually, of course) they feel our caring and our respect for them, and our trust in their own process, pace, and style of recovery. Through our modelling, they learn to accept each other and ultimately to accept themselves. By experiencing this acceptance first-hand, they learn to trust again—this time with safety, and they learn to be responsible for themselves and to take control in their own lives.

As we have worked with adults recovering from child abuse, we have noticed a process emerging which seems to involve seven stages. Some aspects or stages may occur simultaneously with others, or they may be sequential. The order in which we have written them seems to be the most common, but it may vary. For example, some clients may confront (#6) before they orphanize (#4); or they may be rebuilding their new selves (#7) throughout the entire process. Each person has her own style and pace of recovery which must be accepted and allowed. Some clients may drop out of therapy before all seven stages are completed and then we leave the door open for them to reenter. The stages of overcoming the abuse as we see them are as follows:

1. Disclose the Secret

As with many other traumas such as grieving, rape trauma and war horrors, incest victims go through a denial period during and after the abuse. Many of them block it out partially or completely, and thus they must break through the amnesia to recover memories as well as the emotional denial. Some recover feelings along with the memories, others remember experiences devoid of any feelings, and still others have the feelings without the memories to understand where the feelings are coming from. Some will have total recall eventually, whereas others will never recall more than vague memories, especially if they were half asleep during the abuse.

Generally, I have found that those who recover the material slowly are working through each piece thoroughly as it emerges, while those who recover it all at once will work it through later. We have learned to trust each person's natural process without judgement. Clients who recover memories slowly are very tempted to seek hypnosis to get it all at once. This can be very dangerous if it overreaches the clients' natural pace and therapeutic process. A colleague's client had hypnosis and required seven sessions to get to the blocked incest memories. In the sixth session, she pointed to the side of her head saying, "What you are after is right here, but I'm not going to tell you." In the 7th session, she disclosed the incest memories, but was very disoriented and dissociated for months after that. We prefer to let the natural process take its course with gentle prodding, and trust that all the material will emerge in its own time and within the client's control.

Once the memories are available, the clients still tend to doubt the reality of their flashbacks or minimize their severity. One of our clients demonstrated the internal dialogue of self-doubt and realization very clearly as she recovered a memory of her mother anally penetrating her at age 5 or 6. She dreamed of the incident and at the point of penetration, she seemed to scream out in her sleep, "But what happened?!" and the dream was repeated, followed by her question, repeating in this cycle about 15 times before she awoke. Even then, she did not want to believe it and still made excuses for her mother. But a part of her now consciously knew how her mother had deliberately sexually abused her. The part that knows is growing in strength and the doubts have been diminishing since then. To fully accept the reality that this person who was supposed to love, guide, and protect her actually chose to abuse, use, and hurt her requires the breakdown of the fantasy of the perfect family. The loss of this hope is very painful and threatening. Since the victim has grown up being the scapegoat and identified as "crazy" in the family, it is easy to doubt herself. When she dares to share these flashbacks, any feedback which might hint at disbelief or questioning feeds the self-doubt and regresses the process. If, however, she is listened to, believed, supported and accepted, she can begin to trust herself and begin therapeutic process of recovery.

Disclosing the secret in an atmosphere of acceptance and belief is a tremendous relief. Clients may believe that they don't need any more therapy as they ride on the euphoria of this release. They will soon find that the euphoria doesn't last, so they need to know that they can stay in or come back to therapy whenever they need to and are ready. Sometimes they try to maintain the euphoria by telling more and more people, and they seem to get generally favorable responses at this stage since that is what they are looking for and expecting.

Another part of the denial which must end here is the well-it-really-wasn't-so-bad syndrome. In groups this comes out as "but everyone else's experience was so much worse." They must come to realize that the incest was wrong, traumatic, damaging, caused many current problems and that they were *victims*, before they can begin to work through any other issues.

2. Relinquish the Guilt

The next stage continues from the previous one. As these clients tell their stories and are met with belief and acceptance, they begin to see a glimmer of relief from their guilt. Because of the muddled boundaries, crossed lines of responsibility and role-reversals, the victims have shouldered the blame for the incest. As they begin to look at what was done to them, they realize how they were used by the abusers so that now they can appropriately place the blame/responsibility on the perpetrator rather than on themselves. As long as they are protecting their abusers, they tend to avoid the label "victim" because they don't believe in their own innocence. They will go through a period of blaming others (such as the non-protecting parent) who are less threatening and easier to blame than the abuser. Because women are weaker, easier targets, mothers often take a lot of blame for the fathers' actions.

Frequently at this stage they are afraid of catastrophe if they place the responsibility on the abuser, even without a confrontation. Does this mean that the abuser will strike back at them somehow? (Abusers are often seen as having super-human knowledge of the victims' thoughts, feelings, and whereabouts.) Does this mean that they have to hate their abusers? (They usually have a mixture of love and hate, but feel guilty for the hate.) Since this is so foreign to their family dynamics, will somebody die or go crazy? When the victim realizes that she is not to blame for the incest, she can give up her martyr role. She can begin to take control of herself, rather than everyone else. She can begin to understand the appropriate lines of responsibility in relationships.

As a martyr, she has built her self-concept around her guilt and worthlessness. Without the guilt, her self-concept is shattered. The result is a combination of relief and insecurity/uncertainty. This may precipitate an existential crisis: Who am I? Where do I fit in? What is my role in life if I'm not the martyr? What are people really like? Will I ever be "normal"? The old self-concept which was based on negativity is destroyed so that a new, positive, healthier one can be built in its place. This is so threatening that many incest victims do not choose to even remember their abuse much less confront the issues. From our experience, we firmly believe that it is worth the pain and effort, and we admire our clients' courage.

3. Catharsis

As the client accepts the reality of what has been done to her, and that she is not at fault for this abuse, she then experiences a range of emotions: pain, sorrow, betrayal, anger, rage. She must accept that she has these emotions and that she has a right to feel them. She has been well-trained to suppress her feelings so she must now unlearn that suppression and relearn ways to express her feelings. She is afraid that she will lose control of herself if she begins expressing her emotions; yet she dares to open up and let them out in healthy ways she can begin to trust herself, trust her feelings, and find comfortable appropriate means of expression.

In therapy, emotions are brought up continually. The harder the clients fight to keep them suppressed, the harder the emotions will push to get out. Psychodrama or Gestalt dialogues work excellently for appropriate cathartic vehicles. Many of our clients write poetry, journals, unsent letters, stories or express themselves in art work to continue this process of self-expression and release.

In many cases, we have found that incest victims have a clear split between their minds and their emotions. With Gestalt, Neuro-Linguistic Programming or Psychosynthesis techniques are able to bring these parts back together so that the intellect and emotions can work together rather than separately. This further strengthens the individual and begins restructuring the self-concept.

4. Orphanization

As they recognize and express their feelings of betrayal and hurt, victims of incest begin to recognize that their family of origin (at least the abuser and often the non-protecting members as well) has never been the supportive family that was needed. In many cases these people are still incapable of providing the nurturing expected in the familial roles. With that realization, most victims will at first try harder to bring out the nurturing, supportive part of their family members. They keep hoping that they will finally push the right button to transform these people into who they want and need them to be. Occasionally, with a new attitude and if there have been some major changes in the family (such as abuser and spouse divorced, or an alcoholic became sober), then a new relationship can be formed. Generally, these people are too threatened or unwilling to change.

As the former victim realizes that she usually cannot transform her family member(s) into the people she wants and needs, she must make a decision to stop trying to change them. This necessitates giving up the hope that she will someday get the mother/father/sister/brother that she has always needed. Giving up the hope is experienced as a huge loss even though the only losses are a fantasy, the old burden of responsibility for the family, and the frustration of trying to change something out of her control. She must grieve this loss. Then she must break old patterns with the family so that she refuses to be the scapegoat any more, refuses to be the martyr, or to be used and manipulated in other ways. She learns to say no to them. Often the pressure to return to old patterns is so great, that for her own self-protection she must break all ties with the family—no longer attending family functions/rituals, no longer having contact with the family. She will usually feel very guilty about this and the family will certainly promote her guilt; but she must take care of herself, not them any longer. Then she will feel free of the degradations, manipulations and abusiveness.

5. Reintegration

After the loss of the family, there is a huge gap. So the client must find healthy, appropriate people to fulfill her needs for nurturing, support and guidance. She may find these people in a husband and in-laws, friends, church members, or a therapy group. She must also learn to nurture herself, and to accept nurturance—she deserves it and needs it.

She must allow the child within (often a separate personality) whose growth was abruptly arrested by the abuse, to pick up where she left off. She will find that she enjoys being a kid again, making up for lost time—going swinging in the park, buying a doll or stuffed animal for herself, getting a radio she was always denied. She may also need to go through some rebellion as well to find her voice, her ability to say no, her independence, her self.

As she nurtures herself, she listens to her little girl within. Previously she has hated and feared this powerful child, convinced that if she loosened the reins she would run wild. As she grows closer to her little girl, she can forgive her for needing and enjoying the attention given along with the abuse, she can accept the child's feelings, needs, strengths and creativity. Thus she can integrate this personality(ies) into herself and become a whole person. She can love herself and thereby be able to accept love and nurturing from others.

Sometimes the individual has dissociated to the point that these personalities are separate entities with little or no communication between them. These clients report with alarm that they are losing chunks of time, or finding drawings or letters, or at worst, making suicide attempts of which they have no memory. If they are in danger, they may need hospitalization or another supportive, protective environment to give them the freedom to let these personalities express what they need to express, do what they need to do in safety. For the most part, they are scared of each other and convinced that they must annihilate the other in order to survive. The paradox is that they cannot live without each other. If some communication can be established, e.g. through letters or drawings to the other part(s), then they can work out a compromise so that they can work together rather than against each other.

Usually, the personalities are not so split off. They are usually aware of each other, cognizant of their thoughts, feelings and actions; yet they remain distant and fearful of each other. The common dichotomies are the rational being and the emotional one, the child and the adult, the rebel and the compliant one. There may be personalities from different ages—preverbal, five-year-old, eight-year-old, adolescent, adult. The therapeutic goal is to get some communication going between these personalities, then they can see what the other wants and needs as well as the strengths each possesses. They can embrace each other, merge into an integrated self, rather than annihilating the other and the self.

6. Confront Family Members

In order to be able to reclaim the power which was taken away by the abuse and the incestuous family dynamics, it is necessary to confront at least the image of the family members involved in order to express all that has been building up and needing to be said. This is done in psychodrama, an empty chair dialogue or an unsent letter. The client is thus able to express all of her feelings freely without any fear of repercussions or of hurting anyone.

Sometimes this doesn't feel adequate, especially if the family members are still around and harassing the victim. Then the client must assess the safety and feasibility of confronting any or all of these people. Each case is quite different and very difficult to predict. We have known violent, brutal fathers to respond with fear and excuses, and timid fathers to send their sons to kill the woman who is now speaking out. It is extraordinarily rare for the perpetrators to admit to the abuse and take full responsibility for it—they usually deny it, accuse their accuser or rationalize, such as: "I couldn't help myself; I loved you too much." If they are boxed in and cannot deny it, then they want to be punished in some quick, easy way so that they can get it over with. Therefore, the purpose of confronting the abuser is not to elicit some expected, hoped-for behavior from him; but rather to accomplish some relief for the former victim, to assert her independence and strength, and to put an end to the old patterns of secrecy, denial, and manipulation. This can be achieved, and it is most successful if it is carefully planned and rehearsed (role-played) so that the woman is safe and supported as she expresses herself in a calm, clear, assertive manner. Women who confront their former abusers in this manner, are frequently able to make a satisfactory confrontation, may receive payment for their therapy as restitution, may even receive an apology and a short-lived attempt at beginning to resolve the perpetrator's problems (e.g. going to AA or entering therapy). We recently encountered an abuser who, as soon as he was confronted, turned himself in to the police, pled guilty, went to prison, has been in therapy for the year since he's been out of prison awaiting trial and graciously accepts the social worker's supervision as he visits his children (3 out of 6 he abused). In other states that have the backing of the criminal justice system for court-ordered therapy, they seem to have better success.

In those cases in which the perpetrator admits the abuse and asks for forgiveness, the survivor must determine if she is ready, willing or able to accept an apology. Sometimes they think that in order to forgive, they must now trust this person as if nothing wrong ever happened and even let him babysit his grandchildren. Unless the perpetrator has gone through many years of intensive therapy for sexual offenders with continuing support, he is no safer alone with children than an alcoholic is safe alone with a drink. Thus, the former victim may be ready to accept an apology and retribution, but she would be wrong to expect that she can now trust her abuser.

Mothers who actually hear that their child(ren) was sexually victimized within their families tend to react in extremes to the disclosure. Either they are supportive, understanding, sympathetic and protective towards the former victim, or they become hysterical about unearthing the buried problems. For example, one mother nearly threw herself out of the car going down the highway and then later avoided a family counseling session by hospitalizing herself for migraine headaches. Other mothers have faked heart attacks. One set up her sons to ambush their sister when she was due to arrive. This same mother then moved to California with her husband, returned a couple years later and now occasionally asks her daughter, "What ever happened between you and your father?" These women react as if they have more to lose by facing the truth than would their abusive husbands. We speculate about whether these mothers were also incest victims when they were children, to react in such an extremely defensive fashion. Sometimes the women cannot hear the material at all and distort and/or deny it immediately as it is being presented. This is very unsettling to the disclosing survivor.

Siblings who have also been abused by the same perpetrator but who are still in denial, tend to deny or minimize the abuse of their sibling if confronted with it. Others just want to relegate it to the past, and forget it so that they won't challenge the one-big-happy-family fantasy. Siblings or cousins who were similarly victimized and recognize the abuse are by far the most supportive and understanding and may join an incest group with their sister/cousin.

We have repeatedly seen generations of incest victims in extended families as the patterns of abuse are passed down and spread like ripples on a pond. Seeing this cycle, we sometimes feel discouraged, yet we and our clients become more determined than ever to break these cycles now before they spread any farther. Thus we try to protect today's children so that they will not be abused as their parents were; or if they are, that they can bring it out in the open now rather than having to wait until they are adults with more children in danger of being abused.

After the secret is out in the family, some new closer family ties may be possible. Nevertheless, parents who were never able to be close to their children in the past cannot be expected to radically alter their relationships in the present. There may be more honesty and directness from the client who has been in incest therapy, but family members without therapy generally are not capable of entirely new relationships. Thus these "new" relationships must be entered into with a clear understanding of their limitations and possible pitfalls. By this time in the recovery process, the client is relatively independent and thus does not have as great a need for her family of origin. She has found other, healthy supportive relationships outside that family, so anything she can find within the family is a bonus.

7. Rebuild a New Self

Gradually, throughout this process, a new self is being formed. This is a positive, stronger self who has learned self-acceptance, self-confidence, assertiveness, self-expression of feelings and self-love.

One client compared the entire process of therapeutic recovery to a lobster molting out of its old shell which it used to fit, but now is out-grown. When the lobster sheds the old shell, it is very vulnerable and so must find a place to hide away while it grows its new shell. Sometimes it may find a safe shelter (incest therapy group), but at other times it crawls into a lobster pot for shelter. Once the shell is shed, it cannot be put back on. If the lobster survives the molting process, it will have grown a new, larger, stronger shell which fits better and enables it to function more successfully in the world.

Our clients learn to see the world and people in it from a new perspective—they see themselves from a new perspective of strength and self-respect. They are no longer the vulnerable victims that they once were, but now are survivors. They are no longer controlled by external forces, but rather take charge of their own lives, make their own decisions. They are now able to participate in healthy, equal relationships as opposed to their previously victimizing relationships. The process and the results are inspiring and tremendously encouraging.

SUMMARY

We have taken a new look at the many therapeutic issues with which an incest victim must deal, and a seven-stage process of recovery as she becomes an incest survivor.

These issues and stages of recovery have gradually emerged through many years of work with these clients. We gladly share our knowledge and experience so that other therapists may benefit from them and be able to facilitate more clients' growth from victims to survivors.

Speak Don't Eat!
Teaching Women
to Express Their Feelings

Melanie A. Katzman
Lillie Weiss
Sharlene A. Wolchik

The cultural pressures on women to be thin and to diet have been linked to the expression of serious eating disorders such as bulimia and anorexia nervosa (Garner & Garfinkel, 1980). Garner, Garfinkel, Schwartz & Thompson (1980) reported that playboy centerfolds and Miss America Pageant contestants displayed a significant trend toward a thinner standard in recent years compared with past decades. These authors also reported that over the last two decades there was a significant increase in diet articles in six popular women's magazines. In addition, the Neilsen Marketing Report indicates that 56% of women between the ages of 25-54 report being on a diet. In today's culture, thinness is promoted as a symbol of both beauty and success and, unfortunately, weight control for many women becomes confused with self control (Bruch, 1978). "Slimness consciousness" over the past two decades has been coupled with an increased pressure on women in relation to vocational achievement. It has been suggested that these new and often contradictory roles for women may be a potential factor in the increase of eating disorders (Palazzoli, 1974). Women must maintain traditional standards for attractiveness while also meeting heightened demands for professional performance and success. As Orbach

Melanie A. Katzman is a Post-Doctoral Fellow in the Department of Psychiatry, Cornell University Medical College, Westchester Division. Lillie Weiss is Adjunct Professor of Psychology at Arizona State University, Tempe, AZ. Sharlene A. Wolchik is Assistant Professor of Psychology at Arizona State University, Tempe, AZ.

(1978) has observed, in western society, women are expected to "catch a man" by being petite, demure, passive and above all, attractive. Paradoxically, while they are discouraged from being active, assertive and competitive, women are still expected to excel at their vocations.

For some women these stresses may be some of the predisposing factors that result in psychological disorders such as depression or substance abuse. We are most familiar with the food abusers, women who confuse taking control over their bodies with taking control over their lives. What follows is a portion of a treatment program that we have developed following several years of research on the eating disorder bulimia. Our research findings indicate that bulimics differ from control subjects in more than just their eating habits. In fact, bulimia was found to coexist with several personality deficits such as depression, low self-esteem, poor body image, and high need for approval (Katzman & Wolchik, 1984). As a result, we designed a treatment program to help women develop skills in each of these areas.

As researchers we have considered binge eaters, compulsive eaters, bulimics and anorectics as distinct entities; however, as clinicians we recognize that each of these eating disorders represents an obsession with food and physical appearance that helps women avoid the more difficult issues in their lives. Eating-disordered patients are attempting to enhance their self-esteem and increase their control by controlling their bodies and their diets. Unfortunately, many take either the indulgence in or the avoidance of food to the extreme and thus deprive or nourish themselves calorically while failing to develop a means of feeling competent or comfortable with themselves.

Although the efficacy of our program has been validated with bulimics (Wolchik, Weiss, & Katzman, in press), our treatment program comprises excercises developed by researchers and clinicians to deal with a myriad of problems. The general theme underlying the therapy can be summarized in broad terms as helping women to feel better about themselves. We believe that certain aspects of our program can be applied across eating-disordered groups in addition to patients presenting other forms of pathology.

Our program consists of seven weekly ninety-minute group sessions and two individual sessions. Treatment is both didactic and experiential. Although we typically see women in groups, this program has also been used with individuals. Each session of our self-enhancement program focuses on a particular topic that addresses a personality or behavioral deficit associated with research findings on bulimia. These topics include coping strategies, self-esteem, perfectionism, depression, anger, cultural expectations of thinness for women and enhancing body image. Although we use behavior modification to help the bulimic gain control over her maladaptive eating pattern, most of our attention is on developing new skills rather than on the eating behavior. We designed a treatment packet for each session consisting of reading materials, exercises and homework for that particular session. This also functions as a workbook and self-help guide for maintenance after the termination of the program. Although I will be focusing on a subset of our program,[1] one theme which permeates our approach deserves mention. That is the presentation of eating behaviors as learned habits. The emphasis on building skills forces women to take responsibility for their behavior and instills hope for change. We would like to emphasize this point as many of the women who participated in our treatment program were very depressed, a few were suicidal and some could be described as having long-term characterological problems. Our emphasis on building positive skills rather than on pathology helped women make changes.

Sessions 1 and 2 are more specific to bulimics so we will begin with a discussion of week 3.

SELF-ESTEEM, PERFECTIONISM, AND DEPRESSION

In this session, we discuss the relationship between depression, self-esteem and perfectionism and how it applies to both personal and weight goals. Afterwards, women participate in an excercise to help them become aware of the stringent demands they place on themselves, a second exercise to learn to nourish themselves in ways other than food, and a third exercise to increase their self-esteem.

Perfectionism

We use David Burns' article that appeared in *Psychology Today* (November 1980) as a springboard for discussion. We define perfectionism not as trying to do an excellent job but as setting impossible and unrealistic goals. We review research findings that perfectionists are more likely to be depressed (Burns, 1980) and ask group members why they think the perfectionism leads to depression. Many give examples of how they tend to perceive themselves as failures and as inadequate when they fail to reach their goals.

We also discuss how the way one thinks affects behavior. For example, when perfectionists make mistakes, they punish themselves by saying, "I shouldn't have done that. I should have known better." These "shoulds" are generally quite harsh and lead to guilt and feelings of inadequacy. We do a group exercise in which we ask women to list their "shoulds" on the board. Women tend to place very high demands on themselves. We ask women to challenge their "shoulds." How *can* they do everything and do it well? We encourage them to lower their expectations so that they can meet their goals more readily and have a feeling of accomplishment.

Nourishing Ourselves Without Food

We encourage women to replace their "should" statements with "wants" and to discuss how they can "nourish" themselves in ways other than with food. In a second exercise, we ask them to write down situations in which they feel good. Buying clothes or perfume for themselves, taking a bubble bath, listening to music, reading the newspaper from cover to cover and taking a nap were some of the "treats" mentioned by women. Addressing themselves nicely, such as "You did a good job" and "You're doing the best you can," is another way of nourishing themselves. We encourage women to "feed" themselves positive thoughts instead of critical ones. Friends also serve as "nourishers," and women are encouraged to cultivate those relationships that help them feel good about themselves.

Increasing Self-Esteem

We do a third exercise in this group designed to increase self-esteem and to counteract some of the criticalness with which bulimics frequently judge themselves. This exercise is adapted from Morris and Shelton's (1974) "Ego Tripping." Each woman lists five qualities that she likes about herself. After she lists her positive qualities, group members provide her with further positive feedback. This helps to increase self-esteem as well as to encourage interaction among group members.

The homework for this session is basically a continuation of the work they have done in the session. We ask each woman to read the article on perfectionism and to add to her nourishing activities and positive qualities lists. She is also to choose one nourishing activity from her list to do that week. In addition, she is to ask three people (one who knows her at work or at school, one family member and one friend) to tell her what they like about her and for her to record that.

ANGER AND ASSERTIVENESS

During our fourth session we examine anger and assertiveness. Many of the women we saw appeared to have difficulty expressing their emotions directly or assertively. Frequently, they ate instead of focusing on what was "eating" them.

Helping women express their feelings rather than "eating" them is one of the main goals of our program. In view of the bulimic woman's limited coping skills, as well as her depression and low self-esteem, assertiveness skills can help overcome those personality deficits. Assertiveness is one of the coping mechanisms that we emphasize.

Anger appears to be one of the emotions that is difficult to express assertively and directly. Our language has many expressions relating anger to eating behavior. We frequently hear people talking about "swallowing" their feelings or feeling "fed up." "I can't digest this," "he makes me puke," "I ended up eating my words," "swallowing my pride" and other expressions frequently crop up when people discuss their anger.

In this session, we discuss the relationship of anger and assertiveness to overeating. All women in our program keep binge diaries which we review each week. Typically women provide numerous examples of when they have eaten instead of dealing with their feelings assertively. For example, one group member recounted that she had a binge whenever she talked to her mother on the phone. Her mother frequently made comments which angered her. Rather than express her feelings, she would hang up the phone and go to the refrigerator. Frequently, women overeat when they feel overworked and drained because they are unable to say "no" to the demands of others. Sadly, one of our group members lamented: "my best friends are the refrigerator and the toilet."

Assertiveness

Definitions

We provide a brief introduction to assertiveness in this session and review the differences between assertive, nonassertive and aggressive behavior (Alberti & Emmons, 1970). We let them know that at different times and with different people, they may behave in any one of the three styles of behavior.

Human Rights

Since behaving assertively frequently involves exercising one's rights, we ask women to make a list of their basic human rights. Many women are not aware that they have these rights. After listing them on the board, we discuss how they might exercise their rights more. We read over the list of Assertive Human Rights in Manuel Smith's book *When I Say No, I Feel Guilty* (1975). These include the right to judge one's behavior, to make mistakes, to change one's mind, and to say "I don't know," "I don't care," or "I don't understand."

Saying No

One of the rights that many women do not exercise is that of saying "no" without feeling guilty about it. Living up to an image is one of the reasons why many women say "yes" when they would really like to say "no" to requests. We urge women to explore their reasons for saying "yes" instead of "no" to requests. A typical response has been: "I'm afraid that people will think I'm not capable if I say I can't do something. I want people to say: Look at her. She can handle anything." As in the previous session on perfectionism, we encourage women to lower their expectations and not attempt to be perfect. This can be most effective when done with humor.

Another common reason for saying "yes" is to win acceptance and approval. Women report that they are afraid to refuse someone's request; that the other person may stop liking them. We tell them that we don't need everyone's approval, but if we assert ourselves, we may earn their respect, and that is more important. We encourage women to experiment with being more assertive, and they are usually surprised to find that they seldom get the anticipated negative responses from others.

Some women report that they say "yes" instead of "no" to avoid hurting someone's feelings. However, by doing something that they really do not want to do, their unwillingness may become apparent and result in the hurt feelings they were trying to avoid in the first place. Sometimes, the therapist can model effective assertive behavior. When we use role-play, we encourage assertive positive and appropriate body language. We tell them that when saying "no," it is important to be direct and to the point and not to be swayed by guilt, pleading, threats or other forms of manipulation. In some cases, the woman may have to use the broken record technique which is simply saying "no" over and over calmly without being distracted by side issues. The role-play can be fun for group members and can build group cohesiveness.

Expressing Anger

A specific assertiveness skill that is difficult for many women is that of expressing anger directly rather than "stuffing it in" or "spitting it out." We ask women to think of a specific situation when they felt angry and did not express anger the way they wanted to. We ask them to write down their responses to the following questions about that specific situation.

1. To whom was my anger directed?
2. What did I actually do or say?
3. What did I want to do or say?
4. What were my fears about saying or doing what I wanted to?

Women recounted that fears of their own reactions or of other peoples' reactions to anger prevented them from speaking up. They were afraid that they would lose control by crying, yelling or saying something they would later regret. They were also afraid of reprisal if they became angry. In addition, many women have been socialized to think that it isn't "nice" to feel angry and resentful, and they have learned to repress their feelings. For some women, anger was so threatening that they could not recall a single instance when they had felt angry.

The therapist needs to assure these women that anger is a normal and healthy emotion, and can be expressed quietly and tactfully, without being rude or losing control. The therapist can further reassure the women that expressing anger is a choice, and that in certain situations they may deliberately choose not to state their feelings if the consequences can be negative.

Role-play can also be done in this session to help women rehearse difficult situations. Women are encouraged to match their words, voice and facial expression to maximize the effectiveness of their message. Expressing anger with "I" rather than with "you" statements also tends to make the communication more effective and less threatening to the other person.

We teach women to use messages to calm themselves down so that they can express themselves confidently. We have already discussed with them in previous sessions how talking to ourselves and changing the way we think can influence our behavior, and we apply this to anger situations as well. We give them some examples of self-statements in stress innoculation training for controlling anger (Novaco, 1975) and ask them which of these statements they can use. Novaco cites examples of statements to take when preparing for provocation (e.g., "This is going to upset me, but I know how to deal with it," or "Try not to take this too seriously"); at the time of confrontation (e.g., "Stay calm, just continue to relax," or "I'm not going to let him get to me").

For homework, we continue the work on anger by asking them to keep a record of situations in which they felt angry and how they handled them. They are also to review the material on assertiveness discussed in group and they are given an assignment called "Yes's and No's" adapted from Lonnie Barbach (1975). The exercise involves asking the woman to say "no" to three things she did not want to do but would ordinarily agree to do, and to say "yes" to three things she would like but ordinarily would not accept. In both cases, the woman is being given permission to do what she really wanted to do. The "yes's" are essentially an extension of the "nourishing activities," those ways of enhancing herself and telling herself that she is a worthwhile person, one who deserves to do nice things for herself. The "no's" are getting rid of the unrealistic "shoulds" and treating herself more kindly. This exercise affects the woman's self-esteem and sense of power, and reverses her pattern of depriving herself.

CULTURAL EXPECTATIONS FOR THINNESS FOR WOMEN

The focus of our fifth session is on how societal expectations for women to be "slim" and "feminine" lead to food abuse. In this session, we elicit a discussion of these cultural demands for slimness and help women become aware of their feelings about this. Many women are angry at their inability to make their bodies conform to the ideal types presented in magazines, in the movies and on the television set despite stringent dieting and purging.

The "Perfect Woman"

We do three exercises in this session to help women become aware of the unrealistic societal expectations for thinness and how it affects their behavior. We attempt to get a picture of societal expectations of the "Perfect Woman." We ask women to list the qualities of the "Perfect Woman" as depicted by our society. We write down their responses on the board as they say them. Some of the characteristics usually attributed to the "Perfect Woman" are physical. She must be tall and thin. With today's emphasis on physical fitness and exercise, a firm and muscular body is also important. In addition, she must have a tan, white even teeth, as well as "flawless" skin without wrinkles, pimples or blemishes. Other features include youth and smooth legs and arms without any hair. "Perfect" features are important in the definition: a straight nose, large eyes, long lashes and a round mouth. She must always be immaculately groomed, her makeup perfect and her clothes in the latest styles. She just "naturally" looks great all the time, without any work or effort. In addition to physical attributes, a perfect woman is bright and successful at her career and in her personal life. She is a very intelligent woman who is also a gourmet cook and a wonderful wife and mother. To sum it up, the perfect woman should do "everything well" and do it "effortlessly."

This exercise generally brings laughter from women as they become aware of the absurdity of trying to live up to an unrealistic image of Superwoman and feeling depressed and disappointed when they don't.

Payoffs and Price

In a second exercise, we ask women to list the advantages and disadvantages of trying to live up to this Superwoman image, and we write their responses on the board. Attention from men, feelings of confidence and admiration from others are frequently listed as the benefits of trying to live up to this ideal.

While we tell women that these are certainly good payoffs we question if they make the excessive dieting worthwhile. What are the disadvantages of trying to live up to this image? We ask women to list the price they pay in their efforts to reach this goal, and we put their responses on the board. Women list their health, their ability to have fun, their emotions, their identity and their friendships as being affected by their trying to be the "Perfect Woman."

This exercise can serve as an eye-opener at times, as the price of trying to look "perfect" is very high. We stress to women that looking good *is* important. It is the *excessive* time and effort that they spend on this aspect of life that is self-defeating.

Behavior Around Men

We do a third exercise to help women become aware of how societal expectations to be the "perfect woman" also extend to how they relate to men. We ask women to write down how they behave when they are around men they find attractive. Many were suprised to find that they related differently to men than they did to women. Although a number of group members prided themselves on being "liberated" women, they were startled to discover that they frequently did not express their desires and preferences around men as much as around women.

Through the discussions and the exercises in this session, we hope that women will become aware of the self-defeating nature of trying to conform to an impossible image. We encourage them to stop trying to live up to an unrealistic ideal and to learn to accept themselves and their bodies as they are. Rather than try to become the "perfect woman," they can start accepting and loving their bodies, with "unwanted" hair, pimples, wrinkles and all, even if they don't conform to what's "in" this year.

The homework for this week is adapted from Lonnie Barbach's (1975) *Body Mirror Exercise* where women are asked to examine their bodies without any clothing in front of a full length mirror and to list what they like about themselves.

The second homework exercise is to help them become aware that factors other than weight define a person's attractiveness to the opposite sex. They are to ask three men which women they consider sexy or attractive (movie stars and models excluded) and why. The third homework exercise is designed to help them become aware of some distortions in their body image. They are asked to find a magazine photo of someone whose body they think resembles theirs' and one of someone whose body they wish to resemble. They are to bring these to the group for feedback. If the client is being seen in individual therapy, she can ask her friends for feedback.

ENHANCING BODY IMAGE

During our sixth session we focus on how women feel about their bodies. We begin by discussing how designers of women's clothing set different standards of how a woman should look each year. Some years the curvaceous look is promoted, in contrast to other years, where the tall, willowly look is displayed on all magazine covers. If a woman is not this year's model, she feels she's a failure. A body can be in fashion one year and out of fashion the next. Trying to rearrange and remold the body to fit the times is absurd. However, many women go to considerable lengths to do just that.

Many women also report that their feelings about their

bodies interfere with sexual enjoyment because they won't allow their partners to look at them or touch them. Additionally, they believed that their satisfaction with sex would improve if they were slimmer and more attractive. The negative feelings about their bodies and lack of sexual satisfaction may lead some women to binge, substituting food for sex and love. This further reinforces negative feelings about the body.

There are several goals for this session: (1) to enhance body image, (2) to help women realize that weight is not the only physical criterion for attractiveness, (3) to show that *behaviors* and not only *appearance* are important in defining one's attractiveness, and (4) to help women become aware of and decrease distortions in body image.

Enhancing Body Image: Review of the Body Mirror Exercise

Women recount what they liked about their appearance when they looked in the mirror. They are asked to stand in front of the group and tell what they liked about themselves. They are not to mention anything they did not like. If group members have difficulty doing this at first, the therapist can be a model as she stands up and goes through each of her own body parts, starting from the top of her head and ending with her toes. It is important that the therapist does not mention weight when doing this exercise but focuses more on the "functional" qualities of her features, such as "I love my hair because it is so easy to manage," "I like my breasts because they feel so good when they are touched." What we hope to accomplish here is to have women "own" their bodies, imperfections and all, and feel comfortable with them.

After each woman validates her body, group members and therapists giver her feedback on what they see as her attractive features. Women were suprised to find that when they gave feedback to others, it was the *behaviors* they noticed first rather than the appearance.

Correcting Distortions in Body Image

After women review what they like about their bodies, we ask them to show us the photos they had cut out from magazines of what they *thought* they looked like and what they *wanted* to look like. Slim or normal weight women often bring in pictures of obese women. Group members provide them with feedback about their distortions. Frequently, women are unable to see their own bodies realistically but are incredulous at distortions by other group members. This can provide them with insight into their own perceptions.

Showing That Factors Other Than Weight Constitute Attractiveness: What Is Sexy?

Not all women distort, of course, and some women *are* overweight, even by the most objective standards. Is thinness the only way to be attractive? How else can women be attractive or sexy without being thin? The next exercise is designed to bring to their awareness that features other than weight constitute attractiveness to the opposite sex. We ask women to tell us what the men they talked to said they considered sexy or attractive in women, and we write these down on the board. We also ask them to think of what is sexy to them and write that down. Although thinness is sometimes mentioned, personality and behavioral characteristics are noted with even more frequency than physical features. Words used to describe sexiness included, "bright," "in love," "handsome," "athletic," "healthy," "kind," "considerate," "caring," "loving," "sensitive," "musical," "a good personality," "delivery," "a nice tan," "a good voice," "an 'individual'." Very few of these qualities had to do with weight or even with physical appearance.

Our aims are to help women appreciate their bodies and see them more realistically, as well as to realize that weight, or even physical appearance, is not the sole criterion for attractiveness. Women have inflated expectations of what being thin will do for them and many postpone living until the day they reach the "perfect" weight. They delay buying clothes, making friends or doing anything nice for themselves. We try to make them aware of how they have lost perspective, of how dieting has taken over every aspect of their lives. If they spend their energies on other areas of their lives, *even* on other physical improvements, they may get more satisfaction, and others may see them as more attractive, as well. Those "extra" pounds appear to be a burden on their minds more than on their bodies.

For homework clients are asked to write down what they like about their appearance, what others like about it, and what their "attractive behaviors" are. This is to reinforce the feedback they received in the group so that they can refer to it in the future. They are also told to pick one of their "attractive behaviors" from the list and exaggerate it, that is, to change something *behaviorally* that will improve their attractiveness, to smile more often if it is attractive, to exaggerate certain movements, etc. They are to record their reactions from others when they deliberately exaggerated these behaviors. They are frequently surprised and delighted to see how much attention they get from males when they are more verbal, smile more or listen more, while no-one notices if they gained or lost a few pounds! They are also asked to change something in their *appearance* aside from losing weight and to record other people's reactions to this change. Again, a change in hairstyle or makeup is likely to bring more comments than the pound or two that is hardly noticed by anyone.

CONCLUSION

What we have described in the preceeding sections is a subset of a self-enhancement treatment package that has been used successfully with bulimic patients. Some or all of these exercises may be applicable to patients with other eating disorders or women with problems of depression, self-esteem, perfectionism, anger expression, assertion, sex role questions and body image distortions. Although we have focused primarily on the use of these exercises with groups, we have used them with individual patients as well, tailoring the pace to the patient's needs. The women we see are asked to experiment with new ways of thinking and acting during therapy. This approach helps the patient to see that they can control the behaviors they previously saw as controlling them. To feel more competent focuses their attention on changes within themselves rather than on external changes in their appearance. We have found that organizing the exercises into a workbook has helped our patients after therapy, both as a document of their changes and experiences and as a reference as they continue to grow.[2] ·

REFERENCE NOTES

1. The program is described in full in L. Weiss, M. Katzman & S. Wolchik. (1985). *Treating Bulimia: A Psychoeducational Approach.* New York: Pergamon Press.
2. The complete program is available in a self-help workbook. L. Weiss, M. Katzman & S. Wolchik. *You Can't Have Your Cake and Eat it Too.* California: R & E Publisher (in press).

REFERENCES

Alberti, R. E. & Emmons, M. L. (1970). *Your Perfect Right: A Guide to Assertive Behavior.* San Luis Obispo: Impact.
Barbach, L. (1975). *For Yourself: The Fulfillment of Female Sexuality.* New York: Doubleday & Co.
Barbach, L. (1980). *Women Discover Orgasm.* New York: Free Press.
Bruch, M. (1978). *The Golden Cage.* Cambridge, Massachusetts: Harvard University.
Burns, D. (1980). "The Perfectionist's Script for Self-Defeat." *Psychology Today,* pp. 34–52.
Garner, D. M. & Garfinkel, P. E. (1980). "Socio-Cultural Factors in the Development of Anorexia Nervosa." *Psychological Medicine, 10,* 647–656.
Garner, D. M., Garfinkel, P. E., Schwartz, D., Thompson, M. (1980). "Cultural Expectations of Thinness in Women." *Psychological Reports, 47,* 483–491.
Katzman, M. A. & Wolchik, S. A. (1984). "Bulimia and Binge Eating in College Women: A Comparison of Personality and Behavioral Characteristics." *Journal of Consulting and Clinical Psychology, 52,* 423–428.
Morris, K. T. & Shelton, R. L. (1974). *A Handbook of Verbal Group Exercises* (pp. 112–113). Springfield: Charles C Thomas.
Novaco, R. A. (1975). *Anger Control: The Development and Evaluation of an Experimental Treatment.* Lexington, Massachusetts: Heath Co.
Orbach, S. (1978). *Fat is a Feminist Issue.* New York: Paddington Press.
Palazzolli, M. P. (1974). *Anorexia Nervosa.* London: Chaucer.
Smith, M. (1975). *When I Say No, I Feel Guilty.* New York: Dial Press.
Weiss, L. Katzman, M. A. & Wolchik, S. A. (1985). *Treating Bulimia: A Psychoeducational Approach.* New York: Pergamon Press.
Wolchik, S. A., Weiss, L., & Katzman, M. A. (in press). "An Empirically Validated, Short Term Psycho-Educational Group Treatment Program for Bulimia." *International Journal of Eating Disorders.*

Empowering Reentry Women: An Organizational Case Study (The Story of PROBE)

Kathryn Towns
Rie Gentzler

PROBE

Potential Reentry Opportunities in Business and Education

Background

In 1975, many reentry women were on our campus and many were in the "liberal arts" portion of our five curricula. With two graduate students, Towns began a Reentry Women lunch group for peer support. At about the same time a community woman leader asked our provost to help support counseling services for women who were reentering college. The provost named two graduate assistants for Towns and work began to seek funding for just such a service.

With a masters program in community psychology as a base, the three people began a series of community informational and organizational meetings. A successful conference GROW, *G*reater *R*eentry *O*pportunities for *W*omen, was held and together with the reentry women's support group and reinforcing community contacts, the need for such services for women was documented.

Serving as Master's papers, one graduate assistant researched models for services and the other focused on a survey of 600 women students, randomly chosen from three institutions of higher education in the immediate area. The survey helped develop an understanding of underlying family dynamics with the changes that resulted when the woman reentered

---

Kathryn Towns and Rie Gentzler both teach at Pennsylvania State University, The Capitol Campus, Middletown, PA 17057.

© 1986 by The Haworth Press, Inc. All rights reserved.

159

school. Putting these two elements together, with the community-need documentation, a funding search was begun.

In 1978, PROBE became a reality with office space in the main library downtown. There were two thrusts: (1) counseling, information and referral for women and (2) advocacy with business and industry to hire older women workers.

Start-up

PROBE had several philosophical commitments:

1. As a feminist organization, PROBE's practices would be egalitarian and decision-making would be consensual.
2. Counseling would be non-directive and assist in ways to make choices but never in making choices.
3. Placement would be by referral to the client for action and follow-up would center on the client.
4. Advocacy with business and industry would consist of a statistical data base about older workers and information-sharing dutch treat luncheons where PROBE's own older workers would serve as models.
5. Employees would/could be parttime, have flextime, be older, and should have some experience at reentry and/or family trauma.

Some Typical Clients

Sally

Sally was widowed after being married for 25 years. She was a fulltime homemaker whose youngest child was 16. Sally knew that she needed a job by the time her son was 18 and social security payments stopped. She came to PROBE to find out about training opportunities and potential jobs.

Betty

Betty had a college degree in liberal arts. With two small children at home, she wasn't yet ready to find a job, but she needed some help in finding direction, setting goals and exploring possibilities for the future.

Arlene

Arlene had a parttime job but because she was recently divorced, she needed more money. She wanted leads to full-time jobs.

Joan

Joan dropped out of college ten years ago. Now she wanted to return but was unsure of what courses to take and nervous about becoming a student again.

Seven years later we have dealt one-to-one with about 300 clients a year. Overall, 2% have been male. However, in 1982–1984, our percentage of male clients rose to 12% due to all the dislocated workers.

Services to Individuals

1. Counseling
2. Goal Setting
3. Strength Identification
4. Interest Identification
5. Value of Various Work
6. Career Path Planning
7. Assertiveness Training
8. Communication Skills
9. Resumé Writing
10. Interviewing Skills
11. Job Search Skills
12. Referral of jobs/positions to them for action

Services to Groups

1. Peer Support Groups
2. Job Readiness Training combining several of the above for groups
3. Math Anxiety Workshops
4. Tool Recognition Workshops
5. Computer Anxiety Workshops
6. Physical Fitness Groups

7. Blue Collar Skills Workshops
8. Non-traditional Careers for Women

In any one year we provide between 1500 and 4000 workshops. In addition, the director offers a lot of television, radio, and newspaper column work for which we have no estimate of the "audience."

Working Women as Resources

Another PROBE service has been our Working Women as Resources file. Women who are currently employed will do information-sharing interviews with clients interested in their field. They will talk about their jobs, how they got them and their training, how they manage home and career, and sometimes the job opportunities within their firms. Their names, telephone numbers and the information they are willing to share are given to clients who may then contact them. This has been a mutually successful venture and has had a very positive response. Many of these women have been recruited through women's organizations such as AAUW, Soroptimists, Business and Professional Women and other local women's organizations. Some resource women are former clients who are now employed and wish to share their experiences with current clients.

Information Sharing Luncheons

The Information Sharing Luncheons for employers and staff can be extremely valuable in establishing mutually beneficial relationships. Attendees can be asked to pay for their own luncheon.

The president of the company, personnel director, or a department head are invited. Personal contact is always desirable. A luncheon may concentrate on specific areas of employment, for instance: social service agencies, sales careers, manufacturers, business management and so on.

When a representative attended and indicated a willingness to cooperate with our program, we made contact as soon as possible in person, by phone or letter to determine the extent of her or his interest. Will they participate in the Job Availability Service, be a resource person, interview when they have no openings, or so on? The benefit to the employer is that you can send him or her a person who seems qualified for a specific job opening, and the company will be interviewing someone who is really eager for employment.

Funding

For three years PROBE was funded by Title IA Higher Education Act, Community Counseling Section. Since 1981, PROBE has been funded by Vocational Education, Post-Secondary, Displaced Homemakers. The Pennsylvania State University has consistently been a co-sponsor.

Space

In 1981 PROBE moved from the library back to the campus when the library instituted a new computer access program and needed PROBE's space. This has changed the type of client served to some degree but has not reduced the number of people served.

Research Component

Since PROBE is a university-based project, research has been an active component. In 1979, 1981 and 1984 PROBE has surveyed the state's programs for displaced homemakers. As a consequence, we know where all such programs are, whoever the funder is, while vocational education, JPTA, etc. know only "their own."

In 1980, with several books advising various forms of resumé's, staff surveyed 276 business for the resumé style they preferred. In addition we sought information on what women said or did in interviews that was very good or very bad. This information is local and has been invaluable to our clients.

In the current year we are researching and developing a project on peer counseling and/or job support groups for rural areas where it is difficult to help the displaced homemaker or the woman who is exploring returning to school.

Primary Prevention

Each year PROBE offers talks and workshops to women on how to seek non-traditional jobs where the pay is higher and is capable of supporting a displaced homemaker (whose income level falls to 43% of its former level immediately after a divorce) and her children. To facilitate this, contracts are maintained with several labor unions and union men serve on PROBE's advisory board.

To get these non-traditional jobs, math and science are the critical filter. Therefore, the PROBE staff speaks to girls from grades six through twelve urging them to "stick with" math and science. Each of the last two years we have sponsored a math-science day for girls 12–18. Over 50 women panelists whose careers are based on math or science speak. There are also hands-on activities, such as measuring brain waves, playing games on a computer, using a synthesizer for a melody and seeing how emergency help vehicle crews operate their equipment.

The Future

PROBE is at an upper division campus with no training facilities. Currently we are exploring what training that leads to higher pay, could be offered here, under our circumstances.

Evaluation

How well is this all working? Indicators include:

1. 72% placement rate.
2. "Excellent" as rating by over 93% of all group participants.
3. Numerous follow-up calls, letters, offers of help from grateful clients.
4. An excellent regional reputation which puts something of a strain on our speakers.
5. So much volunteer help that supervision and space become problems.
6. Inter placements every semester from both undergraduate and graduate programs.

7. Calls from foundations and other funders seeking pro-
   posals from PROBE (Child Care Information and Re-
   feral has been a spin-off).

SUMMARY

For seven years PROBE has served women who are in the
process of returning to school or to the paid work force.
PROBE is based on feminist and community psychology principles. A primary element in its underlying philosophy is the
empowerment of the people it serves. This paper traced the
course of PROBE from its conception to the present and
speculated on new directions necessary to meet changing
needs and to ensure the survival of the organization.

PROBE grew out of the expressed desire for an information and referral counseling service for women who were in
the process of changing the direction of their lives. Based in
the Harrisburg area of South Central Pennsylvania, the organization began operation as a funded entity in 1978, after
three years of preliminary work and planning. Its institutional
ties are to The Pennsylvania State University, Capitol Campus. Over the years, funding sources have included Title IA
Higher Education Act, Vocational Education's Federal Funds
for services to Displaced Homemakers and The Pennsylvania
State University.

The organization has implemented a wide variety of projects
in addition to its basic counseling and referral components.
Some of these are job readiness workshops, advocacy sessions
for employers, programs geared to helping women overcome
fears about mathematics, readiness training for non-traditional
employment, and a prevention oriented day camp for young
women aimed at encouraging them to keep their future options
open by studying math and science in high school.

These projects and others have served a wide range of
participants, but there has been one population which has
been a primary focus for PROBE—displaced homemakers.
These women who have been dependent upon the income of
others suddenly find themselves without that support because
of separation, divorce, or the death or disability of the wage
earner. For most, especially those who have never been em-

ployed outside the home, this creates a multitude of problems. PROBE addresses these problems through projects which are all based on the concept that the goal is to enhance the opportunities for people to have control over their own lives. In other words, the aim is empowerment.

In addition to direct service, PROBE has an active research component. Through research the organization is not only able to provide up-to-date information to its clients, but it is also able to better understand current trends and future possibilities. New directions must be explored while always maintaining a strong feminist and community psychology philosophy.

Seven years later this organization's overarching goal remains the further empowerment of women.

The Battered Woman

Rosemarie Ieda

The causes of woman-abuse are complex and interrelated in nature. In exploring them, it is useful to look at the problem historically, focusing on how the economics and politics of larger society influence the family, and how this institution has often propagated and reinforced woman-abuse.

Roots of the Problem

With the arrival of the industrial revolution in the 18th century, domestic life and domestic relationships began to change. Essentially what occurred was the privatization of domestic relationships. That is, the industrialist-capitalist forms of production split the general labor process and domestic laborers were divorced from the means of production and exchange. This separation resulted not only in the extreme privatization of domestic relationships but also in the greater physical isolation and segregation of women in the household. Women worked in the domestic sphere but did not earn wages, therefore, their labor was devalued (Dobash & Dobash, 1979). Looking at the family as part of the development of capitalism, the formulation of male supremacy is apparent. Diana Russell (1982) corroborates that the division of labor in the patriarchal family both reflects and perpetuates the husband's power over his wife. That is, while the husband is paid for his labor, the wife is not. This pattern devalues the wife's work and put the husband in financial and psychological control of the family. This foundation provides a basic understanding of the origins of woman-abuse.

Men's greater power in society and specifically within the family is viewed as a specific causal element in woman-abuse.

Rosemarie Ieda is a graduate student in General Psychology, The City College of Liberal Arts and Science, New York, New York.

167

Several theorists elaborate on this point. Russell (1982) contends that husbands do not necessarily abuse power, but are given too much to begin with. There is, probably, an interactive effect between these two elements, that is, an initial overabundance of power may lead to the abuse of the power.

Wherever the origin of the problem lies, power is a common variable which underlies all unequal societal situations. Women in general have less power in society than men. Therefore, they possess fewer resources to prevent violence and have less opportunity to leave when the violence occurs (Giles-Sims, 1983).

The abuse of power by men and institutions is viewed by many theorists as a primary cause in woman-abuse. There are other theorists who contend that the victim causes her own abuse. Though no longer accepted today, the victim provocation hypothesis has served as a justification for the husband's behavior. It has been used as an explanation for woman abuse by some researchers and social service agencies. However, analysis of case studies of actual situations which led to violent outbursts, shows that the woman rarely provokes her abuser (Dobash & Dobash, 1979). Further, to suggest that anyone deserves to be abused takes away the societal responsibility to eradicate the problem of woman-abuse.

I shall now examine what it means to become a wife within modern, industrialized society, since most instances of woman-abuse have occurred within legal and common-law marriages. Within the marital structure, Dobash and Dobash (1979) contend that the woman become increasingly dependent on the man while the man becomes increasingly independent. The woman becomes isolated from outside contacts and becomes increasingly subservient to her husband's demands and expectations within the isolated domestic sphere. These two changes within the life of the couple give rise to conditions under which marital violence may occur.

The process of becoming a submissive wife is a subtle one and a highly valued role for the woman to play. The young girl's movements are constricted and limited as she is taught that marriage is important, if not essential to her identity. Young boys are taught to value themselves in terms of work, financial responsibility, independence and individual development. The young boy, and later the man, is taught to move within the outside world, not the limited inner sphere in which the young girl is socialized and raised. The woman is often left at home and is the second choice for company. Since the man is seen as the primary breadwinner, his contribution to the family is viewed as primarily financial even in households where both partners work outside the home. Thus, once the man makes this financial commitment, he need not make any others (Dobash & Dobash, 1979).

Since the responsibilities of domestic work traditionally have been within the wife's domain, she is responsible for child-rearing, domestic labor and personal service to each member of the family. Though modified, theorists such as Bowlby contend that the child habitually prefers the mother-figure (Bowlby, 1982). There still seems to be the partially held belief that women are more responsible for childcare and other responsibilities involving the household than men are. Often, the man's contribution to the household chores is seen as a situation of choice. It is easier for the man to withdraw his support from these responsibilities, because he is not seen as morally responsible for them as the woman is. In certain professions and occupations, men are viewed as the representatives of the family in the world of work. They move back and forth from this outside world to the relatively isolated world of the family, where, as has been noted, the woman is responsible for the household.

VIOLENCE

The first incident consists of a single blow and usually results in little or no injury. The relationship between the partners changes, however, in that both partners experience shame and guilt. The incident is treated as a single isolated event, rather than the beginning of a vicious cycle (Walker, 1984). The woman is almost always willing to forgive and forget (Giles-Sims, 1983). At this point outside help is often not sought. Not seeking outside control after the first violent incident represents positive reinforcement to the new violent behavior. It increases the likelihood of more violence in an amplifying loop of deviation (Giles-Sims, 1983). Actually, seeking outside control at this point is viewed by patriarchal society as more of a norm-violation than the actual violence.

After the first violent episode, some women may have the tendency to look internally in order to determine in what ways they caused the violence. The woman may believe that she provoked the violence by not living up to her wifely duties. Sometimes, she does not immediately agree with her husband and struggles to establish her own position. Over time, however, the severity of the violence causes the wife to lower her opinion of herself (Walker, 1979).

The attribution of responsibility for violent incidents is seen differently by other researchers. The findings of Giles-Sims (1979) contend that across three violent incidents, that is, the first incident, the most violent incident, and the most recent incident, the women held the men equally responsible for the violence.

The timing of the actual violence in the relationship is of crucial importance. Dobash and Dobash (1979) contend that violence enters the relationship of marriage at an early point. Further, the violence changes in nature throughout the course of the relationship (Walker, 1979). At the beginning stages, the violence seems transient and the problems leading to confrontation seem to be solvable. The man is usually remorseful and the woman hopes that he will change. As time goes on, however, the man becomes less remorseful and is less concerned about changing the violent behavioral pattern. As the physical abuse becomes more prominent, it dominates the course of the relationship. The husband begins to see nothing wrong with what he is doing while the woman becomes more nervous and on guard as she tries to avoid the next violent episode. Usually, the woman will attempt to change it. This is futile, since the woman is struggling to change a pattern of violence by altering her own behavior. She is engaged in an impossible struggle at this point, since the problem of wife-beating is primarily the husband's problem.

A powerful statement is made when a man beats his wife. He is making a statement about her qualities as a good wife. Further, as already noted, he blames her for the violence. Once the violence has occurred, the rules against it within the relationship have been broken (Straus, 1977).

There are certain conditions within the marriage that make the occurrence of violence more or less likely. These conditions have much to do with power positions. If the man is unemployed or underemployed in relation to his wife, or if his wife attains a higher educational level, violence is more likely to occur. Thus, if a man is not in a position of power, he may use violence as a means to achieve this power.

Characteristics of the Battered Woman

There are a variety of characteristics and phenomena which make up the personality and behavior of the battered woman. The battered woman suffers from a growing sense of fear and isolation as the violence proceeds. She will often exhibit a pattern of learned helplessness, a paradigm pioneered by Seligman (Martin, 1976). That is, the abused/battered woman learns that her attempts to stop the violence often fail, especially given the lack of external societal controls. Therefore, the motivation to respond in an active way decreases (Giles-Sims, 1983; Martin, 1976).

The research of Claerhout, Elder and Janes (1982) indicates that different groups of battered women may share similar characteristics. These are low self-esteem, chronic anxiety, learned helplessness, denial, shame, guilt, psychosomatic complaints, withdrawal, vulnerability, and chronically depressed behavioral features. Hartik (1982) has found characteristics similar to these and has observed that these characteristics contrast with those of non-battered women. Hartik has found that battered women possess lower ego-strength, a high apprehension factor, higher ergic tension, lower self-esteem, lower self-satisfaction, and more maladjustment than the non-battered control group. What has not been made clear in the surveyed literature is whether battered women possess these characteristics before the battering or whether they evolve as a result of the battering.

There are also some positive characteristics which battered women possess. Schecther (1982) contends that battered women are often viewed as weak and passive and that it is important to acknowledge their strength, persistance and survival skills. The resilience and strength of the battered woman often goes unnoticed. These characteristics are not merely survival tactics but are sure signs of true strength which may facilitate later treatment.

Characteristics of the Batterer

An important topic within the research on woman-abuse is the profile of the batterer. The batterer has been described as a sociopath or psychopath. This analysis has served to perpetuate the notion that woman-abuse is a remote, isolated event, rather than a common cultural and societal problem. Hartik (1982) also indicates that her research did not find battering to be a remote deviant occurrence. Often, men who assault their wives are living up to the cultural prescriptions which are sustained in western society (Dobash & Dobash, 1979).

Leaving the Battering Relationship

The battered woman is not always able to leave the relationship in which she is being victimized, even if the battering is destructive emotionally and physically. Unfortunately, the problem is not simple. The battered woman sometimes does leave. There are real reasons however, why she has difficulty leaving permanently.

She may think her worth depends on her husband and her children. This wife-status is so essential that she may have difficulty thinking of herself in any other way. The problem of low self-worth and self-esteem is crippling for the battered woman and makes it difficult to leave a relationship, even a destructive one. Further, a woman is less likely to leave if she experienced violence as a child. Leaving the battering relationship is a process which usually occurs over time. Establishing a relationship with another person may be essential to doing this (Giles-Sims, 1983).

There are certain conditions under which the battered woman may be more or less likely to leave the relationship. According to the research of Gelles (1976) the woman is more likely to leave if the violence is frequent or severe.

It is not an easy accomplishment for the woman to leave the battering relationship permanently. She must be able to overcome her personal fears, her ambivalence regarding her husband, and her loss of status. Some women do leave the battering relationship permanently and succeed in beginning new lives for themselves. However, many women leave and then return. Given the lack of societal support, this is not suprising.

Institutional Treatment of the Battered Woman

The institutional treatment of the battered woman shall now be analyzed. This includes the treatment that the battered woman receives from the courts, the police, medical and social service agencies. Many outside institutions according to Schecther (1982) adhere to the victim-provocation hypothesis: that the woman somehow deserved the treatment she received. Schecther cites this as a lack of professional awareness.

The medical doctor is usually the first professional contacted in cases of woman-abuse. The abused woman will usually not share the truth with the medical doctor but invents a story that something else happened to her. If she is truthful, the medical doctor may avoid the problem and simply treat the overt symptoms such as bruises, cuts, and depression. There is a tendency among physicians to overprescribe tranquilizers. Even when the symptoms do not show evidence of clear psychotic or physical disturbances, women are twice as likely as men to receive this treatment (Dobash & Dobash, 1979).

Another institution outside the family which frequently deals with the battered woman is the police. Police were traditionally trained to deal with the battering as a personal dispute, and to believe that the husband is not really committing a crime (Dobash & Dobash, 1979). Therefore, the police were discouraged from intervening on the wife's behalf. However, these patterns have been changing due to the work of individuals such as Bard (1970). Special squads have been trained by professionals such as Bard to use mediation and referral in dealing with domestic violence. Unfortunately, there are still some law-enforcement officials who believe that the woman is to blame for the violence and that the law therefore has no responsibility in dealing with this plight (Schecther, 1982.)

The evolution of the shelter or refuge for the battered woman is one of the few institutions that has actually assisted women. The first shelter was established in England at Chiswhich in November of 1971 (Dobash & Dobash, 1979). With the support of the shelter it was found the women become independent relatively quickly. Shelters provide the battered woman with the opportunity to curb the pattern of abuse. They use the shelter as a temporary respite to negotiate the terms of their marriages with their husbands (Giles-Sims, 1983).

Children are often cited as the main reason for keeping the battered in the home or for her leaving. The children of the battered woman are often not battered. Children are usually spectators to the domestic violence. Society frequently exhibits an overriding concern for the children. This reflects the notion that patriarchy sees the children as a more important concern, and that the concerns of the battered woman come last. This is not to say that domestic violence does not have a significant effect upon the child. However, though certain concerns of the battered woman and the abused child may have some commonality, they are certainly distinct.

The battered woman usually waits until she reaches the point of desperation before seeking outside help. It is usually not until she has been beaten numerous times that the woman will go to a shelter for protection and treatment (Giles-Sims, 1983). In seeking intervention outside the immediate family, the battered woman will first go to relatives and friends. These individuals often refuse to intervene, advising how to cope with the violence instead of encouraging the woman to leave the abusive relationship.

Visions of the Future

There are many changes which need to take place. Alternative structures to the traditional patriarchal family must evolve in order to put an end to woman-abuse. One is a partnership in which husband and wife share equal responsibilities for domestic chores and contribute equally to the finances of the household. If a partner stays home for an extended time period, her or his contribution to the household needs to be recognized as necessary and important. This contribution must also be valued on a real economic level. That is, while the partner who stays at home may not receive a monetary salary for his or her work, this work needs to be recognized as a financial contribution to the household as paid outside labor is.

Perhaps a more fundamenal change in the family would be to establish a structure in which domestic responsibilities are shared among several families. While this more cooperative life-style may not appeal to all individuals, the responsibilities of childcare and domestic support would be more widely shared. Cooperatives or group family living need not lack privacy. Architecturally, building structures can be conceptualized in which common areas are designated, while giving each individual family sufficient privacy.

The most important point to remember in considering these alternatives is that the unequal relationship between men and women in emotional and financial power and freedom needs to be restructured. Men must relinquish their positions of power and control over the family if any true equality is to evolve. Additionally, the superwoman syndrome of the 1970s and 1980s is certainly no answer to this dilemma. Working a fulltime job, and then returning home to all the household and child-rearing responsibilities is definitely not an avenue of liberation, but rather a pervasive form of oppression.

Finally, the treatment modes which are offered to the battered woman must be improved if any serious progress is to occur. The dilemma of battering needs to be treated from an approach that understands and addresses the complex cultural and social factors involved.

The woman's movement and specifically the creation of women's shelters has begun to address these issues. The movement has provided the ideological basis and power which comes from the collective effort to oppose acceptance of wife-battering (Giles-Sims, 1983). However, the commitment to reverse the pattern of woman-abuse should not be exclusive to groups of feminist activists. The burden of understanding and changing this dilemma should fall to all factions of society.

REFERENCES

Bard, M. (1970). Alternatives to traditional law enforcement. *Psychology and the problems of society.* Korten, F.F., Cook, S.W., and Lacy, J.I. (Eds.). Washington, D.C.: American Psychological Association.
Bowlby, J. (1982). Attachment and loss: Retrospect and prospect. *American Journal of Orthopsychiatry, 52,* 664–678.

Claerhout, S., Elder, S., and Janes, J. (1982). Problem-solving skills of rural battered women. *American Journal of Community Psychology, 10,* 606–612.

Dobash, E., and Dobash, R. (1979). *Violence against wives: A case against the patriarchy.* New York: The Free Press.

Gelles, R.J. (1976). Abused wives: Why do they stay? *Journal of Marriage and the Family, 38,* 659–668.

Giles-Sims, J. (1983). *Wife battering: A systems theory approach.* New York: The Guilford Press.

Hartik, L.M. (1982). *Identification of personality characteristics and self-concept factors in battered wives.* Palo Alto: R & E Research Associates.

Martin, D. (1976). *Battered wives.* New York: Pocket Books.

Moore, D.M., (Ed.). (1979). *Battered Women.* Beverly Hills: Sage Publications

Russell, D. E. H. (1982). *Rape in marriage.* New York: MacMillan Publishing Company.

Schecther, S. (1982). *Women and male violence.* Boston: South End Press.

Straus, M.A. (1977). *Normative behavioral aspects of violence between spouses: Preliminary data on a nationally representative USA sample.* University of New Hampshire.

Walker, L. E. (1979). *The battered woman.* New York: Harper & Row.

Walker, L. E. (1984). *The battered woman's syndrome.* New York: Harper & Row.

Women in Prison:
A Case of Pervasive Neglect

SeEtta R. Moss

Female prison inmates are in the minority, both statistically as well as socially. Although isolated from the mainstream, they share many of the problems indigenous to women in today's society, including the following: constituting single parent families; working women; poor women; incest victims; disabled women; lesbian women; victims of violence; older women; and members of ethnic minority groups. This is also a highly abused population—physically, sexually, and psychologically. Female prison inmates suffer a high frequency of abuse during adulthood by spouses and lovers, of both genders, and a high frequency of childhood abuse by individuals both inside and outside the family.

Approximately one-half million inmates are incarcerated in state and federal prisons. However, barely four percent of the state and six and one-half percent of the federal prisoners are females (American Correctional Association, 1984). The paucity of female inmates contributes to the lack of attention focused on them and on their specific concerns. One reason this group is disregarded is that female prison populations have not attracted public attention via prison riots, law suits, and high publicity crimes which arouse the public's emotion. Public attention focusing upon male prisoners after the Attica and New Mexico prison riots has not impacted female corrections.

Ten years ago, Rita Simon (1975) documented the disparity of program opportunities for women in comparison with male inmates, and indicated that this was correlated with the lack of interest in female inmates. Although a recent paper noted that "Special concern for the female offender has surfaced in

SeEtta R. Moss, MS, is a psychologist with the Colorado Department of Corrections, Canon City, Colorado 81212.

recent years . . ." (Glick and Neto, 1982) the authors note that research on the female inmates has been minimal even though a number of publications, as exemplified by Burkhart (1973) based on anecdotal or impressional accounts, have proliferated. The first national study of female inmates (Glick and Neto, 1982) indicated the continued deficiency in program services for this group. Not only are female inmates neglected by legislators, the judicial system and the public, but also by government administrators in general and correctional administrators specifically.

Illustrative of this problem is the disregard for the specific needs of women offenders in planning for correctional facilities. A recent book on this subject by Montilla and Harlow (1979) has specific chapters devoted to racial issues and gang violence, but none to the needs of female inmates. Another indicator of the pervasiveness of this problem involves line staff (non-supervisory personnel) perceptions of female inmates. In a study by Pollock (1982), both male and female correctional officers were surveyed about their beliefs and preferences for working with male or female inmates. Both male and female staff preferred to work with male inmates, with female officers (83%) describing female inmates as "more difficult to supervise" than male officers did (55%) (Pollock, 1982, p.1). These data confirm the experience of this author in the Colorado Department of Corrections. This negative bias directed against female inmates by staff has obvious deleterious effects on their rehabilitation.

Contrary to the level of interest and the program services focused on them, female inmates have many serious needs. In a national study, only 39% of female inmates reported that, at the time of their incarceration, they were married or living with a man. Yet, 56% had dependent children living at home prior to incarceration. These statistics indicate that a large number of female inmates were financially responsible for themselves and also for the support of their children. Furthermore, 56% reported they had received welfare as adults. Yet, vocational training in prisons for female inmates is limited at best (Glick and Neto, 1982).

In regard to educational needs, the limited data available indicates that this is one area in which the basic needs of females are being addressed. The national study by Glick and

Neto (1982) notes a correlation of educational level of female inmates to the state-wide educational level, although at a lower level of attainment. These authors further note the availability of basic educational programs (at least remedial and GED preparation) in all prisons surveyed in their study.

The need for physical and mental health care appears more problematic. Although Glick and Neto (1982) provided significant data on female inmates in a number of areas, they did not survey the inmate needs for health care. They did provide information about mental health and physical health care programs available to female inmates which indicates deficiencies in the provision of services in these areas. In regard to counseling and treatment, Glick and Neto (1982) state, "Treatment in correctional institutions was conspicuous by its absence" (p. 148). They note that most of the "treatment" service was provided by correctional officers while professional staff (psychiatrists and psychologists) were involved mostly in testing and evaluation. They further speculated that psychotropic medications may be utilized in lieu of treatment programs. In regard to the physical health care of female inmates, Glick and Neto (1982) noted that minimal medical services were available. This study seemed to imply that the focus of attention is on the needs of male inmates (" . . . the medical staff spent most of their time on the men's unit and came to the women's side for sick call, pill call, or only on request.")

Some research has been published concerning female inmates who are mothers. Baunach (1982) presents a comprehensive view of the problem and its psychological impact which includes a brief description of the grief many inmate mothers experience over the loss of their children because of incarceration. This article discusses the specific problems in explaining the mother's absence from the home: what the children have been told about the mother's absence, who told the children, legal custody issues and the problem of visitation between inmate mothers and their children. This seems especially significant with inmate mothers since research has indicated that a " . . . substantial proportion of inmate mothers reportedly plan to reunite with the children following release from prison. . . ." (Baunach, 1982, p.107).

Although the problem of prison overcrowding has attracted much attention in the media in the past several years, the focus has usually been on men's prisons. The female population has increased 42% from 1980 to 1984 (American Correctional Association, September, 1984). The rate of increase for female inmates is much higher than for males. When the increase in female prisoners does attract media attention, it is attributed to the women's liberation movement. In contradiction, several recent studies (Smart, 1982; Steffensmeier, 1982; Weisheit, 1984) present data which question this oversimplistic theory and suggest that women who are incarcerated are far from "liberated." This confirms the author's experience which has found the majority of female inmates virtually untouched by the women's liberation movement.

On the positive, the American Correctional Association has begun to recognize the needs of female inmates and recently published "Female Classification" (September, 1984) the first major study of women's specific characteristics and needs. The American Correctional Association has also started addressing the needs of female inmates by including some specific requirements for them in their current standards manual (1981).

FEMALE INMATES IN COLORADO

The ethnic distribution of female inmates in Colorado is somewhat different than the national statistics. The current population at the Colorado Women's Correctional Facility (CWCF) is 44% White; 26% Black; 29% Hispanic; and 1% Indian. The 1983 state and federal population figures indicate 46% White; 46% Black; 8% Hispanic; and 2% Other (American Correctional Association, 1984). (Note: These statistics were taken from Chart 1 of the publication and rounded off. It is noted that they add to more than 100%.) The mean age for female inmates incarcerated at CWCF (this does not include those at the camp) in February, 1985, was 33 years of age with a range of 18–62. Unfortunately, range and mean age were not specified in the most recent American Correctional Association publication, "Female Classification" (September, 1984). However, the statistics provided in the results of their survey (2% 18 and under; 28% 19–24; 44% 25–39; 19% 35–44; 8% 45 and over) appear similar. An informal statistical breakdown of sexual preferences of Colorado female inmates, based on the author's personal knowledge from inmate interviews provides the following percentages: primarily homosexually oriented 14%; bisexually oriented 34%; primarily heterosexually oriented 41%; primarily heterosexually oriented inmates recently introduced to homosexual activities in prison 10%.

The situation for female inmates in the Colorado Department of Corrections is similar to the overall problem described above. Because of the small number of incarcerated females, Colorado has only one major facility for housing female inmates (American Correctional Association, September, 1984). A "camp" was opened in June, 1984, to provide alternative housing for minimum custody female inmates. This was the direct result of the overcrowding at CWCF. Although camps have been available for many years, this was the first such housing available for females. Only a few years ago, the women's population in Colorado remained between 70 and 80. In the summer of 1984, the population peaked at 117 prior to the opening of the camp. This caused serious overcrowding since the facility was built to house 90 general population inmates with an additional six cells for segregated inmates (those convicted of institutional offenses or with problems which necessitated their removal from the general population). To cope with the extra inmates, a temporary dorm was opened in an unused area previously utilized as an infirmary. The use of an open dorm resulted in many difficulties, such as security problems for both staff and inmates, and has been considered undesirable by all concerned. The problem with overcrowding at CWCF has not been as severe since the camp was opened, although the dorm is still frequently used. Few inmates need to be housed in the dorm at any one time. In addition a four-bed "Special Needs" housing area has been built to accommodate inmates with special problems such as physical handicaps.

In regard to educational level, female inmates in Colorado test out at approximately the seventh to eighth level. Colorado provides full-time basic educational opportunities leading to the GED for most who are interested in pursuing academic education (the major exceptions are those with very short sentences or those released by the courts within a few months of arrival). Although vocational training classes are limited, as in other states, inmates at CWCF can work toward vocational certificates in business school (typing, filing, speed writing, and basic accounting are offered) and, subsequently, in word processing. Non-traditional job training is also provided on a limited basis (welding, job training in plumbing, electrical and general maintenance work). On-the-job training, without certification, is also offered in the janitorial, laundry and stewards departments.

The level of health care provided at CWCF is minimal (but apparently adequate by constitutional standards, which are based on the concept of minimal adequacy). In the area of physical health, a nurse is available on-site for 16 hours per day. A physician extender, based at the male facilities, services the women's facility on a twice weekly schedule, with physician back-up and consultation available as necessary. Although Department plans include provision for female care in the new infirmary planned for the system, female inmates who currently require 24 hour care, surgery or specialized treatment are transported to the Colorado State Hospital medical unit. Acute and emergency services, as well as obstetrical services, are provided at local community hospitals. Basic dental services are provided on-site, when feasible.

The provision for mental health services is also based on the concept of minimal care, but apparently provided at a higher level than that reported in the study of Glick and Neto (1982). This author provides the primary mental health services at CWCF, which amounts to approximately 80% of a full-time position. A staff psychiatrist provides consultation and prescribes psychotropic medications (which fortunately are utilized primarily as adjuncts to treatment and not strictly management purposes in lieu of treatment). A substance abuse counselor provides group treatment for drug and alcohol problems approximately eight hours per week. A part-time Alcoholics Anonymous coordinator is assigned who provides an AA study group, coordinates an AA meeting with outside AA members, and regularly participates in multidisciplinary staffing meetings. In addition to AA, services include two substance abuse groups, one stress and tension management group, two psychotherapy groups, psychological evaluation, staff consultation and training, and multidisciplinary staffings. Although the level of provision of mental health services at CWCF appears higher than the overall national average, and is definitely higher than in the past, it neverthe-less receives less attention than the Colorado male facilities which are currently under Federal Court scrutiny.

THE ISSUE OF ABUSE

It is a major contention of this author that female inmates are a highly abused population. A recent study by the author at CWCF provides data to support this thesis. A questionnaire was administered to all available general population inmates at CWCF with specific provisions for confidentiality. Inmates housed in segregation on the day of the survey were excluded. This limits the data to this specific portion of women inmates. Questionnaires were given to 93 of the 100 on-site inmates, and 85 of these were completed (a 91% return rate). The following data were derived from the results of this questionnaire. Re-garding abuse as children, 14% reported physical abuse by someone not in their family, and 27% reported physical abuse by family members (including aunts, uncles, grandparents, and cousins). Sexual assault under the age of 18 by someone not in the family was reported by 28% of the respondents, while 19% reported sexual assault by family members. In a general rating of their childhood as either basically happy or unhappy, 20% rated their childhood as unhappy. In regard to sexual assault as an adult (over the age 18), 17% reported sexual assault by someone not in the family. None reported similar assaults by family members after the age of 18. A large majority (70%) reported physical abuse by a spouse or lover, while 26% re-ported sexual abuse by a spouse or lover. These statistics strongly confirm the theory that female inmates have en-countered considerable abuse, both as adults and children, prior to their incarceration. Female inmates, however, are not only the recipients of abuse, but also the perpetrators. In re-sponse to the question, "Have you ever physically abused your spouse?", 21% admitted they had done so. Five percent admit-ted to sexual abuse of spouses. These statistics do not necessar-ily indicate that female inmates are abusing their male spouses, as sex of spouse was not specified, and it is speculated that much of this abuse was perpetrated upon homosexual spouses. Four percent admitted on the questionnaire to having physically abused their children. None admitted sexually abusing their children (although one female inmate was incarcerated for sexually abusing her children at the time the questionnaire was administered but has denied the offense). In regard to the children of female inmates, a larger percentage (9%) reported their children have been, or they believe they will be, sexually or physically abused while the mother is in prison.

Although the results of this research may not be generalizable on a nation-wide basis, they do indicate that the problem of abuse is significant among females in the Colorado system. They demonstrate the need for services to female inmates encompassing the various factors of "abuse." In recent years in the Colorado Department of Corrections, parenting courses and Domestic Violence Workshops have been made available to female inmates under the conjoint auspices of the current recreation/programs staff member at CWCF and this author (provided on a twice/yearly basis by community volunteers). Given the potential ramifications of the problem of abuse, more intensive programs seem indicated.

SUMMARY AND CONCLUSIONS

In the past, the women's prison in Colorado has been very treatment oriented. It is only very recently that the emphasis on treatment and programs has deteriorated. On a national level, it seems apparent that female inmates constitute not only a neglected, but often abused, population. Although their overall needs have been adequately substantiated, lack of interest and concern for them is apparent. There is an urgent need to overcome the lack of concern demonstrated by feminist professionals whose philosophy and goals are contrary to the results of this neglect. The fact is that all but a small percentage of female inmates will return to society. If their needs and problems have not been adequately addressed, they will be higher risks for committing more crimes. Furthermore, they will be more likely to perpetuate their problems, from criminal behavior to patterns of abuse, through their children. There is a need to not only emphasize parity of program services between male and female inmates, but also to focus on the special problems which effect women who are incarcerated.

REFERENCES

American Correctional Association, *ACA Directory* (1984). College Park, Md: Author.

American Correctional Association, *ACA Standards for Adult Correctional Institutions,* (2nd Edition) (1981). College Park, Md: Author.

American Correctional Association. (September, 1984). *Female Classification,* (NIC Grant #FG-6), College Park, Md: Author.

Baunach, P. J. (1982). *You Can't Be a Mother and Be in Prison . . . Can You? Impacts of the Mother-Child Separation.* In B. R. Price and N. J. Sokoloff (Eds), *The Criminal Justice System and Women.* New York: Clark Boardman Co.

Burkhart, K. W. (1973). *Women in Prison.* Garden City, N.Y.: Doubleday & Co.

Glick, R. M. and Neto, V. V. (1982). *National Study of Women's Correctional Programs.* In B. R. Price and N. J. *Sokoloff (Eds),* The Criminal Justice System and Women. New York: Clark Boardman Co.

Montilla, M. R. and Harlow, N. (1979). *Correctional Facilities Planning.* Lexington, Ma: Lexington Books.

Pollock, J. M. (1982). *Supervising Women in Prison.* Unpublished doctoral dissertation, State University of New York-Albany.

Simon, R. J. (1975). *The Contemporary Woman and Crime.* Crime and Delinquency Issues.

Smart, C. (1982). *The New Female Offender: Reality of Myth?* In B. R. Price and N. J. Sokoloff (Eds.), *The Criminal Justice System and Women.* New York: Clark Boardman Co.

Steffensmeier, D. J. (1982). Trends in Female Crime: It's Still a Man's World. In B. R. Price and N. J. Sokoloff (Eds.), *The Criminal Justice System and Women.* New York: Clark Boardman Company.

Weisheit, R. A. (1984). Female Homicide Offenders: Trends Over Time in an Insittutionalized Population. Unpublished paper.

III. THEORETICAL ISSUES
IN WOMEN'S DYNAMICS

With each decade, scholarship on feminism has matured. Thus, specific issues concerning women have been analyzed in view of global sociopolitical and cultural processes. Clinical observations and research data have added to our knowledge about women's experiences of their lives. Women's studies has moved from a "specialty area" to a legitimate discipline of study. The articles in this section present some theoretical scholarship about women's roles and feminist therapy.

As therapy has progressed from traditional to nonsexist to feminist intervention processes, there has been an increasing focus on the sociopolitical roots of women's distress and on social activism as a means of change. *Dorothe Rigby-Weinberg* discusses the future of radical feminist therapy in light of the current conservative backlash in the United States. She argues that in order for feminist therapists to identify a unified theoretical orientation, it is important to examine existing theories which can be critically evaluated. She specifically describes Alfred Adler's theory of personality and psychopathology as a model of psychotherapy that can, with several modifications, be adapted for feminist interventions.

The next article presents an interpretation of the relationship between fathers and daughters. *Rosemary Dunn Dalton* identifies issues in women's development that are the product of their fathers' roles. As a consequence of the childcare mandate experienced by mothers, fathers may become relatively absent from family matters. Thus, many women continue to "long for" their fathers into adulthood. The author presents case examples to illustrate her discussion of the father's symbolic bond to adult daughters.

The Diagnostic and Statistical Manual of Mental Disorders

187

has contained increasing numbers of disorders in each of its revisions. The current edition (DSM-III) specifies gender ratios of specific disorders, which often correspond with sex role stereotypes. Thus, women predominate in passive, "acting-in" disorders (depression, anxiety, sexual dysfunction); men in hostile, "acting-out" disorders (explosive rage, antisocial personality, drug abuse). *Violet Franks* examines the relationship between gender stereotypes and categories of psychopathology. She describes how sociocultural factors contribute to the prevalence of depression, eating disorders, and agoraphobia in women and how this connection is often ignored by mental health professionals.

On a lighter side, *Barbara Brown* discusses the importance of play for women. Given our society's focus on achievement, status, and maturity, it is easy to omit recreation and leisure from our lives. Yet play has important "side effects" for women, including a chance to network with others, reduction of stress, and learning of group skills. Play can provide women with the self-confidence to continue the serious business of work.

Stress has been a familiar and yet elusive concept to therapists, since it is difficult to define yet ever-present in our clients and ourselves. As women have entered the workforce in increasing numbers, there have been dire predictions (so far not very well substantiated) that women will begin to have the stress-related cardiovascular and other health problems experienced by men. *Carole Rayburn* describes the therapeutic implications of women and stress, given women's roles in the home, the workplace, and with childrearing. She provides recommendations for today's "wonderwoman" who is expected to be everything in a society that still places major obstacles in her path.

Rachel Josefowiz Siegel discusses the issues facing Jewish women today. Antisemitism and sexism are two processes evident in the stereotypes of the Jewish mother and the JAP ("Jewish American Princess"), both of which ridicule the important contributions by Jewish women throughout a history of oppression. These issues are confounded by the assimilation of Jewish women today, and the denial on the part of Jews and non-Jews of difficulties facing Jewish women.

As feminists have begun to focus on women's experiences,

there has been little attention on a feminist analysis of how men in our society perceive women. *Carol Jean Rogalski* describes the male addict's perceptions of women in his life. She describes how Freud's use of cocaine resulted in exhibitions of masculinity and grandiosity toward his fiancée. The author's case examples illustrate the interpersonal skills deficits experienced by male addicts and the resulting impoverished relationships with women.

A Future Direction
for Radical Feminist Therapy

Dorothe N. Rigby-Weinberg

Feminist criticisms of sex bias in the theory and practice of traditional psychotherapy began making their appearance in the 1960s and early 1970s (Friedan, 1963; Millet, 1970; Chesler, 1972). Ten years later feminist therapists had developed powerful critiques of what Kaschak called "the antifemale and intrapsychic bias" of traditional psychotherapy, and efforts to develop an alternative "feminist psychotherapy" had begun (Kaschak, 1981; Rawlings & Carter, 1977: Sturdivant, 1980). Kaschak reflected the optimistic outlook of most feminist therapists in her 1981 review of the development of feminist therapy during the preceding decade. Not only had feminist therapy already "evolved into a complex and differentiated approach to societal and psychological change for women," but Kaschak predicted that feminist psychotherapy would "continue to exercise a profound and revolutionary impact on the institution of psychotherapy in general" (pp. 400–401).

THE 1980s BACKLASH AGAINST FEMINIST PSYCHOTHERAPY

Instead of the hoped-for growth and consolidation, the early '80s have seen a conservative backlash against the original values expressed in feminist psychotherapy, which parallels the general political and social swing toward conservatism apparent across the United States in the early 1980s. This conservative trend is most apparent in the effort of some psychoanalytic thinkers to appropriate the label "feminist." Those attempting to legitimize a so-called "feminist psychoanalytic" approach to

Dorothe Rigby-Weinberg is Associate Professor of Psychology at Northeastern Illinois University, 8521 North Lotus, Skokie, IL 60077.

191

gender development and psychotherapy generally base their work on the newer "object relations" version of psychoanalytic theory (Chodorow, 1978; Eichenbaum & Orbach, 1983; Schwartz, 1984; Smith, 1984). These authors argue that they have freed psychoanalytic theory from its phallocentric bias by dropping Freud's instinct theory and associated emphasis on penis envy as pivotal to women's development, and stressing the importance of the pre-oedipal relationship to the mother instead. The pre-oedipal language of "separation-individuation" or "differentiation of the self from object" (Eagle, 1984, chapts. 7 & 8) is substituted for the Oedipal language of women's wounded narcissism and "sense of inferiority" over "the fact of being castrated" (Freud, 1925/1950).

Unfortunately, close examination of object relations theory shows that it is vulnerable to most of the same criticisms feminists made of Freud's original theory. As did Freud, object relations advocates conceptualize women's distress as intrapsychic in origin, resulting in the same practice of "blaming the victim" of social subordination and economic discrimination criticized by feminists in Freud's work. Further, object relations advocates locate the solution to women's distress in psychoanalysis or psychoanalytic psychotherapy. But the object relations approach does not remedy several of the key criticisms feminists made of classical psychoanalysis. Though increased self-disclosure and an open commitment to changes in traditional sex roles are permitted "feminist psychoanalytic" therapists, the fundamental power differential between therapist and patient remains. The therapist using object relations theory still assumes the role of expert who will define reality for the patient, interpret unconscious resistance and transference, and even provide the conditions facilitating the separation-individuation process which failed to occur properly in early childhood (Eagle, 1984, chapts. 7 & 8). This is not the egalitarian relationship between therapist and patient for which feminists have made such a strong case (Kaschak, 1981; Rawlings & Carter, 1977, chapt. 3). In fact, object relations theory may go even further in blaming women for their own victimization than did Freud. In blaming women's (and men's) distress on intrapsychic problems created by their *mother's failure* to properly nurture them, object relations theorists in effect blame women for all psychopathology. This placing of all blame on women—reminiscent of the myths of Eve and Pandora—is not softened by assurances that women cannot help the way they mother, due to being left solely responsible for the care of infants and young children (Chodorow, 1978, chapt. 12; Eichenbaum & Orbach, 1984, chapt. 10). The blame-the-victim philosophy underlying object relations theory is exemplified in a recent article by Sandra Smith titled "The battered woman: A consequence of female development" (1984). The battering of women by men is attributed by Smith to the excessive dependency of women, caused by their failure to develop beyond the separation/individuation stage in early childhood.

The criticism here of "feminist psychoanalysis" as theory should not be construed as a questioning of the sincere desire of these therapists to end sexism in psychotherapy. It is also evident from their accounts that many of these therapists are doing very good therapy with women. Apparently, personal qualities of caring, empathy, and intelligence enable many of them to help women heal in spite of the theory to which they subscribe. The point made here is that there is a basic contradiction between the original values on which feminist psychotherapy was based (Kaschak, 1981; Rawlings & Carter, 1977, chapt. 3) and intrapsychic theories that subscribe to a deficiency model cf development in women, due to inadequate mothering. Ultimately, use of a deficiency model of women's development is bound to render psychotherapy with women less effective than it might be.

The Vulnerability of Feminist Psychotherapy to Backlash

Why were the gains made by feminist psychotherapy so fragile that, in the few years since Kaschack's optimistic review (1981) an intrapsychic theory which blames women for psychopathology could claim credence under the label "feminist?" Several of the factors supporting a backlash against feminist therapy are obvious. The feminist critique of traditional therapy came from the least powerful and prestigious members of the psychotherapy community—women. Backlash has no doubt also been fueled by the general political and social swing toward conservatism in the United States since 1980. However the most serious vulnerability of the feminist psychotherapy movement has probably been the lack of a specific theory of psychotherapy on which feminist psychotherapists could agree. As Sturdivant has pointed out:

> Feminist therapy is not a clear-cut theoretical stance, nor does it have a group of specific techniques. Rather it is a value system—the feminist value system—around which some female therapists have begun to build new conceptualizations about therapy and women. The degree of congruency among feminist therapists as to what constitutes this value system is all the more remarkable for the fact that feminist therapy has no "name" leader, no professional journal, and few training seminars. (1980, p. 76)

Today the "congruency" among therapists calling themselves feminists seems to have broken down. Professional journals now exist but they publish papers such as the one by Smith (1984) mentioned earlier, in which woman-battering is attributed to women's intrapsychic problems rooted in developmental failure. The fundamental problem seems to be that, lacking a specific theory and technique, the integrity of feminist psychotherapy is dependent upon a set of values that developed within a particular historical context—the United States of the 1960s and 1970s. As the historical context has changed, the foundation for feminist therapy as conceptualized by an earlier generation is eroding. There is no feminist theory of psychotherapy that can be taught in clinical training programs to ensure continuity, and so the newest generation of psychotherapists receives training only in established theories—primarily in psychoanalytic theory (though now it may be the object relations variant), with some attention to behavioral, humanistic, biochemical, systems, and perhaps cognitive theories and treatment techniques. It is not surprising that therapists should seek to "practice what they know," and that women trained primarily in psychoanalytic theory should attempt to appropriate the "feminist" label for their own work, though with an apparent failure to understand the original values and aims of feminist psychotherapy.

At present, only radical action on the part of feminists is likely to preserve Kaschak's vision of feminist therapy as "continu[ing] to exercise a profound and revolutionary impact upon the institution of psychotherapy in general, as well as . . . develop[ing] into a cohesive and conceptually sophisticated school of thought" (1981, p. 401). The radical action suggested here is action by feminist therapists toward choosing or developing a theory of psychotherapy around which they can unite. It is the primary purpose of this paper to call attention to an already existing theory of psychotherapy which meets most of the criteria for a genuinely feminist theory of therapy. It is hoped that serious consideration and study of this theory by feminists will lead to its adoption as a framework for feminist therapy, or will serve to stimulate feminists to develop an alternative theory around which to unite.

ALFRED ADLER'S THEORY
OF PERSONALITY AND PSYCHOTHERAPY

As the quotations below indicate, Alfred Adler was a friend of the feminist movement of his day.

> Women often are presented as the cause of all evil in the world, as in the Bible story of original sin, or in Homer's *Iliad,* in which one woman was sufficient to plunge an entire people into misery. . . . The low esteem of women is also expressed in far lower pay for women than for men, even when their work is equal in value to men's work. (Adler, 1927/1980, p. 7)

In his writing Adler stated explicitly, "We have no reason to oppose the present goals of the woman's movement of freedom and equal rights. Rather we must actively support them . . ." (1927/1980, p. 24). Since Adler, too, was raised in Vienna and was only 14 years Freud's junior, Adler's support of feminism calls into question the common explanation given for the anti-female bias of Freud's theory—that Freud's conception of women's inferior "nature" simply reflected the *Zeitgeist* of late 19th century Vienna. Rather, the different views toward women expressed by Adler and Freud appear to reflect basic differences in their own belief systems.

By way of orientation to Adler's ideas, it is useful to look at the way others have categorized his work. Adler has been named as the first among "third force" psychologists (Maslow, 1962) as the first to develop both the interpersonal and the cognitive approaches to psychotherapy (Ansbacher & Ansbacher, 1979) and as influencing the development of existential psychiatry (Ellenberger, 1970). It has also been argued that the "neo-psychoanalysts" Harry Stack Sullivan, Karen Horney, Erich Fromm, and Clara Thompson should actually be classified as "neo-Adlerians" because of their "adaptation of formerly Adlerian concepts" (Ellenberger, 1970, pp. 638, 641; Hall & Lindzey, 1957, pp. 114–156). However it is not because of Adlers priority in formulating aspects of interpersonal, phenomenological, existential, and cognitive approaches to psychotherapy that his theory is worth study and development by feminists. Rather, Adler's theory speaks to feminist psychotherapists because the issues of human connectedness and cooperation, male domination and female subordination, and the misuse of power are his theory's central concerns.

Theory of Personality

Adler argued that the basic motivation in life is *social*. As infants and young children, we realistically perceive ourselves as weak and dependent relative to the older members of our family, and recognize that our survival depends on having a secure "place" within our family. The need to overcome this self-perception of inferiority and vulnerability is the primary motivation for all humans throughout life, Adler argued. As young children, each of us develops a "life goal" on the basis of a subjective interpretation of what it takes for to "belong" in the family. All our behaviors as children and as adults, including the "life style" we shape, have the purpose of moving us toward that self-selected life goal chosen in childhood. We are usually quite unaware both of our life goals and life styles however.

Adler believed that there is only one life goal which can successfully enable us to overcome our perception of ourselves as weak and inferior. That goal is cooperation with others toward furthering the common good. Adler used the term "social interest" (*Gemeinschaftsgefühl*) for the willingness and capacity to contribute to and participate in communal life—singling out work, friendship and community, and love and sex as the three central life tasks for which social interest is a prerequisite. The central challenge of childrearing for Adlerians, then, is encouraging development of the child's social interest, since this is the only realistic way the child can transcend belief in his/her inferiority (Dreikurs & Soltz, 1967). Social interest involves the capacity for empathy and caring, both for those close to us and for the larger community of humankind. The person with well developed social interest views other humans as "our equals, our collaborators, our cooperators in life" (Mosak & Dreikurs, 1973, p. 43).

Adler, then, viewed the development and quality of our connectedness and cooperation with others as the central issue in psychological development. This same theme has appeared frequently in the work of contemporary feminist psychologists and psychotherapists. Jean Baker Miller points out that "one can, and ultimately must, place one's faith in others, in the context of being a social being, related to other human beings, in their hands as well as one's own" (1976), p. 87). Gilligan has described the central role of care, maintaining connectedness, and "not hurting others" in her description of moral reasoning in women (1982). Kaplan and Surrey emphasize the importance in women's development of what they call "growth *within* relationship"—maintaining connection while fostering growth of self and other. They contrast "growth within relationship" with the separation-individuation model which views development in terms of *dis*connection from the mother (1984, pp. 86–87). Adlerian psychology would view Kaplan and Surrey's "growth within relationship" as the appropriate model of development for men as well as women, since Adlerians believe that both sexes develop according to the same fundamental principle— striving to overcome a self-image of inadequacy which can only be accomplished by developing and maintaining connectedness and cooperative relationships with others.

PSYCHOPATHOLOGY

Adler did not find the traditional categories of psychopathology useful. He viewed what are commonly called neurotic and psychotic symptoms as having a common origin—failure of the individual to develop social interest. Rather than the products of intrapsychic conflict, Adlerians view symptoms as problems in interpersonal relationships and particularly in how the individual goes about trying to achieve "belonging." Inadequate development of social interest can occur under a number of circumstances which include neglect, abuse, or "pampering" of the child, and/or growing up in a hierarchically structured family or community in which power and privilege are unequally distributed. (This last block to the development of social interest will be discussed in greater detail later.) Such experiences tend to lead to the development of self-defeating beliefs and strategies in the common human effort to overcome self-perceived weakness and inferiority. These self-defeating strategies include competitiveness and constant attempts to "put down" and actively or passively defeat others, in order to establish superiority.

Life goals reflecting the striving for superiority include the following: "In order to belong in this world I must always be in control," or "to be a man, I must *always* be right," or "to be accepted as a woman I must always put the needs of others first." The weaker and more inadequate the person feels, the harder s/he strives to "be in control 100 per cent of the time," or "always put others' needs first," or to be "righter" than everyone else. Since realistically these goals are impossible to achieve, those who hold them are constantly experiencing frustration and self-created "failure." Each "failure" diminishes the person's already low self-esteem and s/he responds by redoubling efforts to reach the impossible self-imposed goal. Since most people are not aware of the goal around which their life style has been constructed, the above cycle tends to repeat itself with increasing feelings of inadequacy and failure often the result. Eventually a discouraged person in such a cycle may develop "symptoms." Symptoms serve the individual's purpose in two ways—(1) they enable the person to use covert means in moving toward his/her goal, and (2) they provide an alibi for the person's failure to "carry his/her share" within the family or community, or at work.

Certain features of Adler's theory should be evident from the foregoing discussion. First, neurosis and psychosis represent a failure of learning, a product of faulty perceptions and self-defeating life goals (Mosak & Dreikurs, 1973, p. 43). Second, all behavior is purposive. We are not pushed by causes such as instinctual drives, but rather pulled by self-selected life goals. Third, the person can best be understood from a holistic point of view. We are not divided against ourselves, as a concept such as "intrapsychic conflict" would suggest. Rather we generate our feelings for our own purposes—for example "anxiety" in the case of the agoraphobic or "ambivalence" in the case of the obsessive-compulsive. Current popular beliefs in the primacy of feelings as causes of behavior enable us to avoid awareness of the ways in which we generate and use feelings to implement decisions we have already made.

It was the holistic emphasis of Adler's theory that led him to name his system "Individual Psychology"—"individual" here meaning "indivisible."

Inequality Between the Sexes and Psychopathology

As mentioned earlier, Adler viewed the unequal distribution of power and privilege as a block to the development of social interest in the child. Thus he viewed inequality between the sexes as "the severest illness of our social organism" (Adler, 1914/1980, p. 27). The higher value placed on all things masculine burdens the man from childhood "with the obligation to prove his superiority over women" (p. 27) and, in keeping with the exploitation of men by other men which he observes, he is also likely to develop the belief that "a real man" must prove his superiority over other men too if he is to have a "place" in his family and community. The goal of superiority over men and women prevents men from developing the social interest and cooperation which would yield a secure sense of connectedness with others. Instead, an emphasis on competition, dominance, and open exercise of power become part of the life style of many men, in a vain effort to compensate for feelings of inferiority (Mosak & Schneider, 1977).

The undervaluation of women interferes with their choosing a life goal of cooperation with others too, since true cooperation is only possible between equals. But since, as Jean Baker Miller has observed, "the only forms of affiliation that have been available to women are subservient affiliations" (1976, p. 89) the life goals and life styles of women, too, have been distorted in the direction of power seeking. Living in a society that devalues them, women tend to develop one of two approaches in attempting to insure their social significance—the "male" strategy of openly attempting to dominate and defeat others and prove themselves "as good as or better than men" or, more frequently, indirect techniques such as attempting to demonstrate "moral superiority" or "superiority through goodness and self-sacrifice." Once again, however, the goal is unattainable. One cannot realistically prove oneself morally superior to *all* others, and so the belief in one's own significance suffers, followed by redoubled efforts to prove superiority, or by such severe discouragement that symptoms occur in order to excuse the individual from the stress of competition in what is, indeed, a hopeless quest for superiority.

PSYCHOTHERAPY

Adler's theory has been described as a forerunner of the cognitive, Rogerian, and existential schools of psychotherapy. Thus it is not surprising that there is overlap between Adlerian therapy and these other three approaches. Adler did not consider patients "sick," but deeply discouraged due to the pursuit of an unattainable life goal—some version of superiority over others. The goal of therapy is not to cure the patient of illness, but to help the patient become aware of his/her self-defeating life goal, and to substitute for it the goal of cooperation with others in egalitarian relationships. This can be accomplished only through cooperation between the patient and therapist. And, in turn, cooperation can only be developed when certain conditions hold in therapy—conditions similar to those later advocated by Carl Rogers (1957). Those conditions are (1) an egalitarian relationship between patient and therapist, (2) understanding and appreciation of the patient's view of reality by the therapist, and (3) the therapist's genuine care and concern for the patient.

With respect to an egalitarian relationship, Adler is reported to have felt so strongly about this that he made certain that he and his patient sat on chairs similar in height, shape, and size (Ellenberger, 1970). This is in line with Adler's statement that "the therapist is never to allow the patient to force upon him a superior role such as that of teacher, father, or saviour . . . " (1913/1956, p. 339). Concerning the patient's view of reality, Adler set a high standard for therapists—"We must be able to see with his eyes and listen with his ears" (1931/1956, p. 340).

Given a cooperative, egalitarian relationship between patient and therapist, Adlerian psychotherapy typically moves through three stages. In very brief form these involve (1) the therapist's gaining an understanding of the patient's life goal and life style, and how these have contributed to the patient's conviction that s/he is deficient in some way; (2) the therapist's sharing with the patient what has been learned regarding the patient's self-defeating life goal and life style; and (3) to the degree that the patient then wishes to change, the therapist's facilitating reorientation in the life goal and the life style. The Adlerian therapist plays an active role in the reorientation process, focusing on the *goal* of the patient's current actions. With understanding of the life goal, choice and change in the goal and the life style become possible for the patient.

Adler considered "transference" and "resistance" phenomena to be artifacts created by Freud's method of treatment (Ellenberger, 1970, p. 621). Adler encountered neither, he said, when he maintained an egalitarian relationship with clients, and focused on the *present goals* of behavior, rather than searching for "causes" in the past (1913/1956, p. 343). Contemporary Adlerian therapists often use "multiple psychotherapy" (treatment of patient with more than one therapist present). Among other advantages, multiple psychotherapy reduces transference and patient dependence, thus contributing to equalizing the relationship between patient and therapist(s) (Dreikurs, Mosak, & Shulman, 1952).

EVALUATION OF THE UTILITY OF ADLERIAN PSYCHOTHERAPY TO FEMINISTS

It should be apparent from the brief review above that Adlerian psychotherapy shares many of the most important values of feminist therapy listed by Kaschak in her 1981 review of feminist psychotherapy. These include the following:

Egalitarian relationship between patient and therapist.
Strong effort to erase the power differential between patient and therapist.
"Psychopathology" viewed as a function of both individual development *and* the effects of inequality in sex roles.
"Transference" generated by faulty therapy technique. Considered an interference with therapy.
Goals of psychotherapy include increasing patient interest and participation in community activities, including those aimed at social change and equality among people.
Traditional sex roles viewed as primarily social constructions. Should be abolished insofar as they imply inequality between the sexes.

In contrast to the many similarities, there are also at least two contradictions between Adler's ideas and the values of feminist therapy. They are Adler's anti-homosexual bias, and his assumption that motherhood would be desired by all women in a society in which women were valued equally and motherhood given the support and respect it is due. Adler believed homosexuality was based on rejection and depreciation of the other sex, and that it represented simply one more instance in which feelings of inferiority led to "putting others down" in an attempt to prove one's own superiority. In contrast, most contemporary feminist therapists view homosexuality as a preference for loving members of the same sex—as a positive choice in its own right, rather than a compensatory reaction "against" the other sex. Hence feminists would not share Adler's view that homosexuality is an instance of striving for superiority over members of the other sex. Similarly, most feminist therapists would probably view as patronizing Adler's belief that all women would want to become mothers in a world in which women and motherhood were properly valued. More choices are available to women today than Adler was capable of envisioning when he developed his ideas in the first third of the 20th century. Fortunately, Adler's ideas on homosexuality and on the attractiveness of motherhood to all women are not central to his theory of psychotherapy.

As has frequently been pointed out, no theory is "true" in the ultimate sense—neither the Freudian or object relations theories criticized earlier, nor Adler's theory of personality and psychotherapy which has just been outlined. The only legitimate question we can ask about a theory is "how useful is it for the purpose at hand?" In order to answer this fundamental question of the utility of Adlerian therapy for feminist therapists, a number of prior questions need to be asked. Is the theory on which Adlerian therapy is based closer to feminist values than the theories underlying other models of psychotherapy? Are the goals of Adlerian therapy closer to the goals of feminist therapy than is true of other models of psychotherapy? Are the differences that exist between Adler's ideas and feminist values central to Adlerian theory, or peripheral issues? How effective are Adlerian treatment techniques in achieving the therapy goals valued by feminist therapists? Obviously not all these questions can be answered on the basis of the brief description of Adlerian therapy provided here. In the judgment of the author of this paper, however, feminist therapists who do explore Adler's theory of psychotherapy will find it well suited to providing a method of therapy on which nearly all feminist therapists might agree.

Another important question concerns the likelihood of feminist psychotherapists agreeing to unite around one theory of psychotherapy. Is this a realistic possibility? Certainly many factors stand in the way. The most important of these is the dominance in clinical training programs of already established theories—particularly psychoanalytic and behavioral models of therapy. None of us particularly wants to relinquish that which we already "know" and are used to, in order to learn new approaches. Also, a change in the language and concepts we use in doing and discussing our work can make communication with colleagues difficult. It is often easier to unobtrusively slip small bits of feminist thinking into theories already dominant in the psychotherapy establishment, than to take the more radical stance of seeking a fresh approach that truly embodies the original vision of feminist psychotherapy. It is argued here that the radical approach is the only one that will prevent the erosion and loss of the fundamental values of feminist psychotherapy.

The Adlerian movement in North America is still small enough for there to be ample opportunities for leadership in determining the direction this movement will take in coming years. While many contemporary Adlerians are not feminists,

Adler's theory encourages such a political orientation. No one is better suited to developing and directing the future of Adlerian therapy than feminists, whose cause Adler was championing 70 years ago.

REFERENCES

Adler, A. (1956). *The individual psychology of Alfred Adler* (H. L. Ansbacher & R. R. Ansbacher, Eds. and Annots.). New York: Basic Books. (Original work published 1907–1936)

Adler, A. (1980). *Co-operation between the sexes: Writings on women, love and marriage, sexuality and its disorders* (H. L. Ansbacher & R. R. Ansbacher, Eds. and Trans.). New York: Jason Aronson. (Originally published 1910–1945)

Ansbacher, H. L., & Ansbacher, R. R. (1979). "Introduction" and "Comment" sections. In A. Alder, *Superiority and social interest: A collection of later writings* (H. L. Ansbacher & R. R. Ansbacher, Eds., 3rd rev. ed.). New York: W. W. Norton.

Chesler, P. (1972). *Women and madness.* New York: Doubleday.

Chodorow, N. (1978). *The reproduction of mothering: Psychoanalysis and the sociology of gender.* Berkeley: University of California Press.

Dreikurs, R., Mosak, H. H., & Shulman, B. H. (1952). Patient therapist relationship in multiple psychotherapy. II. Its advantages for the patient. *Psychiatric Quarterly, 26,* 590–596.

Dreikurs, R., & Soltz, V. (1967). *Children: The challenge.* New York: Duell, Sloan & Pearce.

Eagle, M. N. (1984). *Recent developments in psychoanalysis.* New York: McGraw-Hill.

Eichenbaum, L., & Orbach, S. (1983). *Understanding women: A feminist psychoanalytic approach.* New York: Basic Books.

Ellenberger, H. F. (1970). *The discovery of the unconscious: The history and evolution of dynamic psychiatry.* New York: Basic Books.

Freud, S. (1950). Some psychological consequences of the anatomical distinction between the sexes. In J. Strachey (Ed. and Trans.), *Collected papers* (Vol. V, pp. 186–197). London: Hogarth Press. (Original work published 1925)

Friedan, B. (1963). *The feminine mistique.* New York: W. W. Norton.

Gilligan, C. (1982) *In a different voice.* Cambridge: Harvard University.

Hall, C. S., & Lindzey, G. (1957). *Theories of personality.* New York: Wiley.

Kaplan, A. G., & Surrey, J. L. (1984). The relational self in women: Developmental theory and public policy. In L. E. Walker (Ed.), *Women and mental health policy* (pp. 79–94). Beverly Hills, CA: Sage.

Kaschak, E. (1981). Feminist psychotherapy: The first decade. In S. Cox (Ed.), *Female psychology* (2nd ed., pp. 387–401). New York: St. Martin's.

Maslow, A. H. (1962). *Toward a new psychology of being.* Princeton, NJ: VanNostrand.

Miller, J. B. (1976). *Toward a new psychology of women.* Boston: Beacon.

Millet, K. (1970). *Sexual politics.* New York: Doubleday.

Mosak, H. H., & Dreikurs, R. (1973). Adlerian psychotherapy. In R. Corsini (Ed.), *Current psychotherapies.* Itasca, IL: F. E. Peacock.

Mosak, H. H., & Schneider, S. (1977). Masculine protest, penis envy, women's liberation and sexual equality. *Journal of Individual Psychology, 33,* 193–202.

Rawlings, E. I., & Carter, D. K. (Eds.). (1977). *Psychotherapy for women: Treatment toward equality*. Springfield, IL: C. C. Thomas.

Rogers, C. R. (1957). The necessary and sufficient conditions of therapeutic personality change. *Journal of Consulting Psychology, 21,* 95–103.

Schwartz, A. E. (1984). Psychoanalysis and women: A rapprochement. *Women and Therapy, 3*(1), 3–12.

Smith, S. (1984). The battered woman: A consequence of female development. *Women and Therapy, 3*(2), 3–10.

Sturdivant, S. (1980). *Therapy with women: A feminist philosophy of treatment.* New York: Springer.

The Psychology of Fathers and Daughters: A Feminist Approach and Methodology

Rosemary Dunn Dalton

This paper explores the role of the father and how he has impacted the development of some daughters in our culture. As a feminist therapist I hope to present a perspective that will further illuminate the need for a more balanced view of the father-daughter relationship in the psychological literature. I would like to concentrate on a particular daughter disturbance which I am characterizing as a "longing for the father." This will combine feminist writing, traditional psychoanalytic theory, feminist theory and methodology.

For four years I compiled daughters' stories about their relationships (or the lack of them) with their fathers and found that it is common for women to complain that they were let down by their fathers. Many say that their fathers were emotionally and/or physically absent.

As feminists it is in our self-interest to re-examine the relationship of the father to the daughter, first, because it is timely to shift to the father some of the mother-blaming that permeates psychoanalytical theory so that he takes his proper place in the literature. Second, as women explore roles that have been traditionally held by men, the hidden messages of the father are often worth uncovering and may better enable women to view themselves as successful.

Rosemary Dunn Dalton is in private practice at the Cambridge Feminist Counseling and Consultant Services, 127 Lanark Road, Brighton, MA, 02146.

WHAT IS THE CONTRIBUTION OF THE FATHER?

William Appleton, author of *Fathers & Daughters,* in his examination of fathers' influence on daughters, presents the argument that during life's cycles, certain father behaviors are just a part of a sequence. He makes a case for daughters' understanding of the father in the context of his age. Appleton has minimized the rage of daughters. He characterizes fathers as having to put up with abuse from the daughters, for example, during adolescence. However, we need to advocate for daughters who suffer from a longing for a father who will never be.

Nancy Chodorow, in her book, *Reproduction of Mothering: Psychoanalysis and the Sociology of Gender* (1978) uses many references to speak to the underlying assumptions within the psychoanalytic literature that father is seen as an adjunct to the mother; his role has been as the catalyst in the process of separation of the daughter from the mother. After the symbiotic stage with the mother and child unconsciously fears complete merger with her and welcomes the father as a means of breaking away psychologically from complete dependency on the mother. Until that developmental stage occurs, it has been expected that mothers be the primary nurturers while fathers stand by passively and observe the bonding between mother and child. Later, father represents independence and mobility for the child; for the girl-child he provides the first link to heterosexuality—the daughter's first man-love. She competes with mother for the love of the father. The first stirrings of self-hate, feelings of contempt for women (mother) and subsequently for themselves as girls thus occur. If fathers provide "good" parenting, then daughters simultaneously awaken to another avenue of self-love through their relationships with their fathers. It is the fathers' turn to provide for the daughters a basis of love and then to help daughter to develop in ways that cannot be accomplished through the mother.

In my work I found that many fathers have been emotionally absent, cut off from the feminine side of themselves. In the process of their own rearing, their fathers were not emotionally accessible and they were often forced into emotional dependency on their mothers. Men resentfully accepted the emotional support of their mothers while rejecting them as less-than-men and, as a result, they were cut off from the feminine aspects of themselves. Emotions attached to fear, vulnerability and lover were suppressed with the hope of unconsciously winning over their fathers. Young and old men alike emulate their fathers' behaviors in order to become like them, thus to prove that their fathers care for them or that they even exist in their fathers' eyes.

Linda Leonard, in her book *The Wounded Woman* (1983) expounds on the sacrifices of the father's inner feminine side to the "ideal of macho-masculine power and authority." She says; "if the father is not there for his daughter in a committed and responsible way, encouraging the development of her intellectual, professional, and spiritual side and valuing the uniqueness of her femininity, there results an injury to the daughter's feminine spirit." Leonard speaks to the process of reclaiming the feminine in that "women have begun to realize that men have been defining femininity through their conscious and culturally conditioned projections on women," rather than as an "inherent principle of human existence." Leonard refers to the father-daughter wound as a "condition of our culture" which rests in the "patriarchal authoritarian attitude" which devalues the feminine (in whatever form it takes) and doesn't allow it to manifest itself from its own "creative essence" in the world.

In my work I've concluded that within each of us lies the masculine and the feminine and much confusion has evolved because of the role assignments of male and female. Father, the male, is to grant approval to the daughter. Many fathers withhold approval because daughters are female and visibly represent the feminine, a repressed aspect in the male. Another contribution of the father is to give affection. He is in the powerful position of withholding affection or granting it when he sees fit. Many grant it as a form of approval.

In white middle class families, fathers traditionally have been responsible for introducing daughters to the external world, the objective outside the realm of the personal, the world of work.

Father teaches daughter what it means to be a man; he also teaches what it means to be a woman by the way he treats her, her mother and other women.

Father has represented authority; the political and institutional world is run by men. Men represent power in the world.

This paper concentrates on the emotionally absent father; that is, the father who does not represent a balance of the masculine and the feminine and his affect on the daughter's development. The cases I have chosen are three daughters who suffer from a "longing for the father." Case #1 is Morgan who characterizes herself as the "invisible daughter"; case #2 is Cathi who experiences "fear of intimacy"; case #3 is Jane, the "guilty daughter of the vulnerable father." These three daughters are a sampling from over 250 "stories" about fathers compiled over four years.

#1—Morgan, the invisible daughter:

Morgan is the second daughter in a family of two girls, one older brother and one younger brother. Her father never wanted children but conceded on the condition that he not be responsible for their rearing. In fact, the family lived in a home that had an apartment attached so that the father could enjoy a separate space altogether. For the most part, Morgan's father lived as though his children did not exist except when they could serve as an audience for him. It was understood that the children were expected to excel and they always did. Morgan would overhear her father talking about his children's accomplishments, but nothing was expressed directly to her. Morgan recalls:

> As a young girl, about 12 or 13, my role was to sit late at the dinner table and listen to my father expound on life and politics. He was extremely interesting—but it was always a lecture, no thought that I might have something to say. Subsequently, I have spent much of my life being a listener who would rather be a speaker.

The pain of this unacknowleged daughter lies deep. She longs for visibility yet fears it. Morgan continues:

> I flew home when my father died unexpectedly of a heart attack at age sixty-three. I did not know that there were black clouds over his death. I went because I thought it would be a freeing experience for me and to be support-

ive of my mother whose life seemed very sad. My father was a well known political figure in my small town. He had been a city councilman for many years—extremely colorful, funny, dramatic—and then mayor for many years. Although he no longer held office, during a court trial looking into some missing funds, a young policeman testified that he had been ordered to collect $1000 from a businessman and deliver it to my father when he was mayor, as an apparent bribe for a change in a planning zone decision. My father died of a heart attack the evening of the testimony. The following day the policeman testified that he had perjured himself—he had taken the money for himself. At the huge Irish wake that night the theatrics began again. In the outer hall, the policeman was crying and wringing his hands.

Streams of people passed through taking each of our hands and whispering "sorry for your trouble." A tall, black man came through the line and I recognized his name as the first black councilman in my hometown, an accomplishment spearheaded by my father and one of the many exciting political battles talked about endlessly by my father and his friends. When introduced to him, by my married name, he asked my connection with the dead man. I replied I was his daughter—he registered surprise, "I didn't know he had children." Suddenly it hit me clearly. I had always felt that we barely existed in my father's life and now it was confirmed. I knew the story of this man before me—but he didn't even know I existed!

Morgan is a skillful listener. She was neither seen nor heard, right to the end of her father's life. And now, as an adult, she has to live with the fact that she did not just imagine that her father deemed her unimportant, she has proof because his old and loyal friend did not even know about her existence. Morgan will spend her adult life seeking visibility, yet fearing it. As a counselor, she can now practice her well-honed listening skills, but she will not easily achieve the self-confidence of knowing when she is good at her work, aware that she may be right, may be visible.

#2—Cathi and fear of intimacy:

Cathi is the only daughter and oldest child with two younger brothers. Through her eighteen years at home she recalls a violent and ill father who taunted her from a very young age. Cathi's story begins with a description of her father's angry personality.

My father was the type of person that you never knew was going to get angry. The whole house revolved around him. It was when *he* wanted to eat; we went to bed when *he* was sick of the kids; we went where *he* wanted to go. It seemed like everything happened when he wanted it to happen. He was a very serious man. I don't think he ever laughed. He read the newspaper and listened to the news. He was always angry. He would come home and tell stories about how he told the boss off, and I can remember all of us always being afraid that he might lose his job because he was always telling people off. If we had company we never knew if they were going to go away mad because he would tell them to shut up or get out. I was always afraid of my father. What he was going to say, what he was going to do. If he didn't like what was being served he would throw it on the floor. When I was in the seventh or eighth grade he became very sick, and it took him about fifteen years to die from it while he grew progressively worse. So his anger got worse too. He was angry at the world. When I was in high school I used to tell my mother to kill him. I went into the convent. And so I got away from him. And I know that I am like him in the sense of being angry. He didn't take anything from anybody, and I have a hard time taking any kind of oppression from anybody because of him.

Cathi is in a bind. She characterizes herself as being unable to withstand any kind of oppression "because of him." Because he was so abusive, her unresolved anger at her father is conjured up now when she is exposed to anger and animosity and she must flee the situation or the person. The scenario has come full circle and, as her father did, Cathi chases people away. Avoidance of "oppression" is the dynamic that prevents Cathi's maturation but real harmony with others entails conflict, suppression (deference of one's need to another's need, or for the larger good or cause), as well as equanimity.

Cathi decided it was better not to marry and entered the convent directly after high school. There was one thing sure in her mind: that she needed to flee her ailing father's household, and the safest place to go was the convent, a vocational choice that her Catholic father and mother dared not protest.

When her father would berate Cathi's mother in Cathi's presence, her mother would then explain the source of her husband's anguish:

> My mother used to tell me that when the bedroom door was closed, they were trying to have sex, and my father couldn't. And they would cry themselves to sleep. My mother used to say, once you've had it, you can't live without it. I used to get the idea that it's impossible to have it and then not have it.

So, Cathi decided not to have it. During a group counseling session, Cathi and the facilitator simulated a conversation with Cathi and her deceased father. Here she repeats the sentiments of her father, spoken to her when she was a nun:

> I have a lot of respect for you. I think it is because you haven't dirtied yourself with a man. You haven't had sex. You know women, that's all they want, and that's all they make men do. It's not the man's fault, it's the woman's and you're not playing the game. I'm proud of you.

Cathi the sexless daughter, sexless just as Dad is, dying in a nursing home. It will take her years to acknowledge her sexuality and eventually be able to leave the convent. Until then, it is not a good thing to be a woman because women want only one thing: sex. Women are whores, and it is better for Cathi to stay a virgin, a nun wedded to an invisible man, Christ. Mother says, "Once you've had it, you can't live without it" and Dad says, "If you want it, you're a whore—just as mother, just as all other women." Cathi is trapped in a no-win situation. She will need to decide what is right for her. She will need to pursue the adult sexual woman who resides somewhere between the virgin and the whore—no easy task while surrounded by priests who forego sexual involvement for a higher state. In fact, to have sex with a woman is a sin. If Cathi chose a priest, she was a whore; if she broke her chastity vow, she was a whore. No, she needed to stay "pure," maintain her virginity for Dad, and for God, the ultimate father.

Eventually when she leaves the convent, her journey to self-fulfillment takes time, and then she is past her childbearing years. She has no desire to reproduce herself, to reproduce father and she does not birth a child. For many years Cathi is hiding, too fearful that all men are the same as her father. She loathed him. He was a sad and lonely man and she was powerless to help him. The only way she could please him was to be an asexual woman.

#3—Jane, guilty daughter of the vulnerable father:

Jane is the oldest child with a brother very close to her in age. She cannot remember a day in her life when she respected her father. For her, he represented the sad sack, a down-trodden man who experienced a lot of bad luck. Early in her life she was ensnarled in an ongoing battle between her mother and her father. She says:

> My parents were always fighting and leaving or threatening to leave, for almost eighteen years. One time they got in a big fight and my mother was leaving, this was late at night and she told us to get into the car. We went out into the garage and my father was hiding in the back seat of the car. He looked at me, put his finger to his mouth and said, "Don't say anything." But I did. I was always on my mother's side.

Jane will never forget this event—the time she turned Dad in. This is the revenge of a child who resents having to take sides, who resents father for not standing up "like a man" to mother. Jane can connect these guilt and anger feelings about Dad to the times her father abdicated his role as her protector:

I remember in the third grade I didn't like him, I don't know why. I can remember when my uncle was looking for my cousin, and there was a lot of turmoil. He really beat my cousin and my brother; and my father stood and watched. He was laughing because it was a kind of a game and we were laughing too. We didn't think our uncle was really going to hurt us, and then he went into a rage and started ripping our fort apart and really maiming my cousin. Later, my dad took a lot of abuse from us, my mother, and my grandfather because he had stood there and watched his brother beat us.

Jane's father chose the easy way out. Rather than confront the uncle and protect his daughter, he stood by and laughed. From then on, Jane disrespected her father and saw him as a weak man. She "abused" him; she became the parent, he the child. Easier now for him to take on her role than to assert himself and take responsibility for his actions. Jane continues:

He never stood up to me, he never stood up to my mother. I mean, I would do something wrong and my father would say, "Now, Jane, you shouldn't do that," and I'd say, "Shut up. You can't tell me what to do. I hate you." And he would say, "Now, you shouldn't say that."

Eventually Jane's parents did separate and divorce. She recalls the day of the split when once again, she is put in the position of choosing. Only this time, she feels in full force the guilt of the daughter of the vulnerable father.

The furniture was going out of the house, and my parents were arguing over all this crap and the maid was there. My future step-father was there, as my mother was getting ready to remarry. My father was there and the moving van closed the door. I got into a car with my brother and my mother and stepfather, and my father stood there alone. He was standing in the driveway watching us pull away. About two days later I got a letter from him saying that he couldn't say good-bye because he was afraid he'd cry. I think that was one of the few times I saw that he really felt sad, but I didn't do anything about it.

Father is abandoned now by both mother and daughter. Dad shows his sadness, shows his feelings, and Jane does nothing about it. Jane could have chosen sides. She could have stood up to mother for Daddy's sake. But could she? Father had never shown her that he could be there for himself or for her. She was unsafe with Daddy.

Today Jane is married and moved to another state. Her father comes to visit about once a year. Below she journalizes after one of his visits.

> Today my Dad left after a three and one-half day visit. If it had been one day longer I think I would have lost my mind. It was tiring and tense. Perhaps I am angry at all the memories of the tongue-lashings I gave to my father. I, along with so many other people, have beaten him down to this nervous, paranoid man with his forever fleeting eyes and continuous body movement. I want so much to love and accept him. Maybe somehow deep down I want his acceptance of me. Right now I am hurting inside because I can't love him as a daughter should and I can't be proud and hold my head up when I'm with him. All I feel is contempt and pity, and I feel so bad that I feel that. I don't want my father to feel any more hurt from anyone else. I can see where my problem lies. I never really was aware of how deeply my father has affected me. How can I put away all of this? I know it affects so much of my feelings about myself. I must dig down to the bottom of this hurt. I somehow can't write off my dad, yet I can't tell him of my feelings. I must somehow in my own mind get some sort of release from my guilt and anger. It's time to deal with an old wound. I need to cure it instead of patching it up.

Jane says it so well. What is the prognosis for Morgan, Cathi and Jane? What is the treatment plan for these daughters who now, as adults, still long for the father?

These three cases demonstrate that fathers have a great deal of power in their relationships with their daughters. Fathers can be very damaging to daughters' development. Some fathers have seriously undermined the development of self-confidence and self-esteem in their daughters. Surely the goal is to help these daughters reclaim their self-esteem and personal power. What is the process by which these daughters can embrace the parts of themselves that were stolen by their fathers? The task is to go back and review the painful and the joyful times, to explore photographs of daughters with their fathers and their families with the hope of uncovering old forgotten memories and messages. Daughters need to examine the direct and indirect messages from their fathers. It may be helpful at some point to see father in the context of his life and his parents' lives.

Questions of the father can be formulated, such as: what did he feel about me? What were his secrets? His first love? Will he forgive me for not being what he wanted? Can I forgive myself? What did it mean to be a man? What does it mean to be a woman?

For someone such as Cathi who has feelings of revulsion for her father, it may be necessary to engage in some visualizations that actually kill off the father in order for her to kill off the father in herself and begin again.

For Morgan, once she becomes more comfortable with visibility, another examination of the talents of the father may uncover his indirect gifts to her. Eventually she may be able to acknowledge the father in her who is quite visible.

Jane, who is ripe to finally forgive her father may ultimately forgive herself for expressing her power as a young girl well before coming of age. She rescued herself and learned survival skills early in life; how do these work for her now?

I want to close with a passage from the last chapter in Sheila Ballantyne's book, *Imaginary Crimes* (1982), a series of vignettes about a father/daughter relationship.

> Walking through the doors of the King Street Station is hard. It is like leaving all over again, in 1954. I see Ray standing over by the jewelry counter, buying a pair of earrings he plans to surprise me with on the train. I can't suppress the old feelings, maybe they never die. I call to his ghost:
>
> "Did you really love me? Or was that a con job too?"
>
> He doesn't even blink. I try a different angle. This is hard.

"When I was sick and you sat with me all night, when you stroked my face, when we bucked the wind, was it real?"

No response. He really means to have it his way this time. The train is about to leave.

"WHERE IS MY PROOF?" I scream at him.

"It's inside you!" he finally shouts. A trick.

"Why weren't you a better parent!" I cry.

"Why aren't you?" he yells back.

"I do my best!"

"Yes, well, that's the way it goes. So did I."

And then I see. And then I forgive.

REFERENCES

Appleton, W. S. (1981). *Fathers and daughters.* Garden City, NY: Doubleday & Company, Inc.

Ballantyne, S. (1982). *Imaginary crimes.* New York: Viking Press.

Chodorow, N. (1978). *The reproduction of mothering: Psychoanalysis and the sociology of gender.* Berkeley, CA: University of California Press.

Dalton, R. D. Unpublished manuscript.

Leonard, L. (1983). *The wounded woman.* Boulder & London: Shambhala.

Sex Stereotyping and Diagnosis of Psychopathology

Violet Franks

If we consider men and women as separate populations within any culture, an understanding of the psychopathology presented by each will facilitate an appreciation of the many influences which impinge on these two discreet populations. In part, the concept of psychopathology is gender-determined. Cross-cultural psychologists try to understand psychopathology within different social cultural backgrounds (Marsella, 1984). Although men and women grow up side by side in the same country they experience different social, cultural and biological backgrounds. This paper examines some of the many factors which differentially influence men and women within the context of contemporary notions about psychopathology and diagnosis.

Nowadays, the DSM III is the prevailing diagnostic instrument throughout the world. Whenever possible, the manual estimates the prevalence of a particular disorder according to sex. However, little attempt is made to understand the significance of these differences. Why are some diagnoses over-represented in the female population whereas others are over-represented in the male population? Glib answers are easy to formulate and all too readily offered. With the growth of the psychology of women literature, the question "Is anatomy destiny?" is often posed. Certain feminists (e.g., Chesler, 1972) view all diagnoses and treatments as male dominant and unfair to women labeled "crazy" by male judges. In pointing a disapproving finger at "double standards" of mental health, the now famous and much quoted Broverman study (1970) elicited a spate of reports chastising mental health workers who view

Violet Franks is Director of the Psychology Department, Carrier Foundation, Belle Mead, NJ 08520.

such stereotypic female traits as gentleness, emotionality and intuition as maladaptive and the male traits of logicality, adventurousness, assertiveness, and action-orientation as adaptive and non-neurotic. Mental health workers are still accused of judging characteristic female traits as neurotic and minimizing the significance of maladaptive male traits. Broverman (1984) is now replicating her original study and reports some preliminary shifts in attitude. Mental health workers, presumably sensitized to women's issues, are now valuing female traits as healthy and the previous "double standard" for mental health appears to be disappearing.

According to Kaplan (1983), the DSM III is intrinsically sexist. Kaplan's attack on the DSM III was quickly rebutted by such authorities as Williams and Spitzer (1983). While acknowledging the importance of societal difficulties in the etiology of mental health problems, they emphasized that DSM III per se is not sex biased. According to Williams and Spitzer, there is no validity to the belief that women are more frequently given certain diagnostic labels because society views female behavior as more disturbed or because the diagnostician values male behavior more than female behavior. If the prevalence of certain disorders is higher in the female population, it is because females actually do have more pathology. Williams and Spitzer strongly object to Kaplan's conclusion that masculine biased assumptions about which behaviors are healthy and which behaviors are "crazy" are built into the diagnostic criteria. Rothblum and Franks (1983) agree that women are over-represented in certain clinical populations and point out the need to understand why this is so. Women have been brought up differently from men and sex role stereotyped training has contributed to many mental health problems of females. Careful examination of those pathologies which affect women differently from men and those pathologies which affect men differently from women may help us understand those extra pressures and stresses which society imposes upon both men and women.

Arguments about the relative importance of biological and social factors deflect from an understanding of the role of gender differences in the development of psychopathology. Feminists who emphasize social problems to the exclusion of all others, over-simplify as much as biochemically-oriented professionals who see, for example, all depression or agora-phobia as due to physiological reactions to be cleared away with pills. Hence, the pill-giving physician may see women as hormonally different from men and prone to all sorts of psy-chopathology because of premenstrual stress, menopausal dif-ficulties, post-partum distress, endocrine disorders, etc. It is fallacious to think in either/or terms: psychopathology is neither exclusively biologically nor socially determined, it is both.

Marsella (1984), a cross-cultural psychologist, views both pathological and normal behavior as functions of an individ-ual's biological, psychological and social/cultural experiences. The roots of behavior reside not only within the individual but also within the innumerable situations to which the indi-vidual is exposed. To argue about the relative importance of heredity and environment is to sidetrack the real issues. If we want to understand psychopathology in men and women, we must understand the relative impacts of these pressures upon men and women within the society. It is the interactions of all these biological, psychological and social-cultural experiences which determine psychopathology. Even if it is not possible to unravel these complex interactions in full at this time, it would seem helpful to conceptualize psychopathology in terms of some predictive equation. This equation would nec-essarily take into account all major forces pertinent to emo-tional distress.

It is acknowledged that men and women have different biological milestones. Nevertheless, it would be foolhardy to undervalue other components in the equation: cultural and social factors which have differential impacts on women as opposed to men. To illustrate the significance of these factors, I shall choose three DSM III categories which are over-repre-sented in the female population. An attempt will be made to understand the contributions of learned sex role stereotypes and expectations in the development of male and female be-haviors. If we examine anorexia, depression and agoraphobia, we see that there is an overlap between symptomatology and sex role stereotyping. Likewise, DSM III male-loaded catego-ries such as alcoholism and acting-out behavior show a ratio bias towards male stereotypes since it is the male population which evidences more aggressive acting out behavior. It is as if one end of the continuum represents the psychopathology of both groups. In other words, exaggerated stereotypes are pathological for both men and women. For example, a normally aggressive man is not diagnosed as needing treatment until he shows temper tantrums and damages property. Likewise, a gentle nurturant woman is considered normal but she is labeled agoraphobic if she becomes so nurturant and dependent that she stays in the house all the time.

This paper focuses specifically upon three major diagnostic categories which are common clinical entities and over-represented in the female adult population. But first it is helpful to take a brief look at a childhood disorder which appears before the full impact of sex role stereotypes are felt by the sufferer. Attention Deficit Disorder (ADD), currently redefined in DSM III, occurs 10 times more often in boys than in girls. It is characterized by impulsivity, gross motor activity such as excessive running or climbing, low frustration tolerance, temper outbursts and inattention. If we match these symptoms with expectations for the behavior of little boys and the behavior of little girls, it is obvious that it is the little boys who are the ones who are characteristically expected to show more aggression and more activities such as running and climbing. Obviously, ADD more closely fits the stereotype expected for the behavior of little boys.

It is also of interest to note that boys are brought in for treatment of emotional and developmental problems much more frequently than are girls. One wonders, therefore, why in adult life many more women than men seek treatment for emotional problems? What happens to the Attention Deficit Disorder in males when they grow up? Does society reinforce the grown-up ADD male because he is more aggressive and because he is more active or does this complex of symptoms get hidden in other diseases such as alcoholism? As yet, we do not know the answers and it is important to find them out. Could it be that certain excessive behaviors are more detrimental than others, and that we view them differently when we are dealing with a child as opposed to an adult population? Could it be that women begin to face more stress and pressure during and after adolescence and therefore become the target group for emotional problems? Could it be that maturity and biochemical changes help the male overcome the hyperactivity and impulsivity presented by his less mature nervous system as a young boy? The answers to such questions might help us understand what is meant by psychopathology and how we view diagnostic categories.

Let us now focus on the concept of femininity and its stereotypic meaning. Traditionally, we have always understood what a feminine person is. Across cultural groups, adjectives which refer to femininity tend to be universal. These adjectives include such positive words as gentle, kind, understanding, nurturant and also more negative adjectives such as passive, compliant, dependent and emotional. Text books on the psychology of women tend to view masculine behavior as instrumental and female behavior as expressive. In other words, the man is seen as the active agent whereas the woman is seen as a support person who easily expresses emotion and is generally passive and dependent.

Let us look next at the DSM III category, depression. It is estimated that 80% of depressed patients are women and all studies consistently show that women are over-represented in this diagnostic category. Does this have anything to do with the role society assigns to women? Does the depressed patient show more female stereotypic behavior? Certainly, some of the female stereotype traits are demonstrated by depressed patients. For example, depression leads to passivity and the depressed patient shows little ability to cope or use problem-solving strategies. There is considerable withdrawal and much demonstration of emotion. Crying and agitation are frequently manifestations. There is a definite loss of energy. Symptoms usually include feelings of worthlessness and self-reproach or excessive or inappropriate guilt. Within the normal population, it has been shown that women tend to blame themselves whereas men tend to blame circumstances. Intrapunitive guilt feelings are more common in the normal female population. Hence, there is an overlap between the female sterotype and depressive behavior. More important, does behaving like a woman increase a woman's chance of developing depression? If we accept the popular theory of learned helplessness as a model for understanding depression (Seligman, 1975), depression in women can be viewed from this perspective. Little girls are brought up to be dependent and to seek help. They are not considered emotionally disturbed when they are compliant and dependent and it is only when they become women that society punishes them. Particularly in recent years, women are expected to be more independent and achievement-oriented in their adult lives. If they no longer have a protective family support system and they are supposed to "stand on their own two feet," it is not surprising that women suddenly find themselves without adequate coping devices. They cannot suddenly shift from being good, compliant, dependent children to strong, masculine, instrumental problem-solving adults. Blechman (1984) emphasizes the need for teaching women competency skills which are taken for granted by the male population.

Depression may be exacerbated when patients are frustrated because they do not have direct power to deal with life's problems. When society places a higher premium on such passive traits as looking beautiful rather than being competent, learned helplessness is not important since competency is not a desideratum. Unfortunately, looking beautiful is an ephemeral quality which is not always under the control of the individual. It is not surprising that aging women have more problems than aging men. Direct control of one's life has not traditionally been within the female experience. This can lead to depression and feelings of helplessness. Even those women who are competent in managing their lives have been traditionally encouraged not to show their competency lest they scare off men and potential marriage partners. This puts women into a double-bind position which could well contribute to a high rate of depression.

The indirect power which women have traditionally been given, the power behind the throne, is not always satisfying. Women tend to attain personal identification through meaningful others in their lives—their husbands and children. It is not easy to manage gratification in this way and much depends upon luck rather than personal efforts. Hence, many women find themselves in a very vulnerable position. Even if their husband do become successful there is no guarantee that the wives will be rewarded for the success of their husbands and the efforts made in helping the husbands·achieve success. Many women find themselves cast off by husbands who have outgrown their now older wives. The helpless wife finds herself in a secondary position to a new young woman. While acting tough and powerful is frowned upon as unfeminine and undesirable in many cultures, the punishment for acting too passive and dependent can be even greater. It is difficult to rely on others for self-esteem and, as noted, this makes the woman vulnerable, a pattern which is once again consistent with the female stereotype.

Let us now take into account the feeling of guilt, a common symptom in severe depression. Society tends to blame women for many problems and women, as a group, tend to attribute failure to their own lack of competency, mea culpa, whereas men tend to use fewer guilt mechanisms and to attribute failure to the environment. Society capitalizes on women's tendencies to feel guilty. There is even a body of literature which labels mothers for their children's psychiatric problems—e.g., the schizophrenogenic mother. Fortunately, even though the role of the father is still underemphasized, and problems which children develop are still attributed primarily to the mothers, this label is disappearing from the literature.

Biological markers should be carefully examined in our equation. For example, the traditional belief that women are particularly vulnerable to depression during menopause is no longer acceptable. The high risk period for depression occurs in younger women. An understanding of menopause has led to a reduction in the diagnosis of "involutional melancholia" in women previously judged by psychiatrists to be depressed because of biological factors during menopause. However, there is much to learn before we understand fully the many factors which contribute to the high rate of depression in women.

Another diagnostic category in which women are over-represented is eating disorders. All eating disorders, including over-weight, anorexia and bulimia show a high preponderance in the female population. Approximately 95% of the anorexic population is female. Women are concerned with weight and dieting, and approximately 95% of groups such as Weight Watchers are females. What do sex role stereotypes have to do with the weight problem? Zegman (1983) emphasizes the traditional sedentary life-styles of women and their effects on obesity. She also points out that changing sex roles appear to affect eating habits. Successful career women are more concerned with dieting and are less often obese than women in lower social classes. Interestingly, women in the United States have become somewhat thinner during the last two decades and the impact of social cultural changes on women's weight is an area yet to be studied.

The high prevalence of anorexia in the last couple of decades is of concern and requires further understanding in terms of sex role stereotypes. Anorexia is an enigmatic condition. It has been viewed as a refusal to accept femaleness and growing into a sexually mature woman and it has also been viewed as an over-identification with the female role. Hence, the adolescent female who becomes anorexic may actually cause biological stunting of growth at puberty and cessation of menses as well as an immature figure by refusal to eat. By contrast, theorists such as Boskind-Lodahl (1976) contend that anorexia reflects an over-compliant condition. By pursuing thinness so relentlessly, these young women actually seek to achieve the culturally stereotypic ideal feminine form and role. The idealized model in fashion magazines is excessively young, thin and fragile-looking and these are the models which influence the developing adolescent.

Bulimia is not associated with severe weight loss. It is characterized by a pattern of episodic binge eating followed by severe purging or dieting. Statistics show that 30% of the college population experienced all the major symptoms of bulimia as outlined in DSM III (Garner & Garfinkel, 1980). Of these, 87% are female and 13% male. By now, bulimia and anorexia are virtually epidemic within the American culture pattern and they are also highly prevalent within the United Kingdom. In considering the influence of sex role sterotypes upon such conditions, it is important to recognize that females have traditionally established self-worth on the basis of body image. In some societies, a woman's weight and beauty determine much of her future. Perhaps heaviness can be the norm; there are cultures which think of woman's worth as being related to her weight in rubies. However, in American society the over-weight woman is socially undesirable. It is more detrimental for a woman to be overweight than it is for a man, and reliance upon physical attractiveness is more important for women. Hence, obsession with weight purely on the basis of cultural needs is a woman's obsession, and this is not surprising.

In a recent study at the Carrier Foundation, Pettinati and I attempted to understand eating disorders as they relate to the concepts of femininity and masculinity in young women. Eating disorder women were compared with two control groups matched for age: patients without eating disorders and normal controls who showed no psychiatric problems and were free of eating disorders. Using the Bem scale, preliminary results suggest that masculinity scores were significantly lower in the anorexic/bulimic group than in either the matched patient group or the normal control group. However, the Bem femininity scores showed no significant differences between the three groups. Only the depressed patients in the psychiatric group looked similar to the eating disorder patients on the masculinity score. The control patient group, which included other disabilities such as bipolar disorder, drug addiction and schizophrenia, scored higher on masculinity than either the depressed patients or the eating disorder group. Perhaps, therefore, it is not the femininity scores which differentiate eating disorders from other groups. More focus should be placed on their identification with masculine type behavior. It should be noted that the Bem "masculine" items include traits such as self-reliance, defending one's beliefs, independence, athletic, assertive, forceful, analytical, leadership abilities, and willingness to take risks and make decisions easily. These traits are very important adaptive traits and, when lacking, they can cause severe problems. Therefore, those patients who rate themselves very low with respect to these health adaptive masculine traits will be at high risk not only for anorexia but also for depression. Pending further analysis of the data, the preliminary results appear to be consistent with expectations for exaggerated sex role stereotyping.

Another component of the female role is the usual involvement with food and nurturance for the family. Adolescent girls see their mothers as cooks and food providers. Later women spend much of their time and energy with food and, once again, the emphasis upon nurturance is more important for women. Men who go on diets often receive diet lunches from their female partners whereas women must have complete control of their diets, constantly weighing their food and monitoring their intake. Again, this may be an added factor in targeting women for the diagnosis of eating disorders.

Psychodynamic explanations of anorexia view the patient with eating disorders as being relatively passive and compliant. Anorexic women are frequently powerless in their families and, since attention is received from the family by indirect manipulation, eating disorders become the main avenues of control. Family members become very concerned when the anorexic patient is literally starving herself to death. Bruch (1978) explains this disorder in females in terms of the traditional female characteristics of dependency, lack of assertiveness and lack of autonomy. She views the refusal to eat as a way to regain control over the pervasive feelings of helplessness that the female adolescent experiences.

Consider the mixed messages and pressures presented by changing goals for women in the Western world. On the one hand, women are expected to behave traditionally, to be compliant, slim and beautiful, gentle and kind. On the other hand, women in contemporary society are expected to achieve at a high level, to enter positions of management, to become professionals and to make an impact. It is possible that anorexic women have reached an impasse since they are unable to reconcile the conflicts presented by these two disparate images. If they have a need to be compliant, as anorexic girls appear to have, and yet they are still very ambitious, they are presented with a neurotic conflict which could well result in an anorexic breakdown. The adolescent boy has a number of outlets. He can become muscular, active, a team member, and thus enhance his value as an attractive male. The adolescent girl is expected to act "ladylike" and may have to give up her tomboyish behavior and squelch her feelings of rebellion and noncompliance. How will she reconcile her need for aggressive success with her need to be a ladylike, gentle young woman? If she cannot resolve this conflict, psychopathology may result. Although there are biological, somatic symptoms to the condition of anorexia, it is difficult, at this point, to explain this disease without taking into account social, cultural and psychological pressures. A medical model cannot, by itself, account for the high prevalence of this disease in the female population without taking into account the total feminine maturation process.

A third diagnostic category which is highly female is agoraphobia. It has been estimated that as many as 85% of agoraphobics are women. Psychologists such as Fodor (1974) and Brehony (1983) view agoraphobia as a condition which strongly resembles stereotypic female behavior. Agoraphobics develop dependent as well as avoidant behavior. They show obvious fear, are often housebound and have been described as passive, anxious, shy, dependent, fearful and nonassertive (Marks, 1970). The similarity between agoraphobic behavior and the female sex role stereotype is apparent. A recent doctoral study at Rutgers University (Powers, 1983) comparing agoraphobic women with a normal control group, showed that the agoraphobic women in her sample were less assertive than the normal controls. Little girls are socialized to display fearful behavior, little boys are encouraged to become independent and to fend for themselves. It would be considered highly inappropriate for the little boy to be fearful and clinging and, by the time he reaches adolescence, he would be heavily censored and encouraged to be brave "like a man." By contrast, women have traditionally been allowed to cling and even to withdraw from feared situations. Hence, exaggerated withdrawal and phobic reactions are much more likely to be expected in female population and would be considered much more pathological in a male population.

We can also consider the possible dynamics of agoraphobia. Agoraphobia is more frequent in the married female population. Many clinicians have noted the "trappedness" that women agoraphobics feel. They may have little outlet for assertive behavior. With the emerging emphasis on career choice and the conflicts presented by family needs, needs of children, husband and home, the contemporary woman may be feeling much conflict and dysphoria and the danger of agoraphobia as a possible solution is high. One wonders about the conflicts and mixed goals as well as fears of independence which the agorpahobic woman may have to resolve. Clinicians working with agoraphobic women are often impressed by the difficulties these women have in taking responsibility for their lives and by their lack of confidence in themselves as competent coping adults. Hence, it is possible to view agoraphobia as an extension of the cultural sex role stereotype—an extreme condition in which the woman abdicates her autonomy and imprisons herself in her own home, becoming dependent upon her benign prison guards (i.e., husband and children) to care for her.

If such stereotypes are not to impact negatively and produce damage, it is important to understand the mechanisms involved. Only then can modification become a viable possibility. Individual differences are more important than gender roles. Traditionally, psychologists have been concerned about "deviant" behavior and have condemned masculine behavior in women and feminine behavior in men. More recently, there has been a general acceptance of the concept of androgyny for both men and women and this allows a wider repertoire of behaviors. Yet the underlying fear that it is highly unhealthy for individuals to act in a pattern atypical for their own sex is still very prevalent and permeates the thinking of parents, educators and therapists. We pay lip service to the need to appreciate and encourage the individual potential of each child regardless of sex. We are becoming aware that pressure to conform to sex roles can cause mental health problems. But on a subtle level, many professionals as well as lay people still become upset when prevailing sex role stereotypes are disregarded. For example, girls who are more aggressive and boys who are more gentle are often chastised or made to feel different because they deviate from the stereotypic norm. At another level, girls who have a scientific bent and boys with an artistic inclination are often discouraged from developing their potentials. Much more emphasis should be placed on training mental health workers to function without bias. Special attention should be paid to the idea that sex role stereotypes can be damaging to mental health. Although this may appear to be obvious, therapists have traditionally been trained within systems which accepted unrealistic norms for both male and female behavior. Too often, women whose behavior is more masculine are seen as "deviant," "castrating" or having "identity problems." Men are also viewed as being pathological unless they conform to the traditional, macho male image. An emerging literature is beginning to question these values and images. Much of this literature has not reached the main stream of clinical psychology or psychiatric graduate training programs. More position papers, such as that of the American Psychological Association Task Force report on nonsexist therapy (1975) need to reach mainstream professionals. Parents and educators should be encouraged to allow and to reach a wide repertoire of non-sex-role stereotypic behaviors in boys and girls alike.

When feminists criticize psychotherapists for trying to maintain the status quo by emphasizing adaptation to society rather than trying to change society, they provide a much needed challenge to traditional thinking about normality, values and goals. While we cannot all become politically active, all therapists can help patients question their cognitive belief systems, particularly those which contribute to their psychopathology. They can also help their patients question the belief systems of their own families and those of society itself. It is my belief that the prevalence of depression, agoraphobia and anorexia in the female population can be reduced considerably if we understand the components of those pathologies which are related to the role of being female. The interactional equation must take into account psychological and social problems as well as biological determinants. The stresses which many women experience or believe they experience within any society need to be considered in arriving at a valid DSM III diagnosis and in prescribing an effective treatment program.

REFERENCES

American Psychological Association: Report on the task force on sex bias and sex-role stereotyping in psychotherapeutic practice (1975). *American Psychologist, 30,* 1169–1175.

Boskind-Lodahl, M. (1976). Cinderella's stepsisters: a feminist perspective on anorexia nervosa and bulimia. *Signs: Journal of Women in Culture and Society, 2,* 242–356.

Blechman, E. A. (1984). Women's behavior in a man's world: Sex differences in competence. In Blechman, E. A. (Ed.) *Behavior modification with women* (p. 3–33). New York: Guilford Press.

Brehony, K. A. (1983). Women and agoraphobia: A case for the etiological significance of the feminine sex-role stereotype. In V. Franks & E. D. Rothblum (Eds.), *The stereotyping of women: Its effects on mental health* (112–128). New York: Springer.

Broverman, I. K. (1984). Paper read at the American Psychological Association, Toronto, Canada, August 26.

Broverman, I. K., Broverman, D. M, Clarkson, F. E., Rosenkrantz, P. S. & Vogel, S. (1970). Sex role stereotypes and clinical judgments of mental health. *Journal of Consulting and Clinical Psychology, 34,* 1J–7.

Bruch, H. (1978). *The golden cage.* Harvard University Press: Cambridge, MA.

Chesler, P. (1972). *Women and madness.* New York: Doubleday.

Fodor, I. G. (1974). The phobic syndrome in women: Implications for treatment. In V. Franks & V. Burtle (Eds.), *Women in therapy* (pp. 132–168). New York: Brunner/Mazel.

Garner, D. M. & Garfinkel, P. E. (1980). Socio-cultural factors in the development of anorexia nervosa. *Psychological Medicine, 10,* 647–656.

Kaplan, M. (1983). A woman's view of DSM III. *American Psychologist, 38,* 786–792.

Marks, I. M. (1970). Agoraphobic syndrome: Panic anxiety state. *Archives of General Psychiatry, 23,* 538–553.

Marsella, A. J. (1984). An interactional model of psychopathology, In B. Lubin & W. Connors (Eds.), *Ecological models in clinical and community psychology* (pp. 232–250). New York: Wiley.

Powers, J. (1983). *Dimensions of agoraphobia in married women: Assertiveness, marital satisfaction and sex role influences.* Unpublished doctoral dissertation, Rugers University.

Rothblum, E. D. & Franks, V. (1983). Introduction: Warning: sex-role stereotypes may be hazardous to your health. In V. Franks & E. D. Rothblum (Eds.), *The stereotyping of women: Its effects on mental health* (pp. 3–10). New York: Springer.

Seligman, M. E. (1975). *Helplessness: On depression, development and death.* San Francisco: Freeman.

Williams, J. B. & Spitzer, R. L. (1983). The issue of sex bias in DSM III. A critique of "a woman's view of DSM-III" by Marcie Kaplan. *American Psychologist, 38,* 793–798.

Zegman, M. (1983). Woman, weight and health. In V. Franks & E. D. Rothblum (Eds.), *The stereotyping of women: Its effects on mental health* (pp. 172–200). New York: Springer.

Play and the Working Woman

Barbara Brown

INTRODUCTION

The concept of play as a rich source of nourishment for the working woman has evolved from my work with clients in a private practice and my own personal experience. I have found that structured, energetic involvement in play, recreation and personal creative endeavors is helpful in dealing with the crises and dilemmas inherent in living an active life in our complicated society.

According to Webster, play is an activity engaged in for amusement or enjoyment. In our society, play has been negated as a valuable entity. Think of expressions such as "all he ever wants to do is play" and "that's child's play." However, there is growing evidence to support at least four distinctly valuable aspects of play for working women:

—First, play can create an opportunity for networking;
—Second, play can provide a stress-reducing experience;
—Third, play can be a source of education about the work world;
—Fourth, play can be conducive to developing inner strength.

Play and Networking

There is the opportunity for networking as a valuable aspect of play. Many play activities provide a structure for satisfying interactions with others, thereby potentiating personal and professional networks. Traditionally the "old boy" network of business and finance developed through the office

---

Dr. Brown is in private practice at 121 Devonshire Drive, New Hyde Park, NY 11040.

233

golf game or squash at the club. Structured play activities on a regular basis with other women leads to bonding and the development of mutual support systems for women. I've been playing tennis with the same group of women for over fifteen years. There is a feeling of community, and a great deal of networking and support.

Play and Stress Reduction

Play, recreation, whatever you do for fun is probably one of the best tonics for alleviating stress. It is letting out the child in us and becoming absorbed in the moment. There is increasing evidence that creative play, recreational play, humor, fun and exuberance are key elements in a healthful lifestyle (Barbach, 1983; LeShan, 1977; Simonton, 1978; Weinstein, 1983). Instead of the proverbial apple a day, there is evidence that we can also use play.

Many types of play involve strenuous exercise or total focused attention for an extended period of time (minimum 30-40 minutes). This produces what physiologists call a "relaxation response." It works the same as meditation. This prolonged concentration stimulates change in limbic system and autonomic nervous system functioning which leads to increase in body temperature, reduced blood pressure and slower breathing. Many recent studies have suggested that strenuous exercise and meditative experiences lead to the production of norepinephrine, associated with the "rush" or "high" reported by long distance runners and to a reduction in long term depression (Psychology Today, 12/84). In addition, it has been hypothesized that stress reduction inhibits breakdown of our autoimmune system, thereby increasing our resistance to disease (Turkington, 1985).

Play and Learning the Ropes

The value of play as a source of learning goes back to the wisdom of the Greeks. The Greek word for play (paidia) and for education (paideia) are almost identical. ‹

Pearce (1977) writes in "The Magical Child" that what we perceive as play is a superficial experience while important work is happening on a more basic level. He focuses on the passionate intensity with which young animals play and how this play offers a way by which the young can learn the social rules and adapt to them with minimal risks. Play offers a chance for the child to learn to use tools without economic pressure. Play serves survival.

Campbell (1977) states that play is an important learning method. It is central to learning skills critical for survival. Play goes with exuberant, energetic, active, not inert, passive or apathetic. As noted by Pulaski (1971), Piaget found that play was "in the service of intelligence . . . that play serves many vital needs and functions of the child's growth."

In relation to child development, Pearce (1977) writes that the child's driving intent to play all the time must logically be a major part of the biological plan. This suggests an inherent drive to play. A gravitation to what is fun is related to our developmental needs. It follows that what might be one person's play is not necessarily another person's play. And what might be play at one time in a person's life is not necessaily so at another time.

Gail Sheehy (1976) and others have observed that development does not stop after childhood or adolescence but continues into adulthood. And women may have to catch up on some developmental work in order to survive in the work world. Betty Lee Harragan (1978) in "Games Mother Never Taught You" writes about how men take to corporate structure using the same rules and strategies they learned as team members in sandlot stickball, little league baseball or any of the team sports so popular among little boys and so alien to most little girls. Williams and McCullers (1983) reported recently that childhood experiences of women in high success positions include more traditionally masculine play patterns such as sports activities and board games. Concepts conducive to professional success such as competitive tactics, team cooperation and risk taking are all issues confronted in sports and games.

We can make abstractions from play experience. Certain tenets of life become very clear when we engage in activities for fun. In tennis, the object is to hit the ball. But I can't see it if I get too close. My game falls apart if I lose my grip. I know the importance of follow-through.

A novice skier recently related an experience to me. She

had gained confidence on the beginner's slope and moved to the intermediate slope. She fell two or three times initially, became discouraged, didn't want to get up and never wanted to ski again. Back on the beginner's slope, she regained her confidence, increased her skills and felt good about skiing again. So tennis players learn the importance of follow-through and skiers learn not to bite off more than they can chew.

I was in a pottery class a few years ago. Someone was pounding a fresh piece of clay to get out the air bubbles and adding water to make it a good consistency for working on the wheel. It was quiet in the room when he said "Oh shit, first it was too hard and now it's too soft." An Australian woman who was working on the wheel next to me said "Very much like life, isn't it. Never just the way you want it."

Campbell has done a lot of work on interests and their relationship to work productivity. He says that a writer who is also a musician hears rhythms in words that are not evident to others, and an executive who is intimately familiar with the patterns of wood grains may see different possible arrangements of work groups.

Play and Inner Strength

Play is a centering experience, an exercise in inner-directedness. We become sensitized to internal cues.

In sports, we learn about balance and muscle tone viscerally. There are two people doing work in this area: Illana Rubenfeld, a graduate of Julliard and a Gestalt therapist, and Moishe Feldenkrais, a physicist, formerly with the Israeli Army and a Judo black belt. They both work with movement and talk about the interdependence between our emotions and posture-observing life attitudes that are reflected in our non-verbal behavior.

Freud wrote about how a child at play behaves as a creative writer. He creates a world of his own, rearranging the things in his world in a new way which pleases him. He takes his play seriously and expends large amounts of emotion on it. Through play experiences, we enlarge our ability to perceive in our own way. We learn from the gut who we are and what we want. It gives us a sense of substance.

There was an article in the *Times* (Blumenthal, 1984) about the psychological payoffs of physical exercise. Dr. Shontz of the University of Kansas was quoted as saying "The exhilaration of exercise and the good feeling afterward give you a sense of control over being able to provide pleasure for yourself." I would extrapolate and propose that this is a payoff of most play experiences.

REFERENCES

Barbach, L. (speaker). (1983). *Playfulness and sexuality: Uses of humor in sex therapy.* (Cassette Recording No. LP 112). Stanford, Ca: Institute for the Advancement of Human Behavior.

Blumenthal, D. (1984, February 5). Body image. *New York Times Magazine (VI),* p. 64.

Campbell, D. (1977). *Take the road to creativity and get off your dead end.* Allen, TX: Agrus Communications.

Harragan, B. L. (1978). *Games mother never taught you: Corporate gamesmanship for women.* New York, NY: Warner Books.

LeShan,L. L. (1977). *You can fight for your life: Emotional factors in the causation of cancer.* New York, NY: M. Evans.

Pearce, J. C. (1977). *Magical child.* New York, NY: E. P. Dutton.

Pulaski, M. A. (1971). *Understanding Piaget: An introduction to children's cognitive development.* New York, N.Y.: Harper and Row.

Sheehy, G. (1976) *Passages.* New York,NY: E. P. Dutton.

Simonton, O. C. (1978). *Getting well again.* Boston, Mass: Houghton Mifflin.

Stark, E. (1984, December). Exercising away depression. *Psychology Today, p. 68.*

Turkington, C. (1985, September). Endorphins: Natural opiates confer pain, pleasure, immunity. *APA Monitor,* pp 17-19.

Weinstein, M. (speaker). (1983). *Playfulness as a therapeutic tool.* (Cassette Recording No. LP 103). Stanford, Ca.: Institute for the Advancement of Human Behavior.

Williams, S. W. and McCullers, J. C. (1983). Personal factors related to typicalness of career and success in active, professional women. *Psychology of Women Quarterly, 7* (4), 343-357.

Women and Stress:
Some Implications for Therapy

Carole A. Rayburn

As increasing numbers of women enter the work force, there have been predictions that they will be susceptible to the stresses and strains suffered until now primarily by working men. Some research has supported that women are no more prone—and in some cases less prone—to stress on the job than their male counterparts (Haw, 1982; Santy, 1984). In the Santy study, women in the space program seem to adapt to extreme environmental conditions as well as or better than men do. However, such adjustment involves the physical environment. When situations involve dealing effectively with the psychosocial atmosphere, including actions and reactions toward the discrimination of women, women experience higher levels of stress than do men (Holahan, 1979; Rayburn, 1981; Rayburn, Richmond, & Rogers, 1983, 1984).

Stress in women is especially high when women enter nontraditional fields (religious leadership, medicine, the police force and fire fighters, the space program, etc.). Most often stress in women does not involve the job per se but the interface of their job and family or personal responsibilities, their sense of rejection, isolation, and the need for social networks to affirm them in nontraditional or nonaccepting job situations.

Self-reliance may even be more important than social support in assessing stress in women (Funch & Marshall, 1984). Women have been disenfranchised in many settings, not being meaningfully involved in decision-making. As a result, they may see themselves as helpless, dependent, and not having much control over their lives nor over the situations in which they find themselves.

Carole A. Rayburn is in private practice at 1200 Morningside Drive, Silver Spring, MD 20904.

Griffith (1983 a, b) found six major stressors in women between 25 and 65 years of age: physical health (the primary stressor for women over 35, and a major stressor for a fourth of all women); personal time (the second most stressing factor for women over 35); personal success; social relationships; love relationships; and parent-child relationships. Personal time and personal success were major stressors for women of ages 25-34. Women often place family needs and job responsibilities before their own health needs, which might lead to inadequate exercise and poor nutritional habits. Consuming too much food or alcohol are ways that some women cope with stress. In younger women, higher expectations and dissatisfactions were evidenced, and personal success stressors were rated highest. Older women, though, are more likely to have achieved their goals or to see attaining them as less important. Least stress for most women was experienced in social relationships.

Sometimes stress in women is due to their living in what has essentially been a man's world built by and for men. Wysocki and Ossler (1983) found that women workers had more trauma injuries due primarily to tools, machines, and work surfaces designed for the strength and size of the average male worker. Most Threshold Limit Values for toxic substances are set at levels determined by studies on men only. The woman living alone may be doing yard work with a power gas mower with a starter-cord designed for a man's physical strength. She may work with hand-tools built for a man's hands and strength. Her very house may have shelves, built-in mirrors, and other devices built for the height of the average man rather than that of average women. Coping in a world which relates so little to women's needs is difficult at best and impossible at other times. Such an environment places added pressures and thus stress on women.

On-the-job sexual harassment has received a fair amount of attention in the literature. Mendelson (1983) found that women sensed a vulnerability when they could not avoid unwanted sexual advances but they are unsure just what management is responsible for in eliminating the harassment. Women may have particular problems with persistent low-level misbehavior which is hard to prove and to challenge with even the help of the EEOC. Crull (1982) commented that sexual harassment produced some common reactions in women: physical and mental stress symptoms, diminished productivity and lowered self-confidence. Many women find confronting powerful authorities, such as bosses or men in general to be quite stressful. Short-term discussion groups which allow women to ventilate their feelings, provide group support, show women the fallacy in blaming themselves because of their gender, help them to define harassment and its stress and to document the misbehavior, prove most beneficial.

Some Suggestions for Treatment of Stress in Women

Therapy with women experiencing stress takes into account several factors influencing women's lives. Part of the therapy may involve information-giving about various resources that could aid women in lowering their stress. When a multidimensional training program was offered to women on public assistance, women were able to lower stress, depression, anxiety and sense of inadequacy, and to increase ego-strength and self-confidence in 10 weeks of training. Being exposed to traditional therapy and stress management strategies alone was not sufficient to counter learned helplessness in these women. The training program, however, raised their consciousness about stress, coping and problem solving skills (Tableman, Marciniak, Johnson, & Rogers, 1982).

Physicians have at times been accused of providing differential treatment to women and men. Verbrugge (1984) found that both genders are equally likely to indicate to physicians that their main presenting problem is emotional distress. Nonetheless, physicians determined that distressed women have emotional disorders less often than distressed men, and they considered men's mental complaints as more serious than women's. Women may have a tendency to report emotional problems in physical terms and vice versa, and they may be less reluctant than men to seek help for emotional suffering. Verbrugge concluded that, when differential care to distressed women and men occurs, it is likely to be related to psychosocial rather than to medical factors: such care based on physicians' attitudes about women and men is "sex-biased."

The unrealistic idea of the "wonder woman" who can somehow manage everything well and tirelessly was discussed by Parker and Drew (1982) as the hoax that it is, laid down by societal expectations of women. The myth is of an all-giving, ever competent woman who never complains or shows signs of wear and tear. These researchers suggested that occupational health nurses need to be aware of the range of symptoms and signs connected to excess stress, but it would also be wise for such information to be passed on to women themselves so that they could monitor their own symptoms and signs and know how to take measures to prevent high levels of stress.

Stress in women involves physical health problems (such as fatigue, anxiety, depression, and greater risk of multiple sclerosis and anorexia nervosa), problems with personal time management, personal success, and inadequate exercise and poor nutritional and eating habits. Some problems are psychosomatic, such as anorexia nervosa, in which societal expectations concerning female body-image are strong and even determining factors (Orbach, 1981). As increasing numbers of women have entered into the work place and into white-collar careers, particularly into nontraditional fields for women, women have experienced greater demands upon their time and energy and higher levels of stress. Dealing with others' expectations, including bosses, spouses, children, and colleagues, often proves to be very stressful. The highly unrealistic image which some women attempt to maintain of super woman, super wife, super mom, and super employee can be almost totally exhausting and destructive in terms of burnout. Women cannot be expected to give almost everything, get little or nothing in return, rarely if ever complain, and to live their lives as though "love means never having to say you are hurting, tired, and needy."

It is thus suggested that the following be incorporated for remediation into therapeutic treatment for women in stress:

(1) Full support of affirmative action programs. Women need to have information as to how to be most effective in making decisions in policies which will influence and determine their way of living. Those in training programs and colleges need to consider giving full support to affirmative action in the institutions of learning, so as to increase representation of women in less traditional and nontraditional areas. This would include encouragement of women's success in occupa-

tional and professional endeavors. Hardesty (1979) noted that acceptance of women in seminaries was usually achieved by a stepwise progression, with increasing levels of confrontation of sexism, support by other women and then of faculty and students, and finally more real understanding and acceptance as the numbers of women seminarians grew.

(2) Social support groups. Self-help social support group₃ would allow women to share some problems which they incur because of their minority status on many job sites or in training or college programs, especially those in nontraditional fields. This would give women some of the needed support which may be missing in the institutions in which they function. As pointed out by Holahan (1979), women with high needs for support who find themselves in academic surroundings giving them very minimal emotional encouragement experience more stress than women in identical settings who need very little support. Women seminarians and clergywomen, for example, have often discovered that such social networks are invaluable (Rayburn et al., 1984). Adding much stress to women working in nontraditional settings is noninclusive language, sanctioning the sad division of the in- and the out-group in terms of gender discrimination. In the deepest sense, women must know from supportive others that they are acceptable, worthwhile, and capable in what may be a less than friendly atmosphere for women in these times. Support groups allow women the opportunity to share personal frustrations and successful coping devices, learn from each other, ventilate feelings, draw strength from each other, and serve as role models for each other. They can lower their sense of isolation and bathe in the healthy and healing sunlight of others' understanding, concern, and caring.

(3) Suitable work sites and equipment. Stress on the job could be greatly lowered for women if they acquired work sites, perhaps through employee unions, to ensure that more work place tools, machines, and work surfaces were suitable for women's size and strength. Taking such steps would lessen trauma injuries and build self-confidence in women workers. They would not need to adapt themselves to a work place designed for men, an unrealistic and often dangerous proposition.

(4) Time management and stress management. Special time and stress managment workshops could be used to good ad-

vantage to lower stress in women. Overly high expectations, internal and external, often play havoc with schedules and increase stress. Learning to say "no" when necessary and appropriate, recognizing stress symptoms, learning to prevent stress whenever possible and to cope with it when it cannot be avoided, and learning relaxation exercises and biofeedback techniques are important. As Tableman et al. (1982) suggest, starting such corrective treatment with basic issues of self-esteem and life planning is helpful before beginning stress management per se.

While women may not be able to leave their desks or other work sites at the moment that their bodies are demanding that they shut down the system for a bit, they can manage to meditate for a few minutes on a pleasant mental image (such as a warm, sunny day at the beach; a soothing breeze blowing across a boat drifting on a lake; a soft, gentle rain falling to earth, etc.). They might also learn "desk exercises" to relax aching muscles and tired heads and necks. The management element implies that they are committed to taking better care of themselves and their health.

(5) Adequate rest and physical exercise and recreation. Resting when tired or ill is a necessary and preventive measure to lessen stress and other harmful effects on the body. Women have to discipline themselves to get adequate rest, sufficient physical exercise, and relaxation. This is particularly true if women are prone to feeling guilty or thinking that they are selfish when they take the time for themselves for these needed health measures. Sufficient sleep, better plans for sound nutrition and good eating habits, and developing greater self-acceptance while learning to take control of their own lives are important in women's coping with and preventing further stress. Setting up a behavior-modification program to achieve these goals would be helpful. Putting aside a regular time each day to rest and relax, holding such time as sacrosanct, emphasizes the importance of such a regimen and reinforces it in the daily routine. It provides the precious inner sanctum for the recuperation of mind, body, and spirit. A quiet moment reserved for the woman in the midst of the noisy, busy day is a soothing balm to alleviate stress.

(6) Job enrichment and continuing education programs. Displaced homemakers returning to the job market and even

employed women at times may benefit from a referral to a career clinic or a job skill program. In more adequately preparing women for their work, job enrichment and continuing education programs would lessen work stress, work dissatisfaction, and rejection on the work force.

(7) Adequate child care provisions. For working women with children, adequate child care provisions certainly would lower potential stress. Society still tends to instill guilt in working mothers. Support of legislation and other encouragement for on-site day-care programs where women are employed or at day-care facilities near their jobs are important measures in lowering stress in women.

(8) More realistic work hours. Demands on women's time are unrealistic in the context of the schedule of the 9-5 work day. More realistic hours for employed women must be considered. School meetings about their children, visits to health care providers, and other necessary services sought by women require flexible work hours at least once or twice a week. Most schools still expect women employed outside the home and even single heads of households to keep daytime appointments to meet with school personnel, with fathers often not being recognized as the other interested parent for such consultations.

(9) Taking responsibility in the decision-making process. Women need to learn to trust their own judgment and decision-making rather than to accept too readily and automatically the urging of authority figures—of men, society, and tradition. Taking resonsibility in decision-making is a necessary step in establishing themselves as equals in the battle of the sexes, as less stress-ridden in the adult world of reality and in determining their lives.

(10) Assertiveness training programs and consciousness-raising groups. Teaching women to become less passive in their interpersonal relationships is the goal of assertiveness training and consciousness-raising. Such training would help women to be more healthfully independent and resourceful, as well as to provide information on what to do about sexual harassment and confronting gender discrimination in the most appropriate and effective manner.

(11) Professional counseling or psychotherapy with a nonsexist orientation. Professional counseling or psychotherapy is recommended for treating stress when problems have reached

serious proportions or, more ideally, as a preventive measure before a crisis is reached. Guidelines for nonsexist counseling and therapy with women, as suggested in *The Counseling Psychologist* (1979) are indispensible. The treatment could be individual, group, couples, or family counseling or therapy. Therapy should include giving women the information on the aforementioned suggestions for ways of ameliorating stressful situations. Sensitivity about and recognition of the legitimacy of women not taking on unrealistic and unhealthy, demanding workloads—of either the paid or unpaid variety—must be shown by the therapist and communicated clearly to women in treatment. Too, appreciation that women's needs, fatigues, and pains are real and not to be denied in the service of fulfilling an Earth-Mother role must be verbalized by both therapist and the woman.

Women working outside the home would find it especially beneficial to negotiate responsibilities with their husbands or lovers, if they live with someone, and also to develop more realistic expectations of demands for excellence at home and on the job. Other areas women could work through in therapy are: change in management of household finances and thus of sharing power in economic decisions, learning to work through increased independence of working women, considerations of sharing child care, learning to balance dual careers while both partners make time for their own needs and for each other and their marriage or relationship, learning to work through their fears and anger and to network with other women in social and job-related support groups.

Therapy must involve the importance of women's being innately worthwhile and worthy individuals, regardless of the roles that they play, the functions they perform, or the successes they achieve. They do not need to prove anything to society, authorities, men, or anyone else. Further, they need to learn that they are not Rocks-of-Gibraltar, with everyone else laying claim to their help 24 hours a day. Women need to know that they are seriously listened to in therapy; that their opinions, thoughts and feelings will not be denigrated; that they themselves will be taken seriously and treated with respect and concern. Therapy can help women to realize that they are not responsible for others' behavior and happiness but are adults seeking self-actualization and individuals who share in responsibilities, decision-making, and the advantages of life. Women in therapy for treatment of stress must gradually become less dependent on their therapists in the growing process of becoming more their own persons and realizing more emotionally mature womanhood.

REFERENCES

Counseling Psychologist (1979). Principles concerning the counseling and therapy of women, *8* (1), 21.

Crull, P. (1982). Stress effects of sexual harassment on the job: Implications for counseling. *American Journal of Orthopsychiatry, 52* (3), 539-544.

Funch, D. P., & Marshall, J. R. (1984). Self-reliance as a modifier of the effects of life stress and social support. *Journal of Psychosomatic Research, 28* (1), 9-15.

Griffith, J. W. (1983a). Women's stressors according to age groups: Part I. *Issues in Health Care of Women, 4* (6), 311-326.

Griffith, J. W. (1983b). Women's stress responses and coping patterns according to age groups: Part II. *Issues in Health Care of Women, 4* (6), 327-340.

Hardesty, N. (1979). Women and the seminaries. *Christian Century, 96,* 122-123.

Haw, M. A. (1982). Women, work and stress: A review and agenda for the future. *Journal of Health and Social Behavior, 23* (2), 132-143.

Holahan, C. K. (1979). Stress experienced by women doctoral students, need for support, and occupational sex typing: An international view. *Sex Roles, 5* (4), 425-436.

Mendelson, R. (1983). Sexual harassment. *Occupational Health Nursing, 31* (11), 47-49.

Orbach, S. (1981). *Fat is a feminist issue.* New York: Berkley.

Parker, J. E., & Drew, K. E. (1982). Women, work and health. *Occupational Health Nursing, 30* (7), 27-28.

Rayburn, C. A. (1981). Some reflections of a female seminarian: Woman, whither goest thou? *Journal of Pastoral Counseling, 16* (2), 61-65.

Rayburn, C. A., Richmond, L. J., & Rogers, L. (1984). Men, women, and religion: Stress within leadership roles. A study funded in part by a grant from the Educational Foundation Program of the American Association of University Women.

Rayburn, C. A., Richmond, L. J., & Rogers, L. (1983). Stress among religious leaders. *Thought, 58* (230), 329-344.

Santy, P. A. (1984). Women in space: A medical perspective. *Journal of the American Medical Women's Association, 39* (1), 13-17.

Tableman, B., Marciniak, D., Johnson, D., & Rogers, R. (1982). Stress managment training for women on public assistance. *American Journal of Community Psychology, 10* (3), 357-367.

Verbrugge, L. M. (1984). How physicians treat mentally distressed men and women. *Social Science and Medicine, 18* (1), 1-9.

Wysocki, L. M., & Ossler, C. (1983). Women, work, and health: Issues of importance to the occupational health nurse. *Occupational Health Nursing, 31* (11), 18-23.

Antisemitism and Sexism in Stereotypes of Jewish Women

Rachel Josefowitz Siegel

INTRODUCTION

Antisemitism is often ignored as one of the forces that keep women from building stronger bonds with each other. In its subtler forms it is often not recognized or acknowledged. In stereotypic images of the *Jewish Mother* and the *JAP* or *Jewish American Princess,* the dominant socially acceptable prejudice of antisemitism or mother-blaming is used to carry or sell another prejudice, and to convey more subtle discriminatory messages, such as heterosexism, agism, classism, racism and anti-intellectualism. These images obscure the diversity and reality in the lives of Jewish women and keep us from appreciating their strengths, their struggles, and their valuable contributions. These images hook into ancient religious and ethnic prejudices that each of us have absorbed from the culture at large, in the same way that we have absorbed the woman-blaming and woman-devaluing messages of our society.

Jewish and female self-devaluation are involved in this phenomenon. The pejorative and ridiculed images are especially virulent because they are sexist caricatures of the limited traditional roles assigned to women, presented in an antisemitic package. The ambition and self-assertion or aggression that do not fit the female role are labeled Jewish and seen as inappropriate. The images express society's devaluation of the limited roles assigned to women and its ambivalence toward

Dr. Siegel is in private practice at 108 West Buffalo Street, Ithaca, New York 14850.

An earlier version of this paper appeared as Preliminary reflections on the Jewish Mother and the Jewish American Princess: Images of combined sexism and antisemitism, in *Women in the eighties: strategies for solidarity,* selected papers from the 1983 New York State Women's Studies Conference, Ognibene, E. R. ed., Loudonville, N.Y.: Siena College, 1983.

the women who conform or overconform to these roles and expectations. Two sides of the same coin, they are equally harsh indictments of the mother and of the young women who seeks security through marriage. The mother is seen as a selfless, nurturing, overprotective, desexualized source of her children's and her husband's problems; the young woman as a selfish, materialistic, dependent, manipulative sex object.

Why are they dressed in Jewish garb? Why do they speak in Yiddish phrases? Why and when do we say that a woman acts like a *Jewish Mother?* or looks like *JAP?* Why do Jewish and non-Jewish feminists participate in this devaluation of women and of Jews by our silence or by our trivializing the impact of these derogatory images? Images of Jewish women, as they appear in literature, in the arts, the popular media, and in the Jewish tradition, convey an exaggerated caricature of reality. We recognize in them enough of the real Jewish women we know, to make us overlook the inaccuracies, the traits not mentioned, the humanity, the dignity, the suffering, the individuality of the real woman. The image so easily portrayed becomes an inaccurate stereotype, reinforcing existing biases, distancing the real Jewish woman from those who see her and from her own sense of who she really is. When positive, these images are idealizations, they have the power to serve as models of being in the world, of living up to important cultural and ethnic values. When negative, they have the power to serve as models of "the kind of woman not to be," rejecting and avoiding those cultural and ethnic traits which are considered inappropriate or unattractive by the dominant host culture.

The Idealized Jewish Mother, A Positive Image

Throughout Jewish history, and within the Jewish tradition of today, the image of the Jewish woman has been almost exclusively a mother image, conveying an idealization of mothering. She is portrayed as a strong, self-sacrificing woman, who bore the hardships of her oppressed people with dignity. She was a source of comfort for her family, her neighbors and community, a skillful manager of meager resources. She enlisted her daughters at an early age in helping to feed, care for, and protect the men in the family from daily cares as well as from the persecutions and insults of an alien and oppressive environment (Gluckel, 1977; Zborowski & Herzog, 1952). She was often more practical than her husband, maintaining her own sense of worth by making it possible for him to observe and participate in the exclusively male pursuits of education, scholarship, religious ritual and community decision-making. This idealized Jewish woman, although subservient to her husband, was spared the overt domestic violence and sexual degradation imposed on her non-Jewish sisters, for the idealized Jewish man was not a womanizer, a warrior, a tough guy; he was a gentle, pious scholar entitled to special domestic privilege. We all know Jewish families who did not live up to these standards; the reality includes every possible kind of human behavior and interaction, yet these idealized norms were taught and institutionalized. Through generations and centuries of external oppression they were perceived as elements essential to Jewish survival.

The Jewish woman was kept in her well-defined place by the subtle and powerful bonds of affiliation and responsibility to her family, her clan, her people. Her role was important. She knew herself to be essential to the biological and cultural survival of her continuously endangered people. She still feels the weight of that expectation. She had no access to alternate roles or occupations which might bring economic self-sufficiency. She knew that she literally could not survive alone if she moved away from the enfolding patterns of her own community. The walls of her ghetto were not made of stone, yet they were real enough to keep her both protected and imprisoned by the far greater dangers surrounding it.

Value Conflict and Changing Values

A significant change occurred as Jews began to move out of the ghetto in large numbers. In turn of the century Germany, emancipation seemed possible, in America the lure was equality, freedom from persecution and access to quick wealth. Suddenly Jews were interacting with Christian neighbors more openly, exposed to Christian culture and the customs and ethics of the world at large. Assimilation into the mainstream offered attractive possibilities. New values and attitudes were not only available, but unavoidable. Well-intentioned public school teachers and principals took pride in Americanizing immigrant children, with an unquestioned assumption that American ways were better and beneficial. Employers rigidly demanded conformity to American patterns of behavior. The established social and economic institutions of the new world set their own terms and newcomers had to adjust. In the process of Americanization, the boundaries of ethnic and religious differences became blurred, immigrant patterns were unlearned, rejected, or confined to the home. Immigrant children learned to be ashamed of their parents, to ridicule their ways. The urge to move up and away, and to discard the old patterns was intensified by the extreme poverty of early immigrant life.

The Jewish mother, struggling to maintain the old values and familiar patterns while wanting the best for her children in the new world became an easy target for blame, ridicule, and rejection. Her role and her performance were not judged by a set of strange, ill-fitting standards. Jewish comedians, novelists, psychiatrists, all sons of Jewish mothers, contributed to blaming their mothers for a culture conflict that was much deeper and more complicated than they understood. Their depictions of intergenerational conflict focused primarily on mothers and sons. Sonya Michel (1976) gives a rare and sensitive account of mother/daughter interactions and how these were perceived by a Jewish male psychiatrist:

> Psychiatrist Alexander Grinstein (1967), described the identity problems common to a small group of his patients who were all second-generation women: "Their own crudeness and inappropriateness in their dress, the excrescence of harshness in their behavior toward their children, loudness in their manner, the lack of accepted values—all speak for an identification with some of their mothers' striking characteristics. Their sense of identity is thus seriously disturbed and they are constantly dissatisfied with themselves in the role that they are playing. . . . It is as though one can see the middle European ghetto community living within the 'modern personality' of these women, like Williamsburg in the middle of New York" (p. 86). Grinstein's identification of the elements of the conflict of these women seems accurate; but the language

of his description and analysis reveals, quite inadvertently, something far more profound: the reason there is a conflict in the first place. By characterizing immigrant women as " primitive," and their daughters as "crude," "harsh," "loud," "inappropriately" dressed, and lacking "accepted values," Grinstein is imposing conventional American standards on Jewish women and their daughters. He assumes that the "normal" female will be ladylike—quiet, cultured, refined, and well-dressed, when in fact East European women were revered for being strong, practical, and nonmaterialistic: qualities Grinstein considers "primitive" (p. 278).

NEGATIVE IMAGES

The fairly recent negative images of *Jewish Mother* and *JAP (Jewish American Princess)* emerge in the context of these conflicting definitions of acceptable ways of being female. The self-asserting nurturing that was essential to Shtetl[1] life and early immigrant days now appears out of place when measured by American mainstream standards of propriety. The nurturing is now devalued, the self-assertion seen as pushy. In a setting in which the subtler, covert forms of anti-semitism can easily be denied, and the memories of Holocaust survivors are shunned and discounted, the self-preserving strengths and coping patterns of Jewish women are interpreted as aggressive, greedy, paranoid and comical.

The new negative image of the *Jewish Mother* emerges as a caricature of the nurturant, overprotective aspects of mothering that were idealized in the earlier Jewish tradition. The image accurately depicts the reduction and devaluation of her former role. She is reduced to a clinging figure, hopelessly holding on to earlier folkways, living through her husband, her sons and daughters, preventing them from achieving the American male-defined goals of autonomy and independence, and causing them guilt, neurosis, and other discomforts. She is the scapegoat, the recipient of all ambivalent feelings toward mothers and toward the Jewish presence.

It is difficult to find anything positive in the *JAP* stereotype. This negative image of the *JAP* has no idealized precursor. The traditional *Nice Jewish Girl* was unsung and modestly invisible. The negative *JAP* image emerges as a caricature of the over-protected, overdependent aspects of the idealized American sex object, the woman whose future depends on marrying well, on being selected by Prince Charming or today's ambitious young man with an upwardly mobile future. She is a conglom-erate of Madison Avenue advertising and non-Jewish fairy tales of womanhood, but unlike a fashion model or a beauty queen, unlike Princess Diana, she has Jewish features and the "negative," "crude" qualities described by Dr. Grinstein. She embodies the antisemitic, sexist, heterosexist, ageist, perfec-tionist, racist, and role-limited biases of American culture. For her parents, she represents the successful, beautiful daughter, her female role defined in a blend of Jewish and American terms. Her "hard working, ambitious Jewish father" and her "self-sacrificing Jewish mother" want only "she should be happy." She is their naches[2] (Schneider, 1984). She is also the product of a generation of post-Holocaust Jewish parents who may be trying to cover up their own and their parents' deep seated insecurity, survivor's guilt and fear by valuing material possessions, upward mobility and a frantic search for happi-ness. The *JAP,* like the *Jewish Mother,* is an image caricaturing a deep and complex culture conflict and generational conflict. The young woman who is seen as a *JAP* is struggling to make some sense out of the rapidly changing Jewish, feminist and mainstream American values of her environment.

These negative images of Jewish women are typical of the internalized oppression and devaluation experienced by mem-bers of minority groups, when they absorb the values of the dominant culture (Klein, 1980). When Jews lived in ghettos, their only contact with the dominant culture was through bru-tal victimization. Now that the interaction of the two cultures offers the possibility of equal co-existence or assimilation, we must remember that the terms are still set by the dominant culture. The victimization, now subtle and denied, still exists. Equality too often means conformity, and the price is rejec-tion of those parts of the self or of the other that are asso-ciated with the minority, in this case the Jewish traits, and overvaluing those traits that are associated with the majority, in this case the feminine role.

For the Jewish woman, the devaluation is multiple and

complex: she no more fits the artificial standards of American femininity than most other woman, she is excluded from important aspects of Jewish ritual and communal achievement (especially in Orthodox communities); her feminist sisters are quick to attack the Jewish roots of the patriarchy or to perceive her as pushy and privileged but slow to validate the pain she suffers from memories of immigrant poverty, antisemitic persecution and present antisemitic stereotyping. In the confusion of Jewish values, American values, and feminist values, she can try to live up to all of them, but she is more likely to reject the ones that are most troublesome, and the people who represent these.

An integration of Jewish and feminist values needs to be explored within the context of our predominantly non-Jewish and male-centered value system. Recent Self-in-Relation developmental literature recognizes and begins to value the "centrality of relationships and connectedness" (Surrey, 1983). The work of Gilligan (1982) and Miller (1984) leads to a reevaluation of the relational qualities of mothering that convey a relational ethic as opposed to the separation/autonomy ethic of American society. When the mothering role exemplified by Jewish mothers is stripped of the distorted and exaggerated aspects that were the by-products of persecution, enforced migration and role limitation, we uncover a core of relational strengths and abilities whose value is now being rediscovered by feminist thinkers.

Impact of the Stereotypes on Real Jewish Women Today

The real Jewish woman in America today is as complex and diverse as her non-Jewish sisters. She portrays herself in the emerging feminist Jewish literature with a new sense of her own worth. Confronted with the stereotypic image, she measures herself by it and finds grains of truth in it, yet the distortions and exaggerations are painful to her and confusing. She does not know whether to laugh or cry at the caricature, to reject or embrace it. These issues were discussed at a New York State Women's Studies Association Workshop and two succeeding workshops for Jewish women. Many women had never before talked about their Jewish identity in terms of being women. The issues were obviously of immediate and very personal concern. Jewish women felt divided from each other by the negative stereotypes and were troubled by the impact of these images.

"What you are describing is not true anymore. Things have changed. I am not that kind of a *Jewish mother* and none of my friends are. My daughters are not like that. They don't call me a *Jewish Mother*," said a woman in her late forties. "I stayed away from this woman in my dorm because I had her figured as a *JAP*. I didn't want people to think that I was like that. When I did get to know her we had some things in common, she wasn't the way I thought she would be. I felt badly that I had missed knowing her for so long," said a young college woman. Each woman had experienced the impact of the stereotype and expressed a need to defend herself against it. These Jewish images were felt to be different or more harmful than stereotypical messages about Italian mothers or other immigrant mothers, because Jewish women of today are deeply affected by the Holocaust. The enormity of that historical event and the possibility of future persecutions, based on historical reality, made antisemitic messages more frightening.

Some women said that the stereotype and the denial of its impact caused them to feel badly about being Jewish and female. It made them wish to avoid their families who were blind to their feelings, and to reject their Jewish background, and that this avoidance was painful for them.

Anger was expressed at Jewish men, fathers, brothers, partners, sons who colluded actively or passively in maintaining the stereotypes. Why are there no such jokes about Jewish Fathers or Jewish American Princes?

It seemed that the *Jewish Mother* had some positive qualities that could be reclaimed and revalued, but it was difficult to do this with the JAP image.

Working with Jewish women individually or in workshops, I have found it useful to examine the ways in which these stereotypes affect each individual woman; what part of the stereotype fits into her own self-concept and why; and how much of the stereotype she sees in her own mother or her own daughter. I have also asked women to identify and reclaim those aspects of being Jewish that felt valuable and comfortable for each individual woman, to reject the negative aspects of the stereotype, and to reevaluate those aspects that were positive but simply differed from American middle class norms. Such discussions have led to an increase in self-esteem and a clearer, stronger sense of Jewish identity.

Among Jewish and non-Jewish therapists, my presentation of these issues has led to greater sensitivity and awareness of the therapist's own participation in perpetuating the stereotypes and in judging Jewish women by non-Jewish standards.

REFERENCE NOTES

1. *Shtetl:* the Eastern European Jewish village or ghetto within a town.
2. *Naches:* a Yiddish term meaning satisfaction, pride, pleasure.

REFERENCES

Gilligan, C. (1982). *In a different voice: Psychological theory and women's development.* Cambridge, MA: Harvard U. Press.

Gluckel. (1977). *The memoirs of Gluckel of Hameln.* New York: Schocken Books.

Grinstein, A. (1967). Profile of a doll. In N. Kiell (ed.), *The psychodynamics of American Jewish life.* New York: Twayne.

Klein, J. W. (1980). *Jewish identity and self-esteem.* New York: Institute on Pluralism and Group Identity, Am. Jewish Committee.

Michel, S. (1976). Mothers and daughters in American Jewish literature: The rotted cord. In E. Koltun (ed.), *The Jewish woman: New perspectives.* New York: Schocken.

Miller, J. B. (1984). The development of women's sense of self. In *Work in progress.* Wellesley, MA: Stone Center, Wellesley College.

Schneider, S. W. (1984). *Jewish and female.* New York: Simon and Schuster.

Surrey, J. L. (1983). The "self in relation": A theory of women's development. In *Work in progress.* Wellesley, MA: Stone Center, Wellesley College.

Zborowski, M. & Herzog, E. (1952). *Life is with people.* New York: Schocken Books.

The Male Addict's Consciousness of Women in His Life

Carol Jean Rogalski

Freud had made the query "What do women want?" (Jones 1955, p. 421; Strachey, 1961, p. 244) suggesting that the concerns of women in life and relationships were not understood by him and were perhaps vastly different, unrealistic, and inferior from the concerns and expectations of men. The question "What do men want?" is now being asked by women scientists, scholars and humanists. While I do not have the answer concerning what "generic" men want, I will present how some individual men—drug users and abusers—describe themselves in their relationship to women.

Freud had suggested in *Civilization and Its Discontents* (1930) that the male moves into a mature psychological position when he no longer expends energy in extinguishing the fires of his adolescent peers, but determines to possess his own fire, and a woman to tend it. He selected a woman to tend his fire not because he sought lively companionship and a family, but because he wanted his own fire. The woman was the logical choice not because he had given up competing, but rather that she couldn't compete with him since she was anatomically not built to put out his fire. The woman was psychologically "safe" in preserving what he owned and controlled. She did not interfere with his desires. He could be proud of himself, his possessions, and his goals and ambitions. In Christian moralistic terminology his hubris could simply be labeled "pride," one of the seven deadly sins, while the Greek philosophers spoke of narcissism or self-love. In one version of the myth of Narcissus he is so absorbed in his own image in the water that he does not turn to look at Echo who

Dr. Rogalski is Adjunct Assistant Professor at the University of Illinois College of Medicine and Staff Psychologist at the West Side Veterans Administration Hospital, 820 S. Damien Avenue, Chicago, IL 60612.

entreats him to notice that she loves him. In another version of the myth, a virginal young woman is drawn away from her female companions by the beauty of the flowers that she sees in the meadow, only to find the earth open to let forth the passion and energy of wild horses. Modern self-psychologists speak of grandiose-exhibitionistic tendencies, and there is a growing recent literature concerning narcissistic issues in our society and in psychotherapeutic treatment (Kohut, 1971; Lasch, 1979).

In modern lay terms, the man was assured that the woman would not "rain on his parade" and that she would protect his interests as if they were her own. He could adore himself in the mirrored adoration he found in her eyes, never becoming the reflecting mirror for her own perhaps contradictory and distinctive desires.

The empirical work of George Vaillant and his colleagues over more than a decade (1966; 1976; 1981) on male psychological health reports that unhappily married men were "delayed in establishing independence from their own mothers" (1976) and that the capacity to love was associated with physical and mental health. Some men might have career success or closeness to children, but fearfulness of life ran parallel to the inability to have formed an intimate relationship. Daniel Levinson (1978) in his study of men from their late teens to late forties, does not write in depth regarding the psychological processes through which the man leaves his mother as a source of esteem regulation and forms an intimate, mutual relationship with a peer. He does state, however, that the wife chosen early in adult life serves the same psychological functions as did the mother. The initial "mother-mate" may be a self-esteem regulator but may not be the ideal woman. His capacity to now form a relationship to an ideal woman is cruicial to man's happiness. It is unclear in his writing whether this ideal woman is a different woman from his mate, either the ubiquitous "other woman," or a second wife, or a modification in intrapsychic functioning which transforms mate as mother, self-esteem regulator and part-object, to mate as loved whole-object.

While both Vaillant and Levinson trace the development of the biological man, neither traces the development of psychological man, and Vaillant (1976) states that in spite of extensive material, Anna Freud writes that "the chronology of psychic processes (defenses) is still one of the most obscure fields of analytic theory" (1937). Lample-de Groot (1957) suggests that "the pathological defense mechanisms seen in neuroses : . . . are the very same mechanisms that served normal development in early childhood." Haan (1969) finds that reaction formation and fantasy decline from adolescence to adulthood, with altruism and suppression taking their place. Carol Gilligan (1982) suggests that the morality of caring for people may be developmentally higher than the morality of caring for a thought or idea.

While we know intuitively that aging alone does not bring wisdom or psychological maturity, research does validate our intuitions that over time the normal adult enhances his or her own ability to work and to love, in keeping with Freud's own reflections. In addition to possessing the ability to work and to love is the belief in something to hope for.

I have been employed for the past eleven years in various capacities with both inpatient and outpatient male veterans who have long histories of drug abuse. I have interviewed thousands and have attempted to understand how I might be of service to them. I consider and reconsider the data—in the form of verbal reports—that they bring to me in order to understand and to intervene therapeutically. If my empathy is accurate I find them concerned mainly with control issues—control of their desires, the drugs they use, the staff, and the persons, if any, in their lives. Repeated helplessness to control leads to self-image distortions that they must be independent, that they don't really need anyone, that they possess common sense, that they are reasonable, fairminded and logical. They are convinced that all people are the same and deny the uniqueness of the individuals in their surroundings. They appear particularly troubled and unrealistic in their relationships to adult women, and sustain a dependence upon their mothers for both money and unconditional positive regard. New females—and I specifically say females because there appears little consciousness of the women as women—are approached quickly, seemingly without regard for their psychological space. If the intrusion is not met with acceptance, there are very hurt feelings, and often an immediate volley of psychological abuse and hostility. While I said that I did not wish to speak of "generic" behaviors, bear with me a moment longer, since the group behavior of the addict does disservice to any individual addict. The reputation within the hospital of the addict population is that they are to be avoided since *as a group* they are often offensive to women. At an average age of 35 years the impression given is that they have just recently learned about the "birds and the bees." Alongside the sexualized behavior is an idealization—these contradictions are certainly represented within the group behavior and are sometimes found within the individual.

I will give you two examples of this behavior. I had entered an elevator at the Veterans Administration Hospital, tired from a day's work, with much on my mind to think about. An ex-drug patient, now on a medical or surgical unit by the looks of the pajamas and robe that he was wearing, greeted me. I responded tentatively—his face was familiar, but I was unable to generate any specific memories of this person. As I became somewhat embarrassed by my memory failure he became immediately offensive, turning to another person in the elevator and, changing his facial expression from a smile to a sneer, said—" she just thinks I want to get into her pants."

This scenario is played out daily within the hospital. Alongside the impulsive reaction to the disappointment of not being recognized—or the annoyance at being reminded of the reality of our relationship—there is a "respect" which is equally demanding. For certain periods I have been unable to enter a patient/staff meeting without all eyes being on me, with chairs being offered, and comments such as "watch your language, a lady is present" being said. For a period I could not leave the room without chaos developing with insistence that I remain. Staff, too, joined the group of the patients, with their attempts to regiment and control comings and goings. While the male staff apeared to have the freedom to come and go at will and to remain relatively anonymous, the women's responses were highlighted and she was credited as the one who would raise the standards of interpersonal conduct, yet was to be under the control of both the male staff and the patient government. They found it easier to refer to me by my body parts than my role as doctor, and preferred to have me reveal personal accounts of husband and children rather than report the details of their lives. It was a usual occurrence for people to get anxious when I left the room.

With a woman on a pedestal to admire the exhibitionism of the group members, her power to approve or disapprove is out of proportion to reality; alongside her power to approve is the fear in finding her less than ideal. Her imperfections are spotlighted, whereas the flaws of the male staff are lauded as aspects of their humanness. Her behavior is viewed as that of a "goddess" and not viewed realistically, and whether or not she smiles or nods her head approvingly or remains passive and decorative determines the self-esteem of the men present.

What is observed daily in the hospital—that is, gender-related responses toward women which expect higher standards as well as intimacy—is reflected in the reports that are made of their lives. I believe that I have found a disproportionate number of primarily negative or idealized internalized representations of women while the images of men are less emotionally charged.

As you may know, drug abuse—both alcohol and hard drugs—is primarily a male mental health problem. To my knowledge, women were not included in smoking even the peace pipe originally, and male addicts will often state that drunkenness or drug abuse are less tolerable for a woman. It is definitely not a womanly thing in which to engage. Does that mean that drug abuse is a masculine/manly thing in which to engage? Statistics reveal that males take drugs primarily in the companionship of other men, and they are the prime distributors of drugs. Pharmaceutical salesmen, physicians and street dealers have historically been men.

It is my belief that there is a connection between gender and drug taking not just on a statistical and biological level, but on a psychological level. Freud had said that intoxicants are taken to produce pleasure and avoid pain. Man's desire to control and to avoid certain aspects of reality are at the base of drug usage. Helplessness is historically psychologically feminine. Potency is historically psychologically masculine. While drug abusers may be acting very "macho," their inner experience is one of loss of control and impotency; they have never come to terms with their passive-dependent strivings. Not only don't they have a woman at their disposal permanently to tend their fires; whoever is around tends not to be impressed.

The psychologically "masculine" desire to control, not just

primitive fire, but bodily reactions and sensations, emotions and thoughts, as well as the persons in their lives, is a real fear of life itself. This desire to control natural life processes and substitute artificial chemicals has resulted both in the development of civilization as well as the destruction of freely living life forms. When Freud rejoiced that cocaine had taken away the pain of one of his patients and he stated that he now "felt like a doctor" (Jones, 1953), Freud had not thoroughly understood either the gastric condition of the patient nor the chemical action of the drug, but noticed only his ability to control discomfort.

I will now present some clinical examples of various levels of consciousness which addicts possess concerning the women in their lives. I will begin with two vignettes, those of Sigmund Freud and his colleague, Ernest von Fleischl, and then illustrate from among patients I have seen.

Clinical Example #1

A prototype of drug-taking behavior and its internal psychology is that of Sigmund Freud's own cocaine episode. When he was hired in 1884 by Merck Pharmaceuticals to study the physiological action of cocaine, he was 28 years old. He was working in a laboratory and engaged to Martha Bernays. He "hastily" closed his scientific investigation to visit his fiancée from whom he had been parted for two years. He had written to her prior to their reunion:

> Woe to you, my Princess, when I come. I will kiss you quite red and feed you till you are plump. And if you are froward [sic] you shall see what is the stronger, a gentle little girl who doesn't eat enough or a big wild man who has cocaine in his body. In my last severe depression I took coca again and a small dose lifted me to the heights in a wonderful fashion. I am just now busy collecting the literature for a song of praise to this magical substance. (Jones, 1953, p. 84)

When he returned from his vacation he found that an idea that he had shared with several colleagues concerning the anesthetizing effect of cocaine had been researched by another. This colleague, Carl Koller, had made decisive experiments upon animals and was credited with being the discoverer of the use of cocaine as a local anesthetic. Freud was angry and resentful and wrote "I bore my fiancée no grudge for her interruption of my work" (Jones, 1953, p. 79). While at this point his social and occupational functioning were not impaired by the use of cocaine his problems in concentration precede drug usage. In terms of his psychological structure, he was unable to maintain his work as a scientist. His thinking was interrupted by sexual fantasies, and he desired to exhibit himself in a gradiose fashion to his fiancée to insure both his masculinity and a merged psychological experience. He subsequently had difficulty sorting out appropriate boundaries for himself and Martha in his inability to be responsible for his own thoughts and actions. He credits her with his own failure to be famous at an early age. In addition, in prescribing cocaine to patients his self-image was not as a physician-scientist who understands, but as a healer who removes pain.

Clinical Example #2

A second example of a person whose psychic structure was considerably more defective than Freud's was that of his friend and colleague, Ernest von Fleischl. He was Freud's senior colleague with whom he had worked on animal experiments. Von Fleischl was noted as a distinguished looking man, handsome, gifted, and a creative thinker. He inspired admiration from his colleagues—or at least from Freud—even though he was noted for being irregular in his work habits. The man was a perennial bachelor, having been engaged for ten or more years to a woman willing to wait for him indefinitely. He suffered the pain of trigeminal neuralgia associated with an amputation of his hand, and was a periodic, then regular user of morphine. He said that his parents viewed him as a "savant" and he worked to uphold their image of him though he desired to shoot himself and refrained from doing so out of respect for them. He reported doing everything with "three times the effort that others use" (Jones, 1953, p. 90). Freud substituted cocaine for morphine and while both were initially optimistic, von Fleischl subsequently became hopelessly addicted, with periods of cocaine intoxication leading to increased agitation and talkativeness as well as fornication. His parents sought Freud's help to care for him, but von Fleischl withdrew both from work and social contacts, and died a cocaine addict six years following his initiation to the substance. There is no significant data about his fiancée and his feelings for her, and one wonders whether the "engagement" was a cloak of Victorian respectability, though there is no data.

Now, let me turn to the patients that I have seen.

SUBJECTS AND METHODS

Every patient who enters the drug detoxification unit at the West Side Veterans Administration is interviewed by myself at least once, generally three times. In the 11 years at the facility there have been only about five women and three to four thousand men. Ninety-five percent are black, the remaining are white of mixed ethnicity. Their ages range from 18 to 65 years, but the majority are in their mid to late 30s. Only 20% are employed, the remaining survive in various forms of legal and illegal "hustles," gambling, pimping and drug dealing.

The interviews are open-ended and are not recorded. Notes are taken during or after the sessions, dependent upon the rapport established. The patient is asked to tell me his concerns— those things that are on his mind—including thoughts, feelings, and bodily sensations. He is not led to talk either about relationships or career, people or work, but rather his experience of himself. I have distilled what I consider to be the essence of their inner experience of themselves as well as their relationships, highlighting their attitudes toward and behaviors with women.

Clinical Example #3

This man had no consciousness either of men or women in his life. He simply wanted the veterans' benefits, recreation, and daily variety in the environment to stimulate him.

Clinical Example #4

This patient had no specific consciousness of women in his life. He viewed generic "others" as not understanding him, and his self-representation was as a man who feared "AIDS, herpes, and the streets." Yet his whole life had been in the streets, with one sexual partner after another.

Clinical Example #5

He had six wives, though he did not speak about them with any individualized identity. The women were never unique, and all the marriages ended when he could not "be responsible" and govern his behavior in keeping with his fantasy of what a husband should be. The information that he never loved his mother was volunteered apologetically, and the term "love" was not used in relation to his wives. Why he was so apologetic for not loving his mother when he later added that he never knew her and was never raised by her was only to be understood from an empathic viewpoint, since the psychological processes were never articulated. His self-representation was as a man "without zing—I can't work—I can't love—and I'm getting old."

Clinical Example #6

As a child, this man always preferred to play with girls, yet as he grew older he could never converse with them. He reported an attachment to an older sister who he "wanted to protect," but she would "embarrass" him by being loud. He likewise no longer liked seeing his mother, and had grown disappointed in her and couldn't live easily with the devalued image he had of her when she "lost face" at a family gathering. He and his wife were "tired of each other" and beyond this bored feeling was concern that she was upset with him because he spent all his money on drugs. All his concerns and attractions to women seemed to have burned out and become lifeless and negative, whereas he had kept alive an internalized idealized image of a brother whom he hadn't seen for years about whom he felt "I should be with him."

Clinical Example #7

This man stated that his wife was always jealous of him as well as that she wanted to go out more. Her verbalizations of her needs and feelings led to a reaction in him that he was "bugged" by her, and he would walk out of their home, straight to his drug-dealing "partner" (the drug addict's hold-over from his adolescent "best friend" or "buddy"). His "partner" would give him drugs to take. There was not enough time to explore what advice, if any, his partner volunteered concerning the marital problems. During his hospitalization he would forget his sessions, transformed the time for attention to his needs into distaste and distortion that he "must" see me, and then would walk out of the session to watch television or play cards with peers.

Clinical Example #8

This attractive man came into the office sporting a noticeable gold watch and chains, unusual for many drug addicts who come for detoxification only after having spent all their money and sold all their possessions. He was quite articulate concerning his plan to leave his fourth wife, though must have had some reservation since he had come to a hospital to seek help for the first time. He couldn't program his wife in the way that he wanted, particularly in relation to being home with their children. She would be in bars till early into the morning hours, and he was quite vague concerning who took care of the children and whether there were any stable arrangements for child care.

He reported that in his childhood he never knew his own mother until the age of six when one day he was told to pack his bags and leave with the stranger who appeared at the door. For the previous six years he had lived first with one aunt and then with another, as well as with one particular uncle whom he feared. Presently he was quite successful monetarily as a dealer in drugs, and though usually not a drug user, had recently become addicted when he began to use drugs as a marketing tool for his customers . . . "See, it's really great . . . I take them too."

In his three previous marriages he would just pack up his things in a suitcase and walk out without warning, leaving the material possessions in the apartment for his wife, denying any emotional regret, to completely start the cycle over again with a new woman. And he always had one or two of them "on the side—if the marriage fails, I have a substitute."

While showing no tearfulness or anger, and presenting an image of being in control of his situation—since he could walk away whenever he decided—the lack of control over his wives' behaviors was evidenced. He didn't understand what occurred between himself and other people, and he had become a drug dealer because he couldn't get along with his peers and superiors at work. He had been fired from a large corporation for being "competitive—even the union couldn't help me—I lost faith in them—they didn't tell me what to do." These experiences were told with pathos, some bravado, and surface charm. While he had come for professional help, there was no emotional opening to provide the assistance he was craving. He was not willing to work on his marriage as he was preparing to leave both his wife and the hospital.

Clinical Example #9

This man was raised by foster parents, yet almost "went to pieces" when his real mother, whom he did not know, died. He reported that he was always "into girls" since the age of seven, and that he was proud of his own seven year old son who was also "into girls." His early attention-seeking from girls changed as he became a teenager, and he reported a loss of interest in them. He would spend all his time and interest in body building as well as in drug taking. He became an abuser for over a decade, and then through his own efforts controlled the drug usage. Shortly before seeking admission to the hospital for detoxification he had gone out of control and had become re-addicted by the women with whom he spent his time. He liked "to party" and the world was described as being "filled with so many beautiful women with cocaine." He came into the hospital in a state of psychological disequilibrium, speaking of how he had "gotten so low" that he was "taking another's 'rinse'," which meant that he was using a syringe which contained blood and left-over drugs from another addict.

Clinical Example #10

This man entered the program for detoxification for the tenth time. During his previous admissions he was arrogant, did not establish any rapport, and ignored my presence. In a typical fashion for a detoxifying addict, he wished medical service and the material resources in the environment but did not acknowledge his troubled emotional life. Treatment was performed by "the program" and by controlling the services provided, not by human involvement or self-understanding. In his usual independent fashion he would become a leader of his peers, offering them advice. His manner was one of disdain and self-confidence. During his previous admission he had stood for twenty minutes in my office ranting and raving about how he would rather sit and listen to addicts than be in the room with me and talk about himself. He couldn't sit still in the educational group which I conducted, and would walk out criticizing me openly. During this admission he had a complete change in his relationship to me. He would sit attentively and listen to what I had to say in the educational group which I conducted daily. He made and kept individual appointments with me. He told me of his marriage to an addict who he had met because of his drug usage. An unexpected, unplanned daughter had been born and recently "something just happened" to him. There were feelings that he was having in relation to the child that were unexpected. He felt frightened about his adequacy to care, but was caring in spite of himself.

He recognized that his marriage was a confusion to him. He wanted to fight for his wife—not because he loved her, but because she was his—he owned her. "There was no love—I held her hostage—I've never loved myself—I used to try to do what I couldn't do and feel what people told me to feel." He described himself as marrying accidentally: "I don't feel what love is supposed to be—she was a car—a possession—I didn't see her as a person."

He described his early years filled with whippings and beatings from both his parents. He said that he never loved his mother, yet sought her acceptance and attention, and began to realize that whenever he had tried to talk to her to get attention for himself, she would change the subject to talk about someone else—her friends, their relatives, his other siblings. His own needs and wants were over-powered by her. He felt placed in that role—that of the listener and advice giver—though he never formed a stable and rewarding internalized image of himself in this role.

As we worked together, he found himself becoming more

aware of his relationship to his mother and subsequently he was becoming more aware of his emotional instability. One phone call to her would go well, but he would get off with a headache. At another time he was conscious of having to lie and would hang up the telephone. He always felt a need to present a false image to her as well as to others. At the time he left the hospital he experienced himself being honest with himself and felt that I had "put him in touch" with his authentic self. The future with him is to unfold.

Clinical Example #11

This patient arrived in the hospital in a state of psychotic fragmentation or drug toxicity or a combination of both. He was unable to speak in sentences, rambled and asked for constant reassurance. He had come from another hospital and he reported being given increasing dosages of medication which exacerbated his feelings of being out of touch with himself and external reality. He established an immediate positive bond with me, and during the month of hospitalization and detoxification sought me out frequently during the course of a day to speak with him and offer reassurance that he would soon calm down. He was having intrusive thoughts concerning the suicide of his brother which had occurred within the year. He blamed himself, not only because his family had implanted this idea during their emotional outbursts at the time of his death, but because he had tried to offer his brother relief from his distress in providing him with a "good lay" to substitute for the brother's ruptured relationship to his wife and subsequent disequilibrium. Sexuality to heal the impaired bond did not suffice, and his brother returned from the encounter in greater disequilibrium than when he had sought the healing ingredient for the failure in psychic cohesiveness. The woman had "rejected" him, which possibly meant that he had failed to perform sexually with her. His brother returned home, knocked out all the windows in his home, and shot himself.

In describing his parents, the patient said that his mother was "spacy" like himself, that he remembered times when she would "go into hysterics" when driving in the family car. While having an argument with her husband, the patient's father, she would leave the car in the middle of traffic, endangering her life and creating a rapid loss in the secure and idealized bond to her. My patient at first was unaware of any empathic failure occurring within the interpersonal environment, though later he acknowledged the demeaning and dismissing attitude which his father possessed toward his wife. My patient had considerable affection toward his mother, but could not get close nor admire her and idealized his father, who became the center of his preoccupations. His father was viewed as "stable," though he was more concerned about a loan his other son couldn't repay because he had committed suicide rather than that his son was dead.

There were serious problems within this family in maintaining empathic bonds, and my patient reported significant incidents of his father shaming and beating him when he was a little boy because he enjoyed playing with his sister and dolls. He relived incidents of his father grabbing a doll away and stating "you *will* grow up—only girls play with dolls." He recalls: "I was real young—I'd play with my sister and he'd come and beat me up—I didn't know what to expect."

He was unable to feel sexually with women friends, was aroused by "pretty women" that he did not know, and feeling inadequate in his relationships, would serve as a drug dealer in order to have access to them sexually. He would give them pills to render them semi-conscious, not unlike the common practice of the insecure male to get his date drunk so that her standards might not interfere with her impulses. Some of the women to whom my patient provided drugs would have seizures, and he would then call them "stupid" and search the *Physicians' Desk Reference* over and over again to learn about drug side effects and how to control the situation by using yet another drug. Successive treatment episodes have revealed the maintenance of longer periods of personal cohesiveness with self-understanding and empathic contacts with friends which enhance rather than demean.

SUMMARY

Freud had begun his young adult life desiring to be famous and better than his colleagues, attempting to bring pleasure to his fiancée and to himself through sexual play heightened by cocaine, and removing his own pain and depression and loss of vitality. During the span of his life he investigated his own mind and the minds of others. He suggested that man's psychological maturity began when he stopped competing and desired to possess a work and woman of his own. However, in his final years he was doubtful whether he had, indeed, accomplished either the heights of love or work. He didn't understand women, and he doubted whether his "talking cure" worked. Freud did meet one of his desires—he did become famous.

When I began this paper and my investigation by checking data against opinion, I felt certain that the addicts' relationships to women were particularly disordered, but I believe that I thought so for the wrong reasons. I had questioned Freud's premise that psychological maturity developed when the man stopped competing and began to seek personal narcissistic gratification and a woman as a self-esteem regulator. I now believe in the accuracy of what he wrote, though recognize it as a necessary developmental stage. The movement from peer competition to focus on the self is necessary, and it is at this stage that men marry their mother-mate. Some men who abuse substances fail to enter the stage of mate as self-esteem regulator. These men are uniquely damaged, never possessing either woman, work, children, or material possessions. Others enter this stage but are unable to transform the internalized images of mother-mate to peer-mate. These men never move forward psychologically but revert to a level of twinship with a male "partner" or merger with a gang. Those who remain in a heterosexual relationship with their mate as mother remain feeling weak, powerless, and in the presence of one who is a constant reminder of their human needs and inadequacies as both a husband and father.

REFERENCES

Freud, A. (1937). *Ego and the Mechanics of Defense.* London: Hogarth Press.
Freud, S. (1930). *Civilization and Its Discontents.* London: Hogarth Press.
Gilligan, C. (1982). *In a Different Voice.* Cambridge, Mass; Harvard University Press.
Haan, M.A. (1969). Tripartite model of ego functioning: values and clinical research applications. *The Journal of Nervous and Mental Disease, 148,* 14-30.

Jones, E. (1953). *The Life and Work of Sigmund Freud: Volume 1.* New York: Basic Books.

Jones, E. (1955). *The Life and Work of Sigmund Freud: Volume 2.* New York: Basic Books.

Kohut, H. (1971). *The Analysis of the Self.* New York: International Universities Press.

Lampl-de Groot, J. (1957). On defense and development: Normal and pathological. *The Psychoanalytic Study of the Child, 12,* 114-126.

Lasch, C. (1979). *The Culture of Narcissism.* New York: W.W. Norton.

Levinson, D.J. (1978). *The Seasons of a Man's Life.* New York: Ballantine.

Long, J.V. and Vaillant, G.E. (1984). The natural history of male psychological health: XI: Escape from the underclass. *American Journal of Psychiatry, 141,* 341-346.

Strachey, P. (Ed.) (1961). *The Standard Edition of the Complete Psychological Works of Sigmund Freud: Volume 19.* London: Hogarth Press.

Vaillant, G.E. (1966). A 12-year follow-up of New York narcotic addicts: IV: Some characteristics and determinants of abstinence. *American Journal of Psychiatry, 123,* 573-582.

Vaillant, G.E. (1976). The natural history of male psychological health: V: The relation of choice of ego mechanisms of defense to adult adjustment. *Archives of General Psychiatry, 33,* 535-545.

Vaillant, G.E. and Vaillant, C.O. (1981). The natural history of male psychological health: X: Work as a predictor of positive mental health. *American Journal of Psychiatry, 138,* 1433-1440.

IV. RESEARCH IN WOMEN'S ISSUES

Few research areas have developed as quickly in recent years as issues concerning women. Sex differences and similarities are being investigated as they relate to biological, personality, cognitive, and developmental factors. Women are studied as they enter new roles at work and in personal relationships. Research on the effects of therapy has changed the way therapists interact with their clients. The articles in this section contribute to the growing body of literature on sex roles, professional roles, and on shifts in male-female relationships.

As each of the helping professions establishes journal issues, conferences, and network groups that focus on women, increasing numbers of women are regarding themselves to be feminist therapists. *Denise Webster* investigated feminist therapy among nurse psychotherapists in order to determine the prevalence and content of such therapy. Her article describes the results of her survey: the characteristics of respondents, their clients, and the specific feminist nature of the therapy process.

Although the media portrays our society as undergoing a "sexual revolution," it is clear that attitudes and behavior regarding sex are often unrelated. *Christina Taylor* examined women's and men's beliefs about extramarital sex. She varied the gender of the person having an "affair," her or his physical attractiveness, and the frequency of that person's past affairs. Her results have implications for the degree of support and acceptance experienced by individuals who are non-monogamous in marriage.

There has been little attention paid to the effects of the women's movement on the multiple ethnic and cultural groups in our society. *Shamita Das Dasgupta* analyzed the experiences of Asian Indian women in the United States. Given the gender dichotomy and traditional family values of women in India, how are these affected by immigration to the United States? Dasgupta examined Asian Indian women's sex role attitudes as a factor of their occupation, education, and length of stay in the United States.

As women have entered the workplace in increasing numbers, the majority have been married women. What changes are occurring as both marital partners are employed? *Sara Yogev* examined the relationship between stress and marital satisfaction among dual-job couples. She investigated the degree of involvement that spouses reported in their family and career. Clinical implications of the results are discussed.

How do women—and men—perceive the consequences of women being approached by male strangers on the street? In the final article, *Jaclyn Packer* asked females and males to rate women's reactions in a street harassment situation. Her results have implications for the area of definitions of sexual harassment.

Models of Therapy Used by Feminist Nurse Psychotherapists

Denise Webster

This study had two purposes: to identify those nurses at any level of training who consider themselves to be doing feminist psychotherapy and to describe the models of therapy they use. Since nursing is generally viewed as a traditional female profession, many would consider the term "feminist nurse" to be a contradiction in terms. Yet interest in the sources and consequences of sex-role stereotyping has grown within nursing in recent years (McGrory, 1980; Muff, 1982). Articles on women's health and women and mental health have become more common topics within nursing literature.

Nevertheless, the public perception of feminist therapists as psychiatrists, psychologists or social workers persists. To some degree this seems to be due to a reticence of nurses to identify themselves as nurses when they are writing about feminist therapy. For example, the classic article on feminist therapy which appeared in *MS Magazine* was written by a nurse but her professional background was not reported (Fishel, 1979). Similarly, most studies of sex-role stereotyping among therapists or studies seeking to identify models for feminist therapy have omitted nurse psychotherapists from their sampling (Sturdivant, 1980; Thomas, 1977). Those which have included nurses have found that psychiatric nurses hold *fewer* stereotypic views about women than do therapists from other professions (Brown & Hellinger, 1975; Kjervik & Palta, 1975).

Denise Webster is Assistant Professor at the College of Nursing, University of Illinois, 845 S. Damien, Chicago, IL 60612.

An earlier version of this paper appeared in B. Hagerty (Ed.), *Proceedings of the Fourth Annual Psychiatric Nursing Conference,* Ann Arbor: The University of Michigan Hospitals.

277

HISTORY

There are many definitions of feminist therapy which contrast it with traditional therapy and non-sexist therapy. Each author stresses different aspects of the therapy process, but most agree that feminist therapy is that which was developed in response to criticisms of traditional therapy, by incorporating the goals of the women's movement in clinical practice. Rather simplistically it's been called "therapy that attempts to unravel the unconscious and social causes of conflict in order to open up more choices to women and men within a sexist society" (Fishel, 1979). Johnson (1980) has written that traditional therapy has tended to tell women that "that's the way the world is, so learn to live with it"; in other works adaptation would be the therapy goal.

Feminist therapy is seen as differing from traditional therapy in its definitions of what constitutes healthy behavior in a normal adult woman, in its interpretations of the problems clients present, and in a concerted effort to decrease the power discrepancy in the therapy process (Kaschak, 1981). The definitions, interpretations and interventions can take many forms. Indeed, Sturdivant, in her study of feminist therapists found that modalities varied considerably; that it was a philosophic agreement with feminist principles which characterized those who practiced feminist therapy (Sturdivant, 1980).

Since most therapists identify their therapeutic orientation as "eclectic," it would be helpful to obtain more specific information about how nurse psychotherapists working with women clients see their own value systems, their socialization within a female profession, and their specialized preparation (within and outside nursing) affecting their interactions with clients. The impetus for this study came from the enthusiastic response to workshop offerings on feminist nurse psychotherapy and from requests for information about feminist nurse psychotherapists.

While there has been considerable controversy about if and how nurses should be practicing psychotherapy, there has been relatively little data reported about how nurses actually do practice psychotherapy (Bird, Marks & Linley, 1979; Hoffer, 1983; Huey, 1975; Lego, 1973). The findings of this study may be best compared with those recently reported by Hardin and

Durham (1985) who studied the structure, process and effectiveness of 82 psychiatric nurses with master's degrees along
with 95 of those nurses' clients. Where relevant, some of the
differences between the findings for feminist nurse psychotherapists and those in this study will be noted.

METHODOLOGY

The questionnaire developed for this study utilized questions from the Hardin and Durham study (1985) and from
literature on feminist therapy, as well as from feminist therapist questionnaires which are used by psychologists in the Mil-
waukee area and by a local Chicago hotline called WICCA
(Women in Crisis Can Act). Other questions evolved from my
own practice as a feminist nurse psychotherapist.

Random sampling ewas not possible since there is no central
listing of nurses doing psychotherapy. Therefore, purposive
sampling was done using a variety of approaches. The first was
to send letters to all those listed in the ANA directory of the
Council of Specialists in Psychiatric Mental Health Nursing
who indicated that they were in private practice and saw adult
clients. A second approach was to seek referrals from those
responding to the letters and/or cards whether or not they
themselves qualified to be in the study. This resulted in an
additional 52 names. One subject was a self-referral following
a presentation at the National Women's Studies Association.
All those potential subjects were sent questionnaires. These
results represent the responses from the above groups. It is
possible to determine that the percentage of those nurses who
see themselves doing feminist nurse psychotherapy (30%) is
similar between all the groups identified thus far—those in the
directory, those identified by referral and those on the list
which Hardin and Durham generated.

The question which determined eligibility was "do you consider yourself a feminist therapist?" Gilbert (1980) pointed out
that the best measure of this variable is self-identification, but
many nurses were unsure of their self-definition in this respect.
The intent had been for nurses to define what *they* considered
feminist therapy to be, but those few who went to the trouble
of writing back to ask or calling long-distance were told "if you

consider yourself to be a feminist and believe that affects what you do in therapy, you would qualify for this study." By including all those who took the time to answer this rather lengthy questionnaire and who did not say *NO* a total of 57 nurses was identified.

DESCRIPTION OF RESPONDENTS

The ages of these subjects indicate that they were in their 20s or 30s when the resurgence of the feminist movement began; their mean age is 42.5 years old. While a few males completed questionnaires, none considered himself to be a feminist therapist. The sample was similar to Hardin and Durham's geographically, representing all areas but the Plains states. Contrary to conventional wisdom, 61% are married, and 63% have children. Even the national mean of children—2.16—was evident. Since some respondents only indicated their advanced degrees, and the sampling was biased toward those who were master's prepared and/or in private practice, it's not surprising that most had master's degrees and 25% have doctorates. More suprising, given the conventional wisdom and the reasons listed by those who said they were NOT feminist therapists, 28% of the sample had advanced preparation and/or certification as family therapists.

STRUCTURE OF THERAPY

It was found that 84% practice privately, and 80% practice alone, compared with 62% and 54% in the Hardin and Durham study.* Fifteen percent practice in more than one setting and with a group on some occasions. The backgrounds of those with whom nurses in groups practice look very much the same as most interdisciplinary settings, rather evenly divided between nurses, social workers, psychologists and psychiatrists. The source of clients is similar to those of most therapists— former clients, other health professionals and clients that they attracted through public speaking and workshops.

---

*This difference was probably because of a sampling bias.

In contrast to the findings of the Hardin and Durham study (which found 20%), more feminist nurse psychotherapists (40%) reported that their private psychotherapy practice constituted their primary source of income. Of those who didn't, a large percentage (42%) also have academic appointments, many presumably part-time. Ninety-five percent of respondents identified themselves as experienced therapists, and nearly half used all modalities of therapy. Contrary to some theoretical assumptions about what is desirable in feminist therapy, the least-practiced modality (at 62%) was group therapy. Individual (96%), couple/relationship (91%), and family therapy (82%) were more common modalities.

Ninety-seven percent of the respondents believed that their clients improved "pretty much" or "greatly," while no one saw herself as entirely ineffective. Most of the nurse therapists seemed comfortable with their current repertoire of interventions, although nine indicated that they would like more preparation in hypnosis.

The length of therapy for clients was consistent with the bimodal tendencies found in the Hardin and Durham study. While the tendency seems to be for therapy lasting less than 6 months, it is clear that many clients are seen for longer periods.

The average cost per session ($40.00) was almost identical to that found in the Hardin and Durham study ($37.00). Fee scales were based on need, the "going rate" in the geographic region and/or by negotiating with the client.

The vast majority (90%) of feminist nurse psychotherapists have ongoing supervision from another professional. Since the largest number of these supervisors were psychiatrists, it would have been helpful to ask what the sex of the supervisor was and if and how supervision was related to the practice of specifically feminist therapy. On the other hand, nearly half indicated at least one of their supervisors was a nurse, while there were few nurse-supervisors in the Hardin and Durham sample.

Questions about medication and admitting privileges demonstrated vividly the relativity of perception. Both those who said they *did* medicate and *did* admit and those who said they *didn't* medicate or admit qualified their answers to such a degree that it was impossible to discriminate absolutely. It seems likely that most nurse therapists are able to *arrange* for medication and/or hospitalization, should they see the necessity.

The same sort of overlap in answers probably exists for those who say they do or do not receive third party payments. For some, "yes" may mean they once received such payments, while for others it may be the major source of income. This is an area which will be of increasing concern to all nurses whose independent practice is their primary source of income.

Who Are the Clients?

Obviously most respondents work largely with women. The sampling bias is present here, again, since cards were sent to those who worked with adults but those who responded were those mainly working with women. Of course since women make up the majority of those seen in private practice, this would not be an unexpected finding in *any* sampling of client populations. The complaints for which clients were seen were similar to those found in most studies of female clients and in the Hardin and Durham study: low self-esteem, depression, poor relationships and marital/family difficulties. Other feminist nurse psychotherapists reported clients had problems with jobs and role conflict.

As in the Hardin and Durham study, the largest categories nurses would refer elsewhere are those who other professionals would prefer to refer: psychotic, sociopaths, and substance abusers. Given the minimal tendency to be pathology-oriented, these nurses might actually be seeing some of those clients others would diagnose more harshly. Of course, the issue of reliability of psychiatric diagnosis is a topic which underlies most of the assumptions in the feminist literature.

What Makes It Feminist?

The variety of ways nurses described the work they did was reflected in the fact that many described a modality, while others described theoretical orientations. The largest category (36%) called what they did "psychotherapy," while the next largest category (which was only 14%) called it "feminist therapy." As has been the case in other studies of therapists, it seems most nurses do eclectic therapy. One hundred and fifty-four responses from the 54 responding subjects about the theoretical approaches used most in their therapy included 44 separate categories—by theory, technique or modality. The largest numbers of responses were (again contradictory to conventional wisdom and some other literature) those of family systems and analytic. Those specifying a nursing theorist tended to use Orem (1980) or Peplau (1952).

The responses to the question about how they would define feminist therapy tended to focus on what the therapist brought into the therapeutic situation as well as what she did and what she saw as a therapeutic "success." The responses to this question were varied but most believed they used an awareness of the oppression of women to help clients counter sexist/stereotyped role beliefs which may be blocking clients' effectiveness at defining or becoming that which they would like to be. Eight respondents made a specific point of saying that the therapist *must* like and respect women to work effectively with them.

The question "how do you see your own value system affecting what you do in therapy?" was intended to determine how conscious the subjects were of the effects of their value system. One charge which is often leveled at feminist therapists is that they are biased. The response to that charge has usually been that *all* therapy is biased, and that feminist therapy differs in stating upfront what the therapists' biases are—a sort of truth in advertising message. Only nine respondents indicated that they worked to avoid having their value system affect their therapy—that they tried to be "non-judgmental." The largest single category response (16) was an awareness that it was impossible to divorce one's practice from one's beliefs.

Since *knowing* the therapist's beliefs is a factor in decreasing mystification and power differences in the therapy, therapists were asked how they felt about having a client interview them. The responses indicated that definitions of what constitutes "client interviews" are probably variable and point to a need to revise this question. It may well have been interpreted that the interview would cover only the structural aspects of therapy, such as time, length of sessions, cost of therapy, etc. The qualifications some respondents listed included the caveat that questions of a "non-personal nature" were seen as appropriate.

Another important question asked how their professional socialization, especially in nursing, had affected what they did in therapy. The most common response was that nursing preparation had made them "sensitive to women's issues and oppression." What's *not* clear is if they learned this by looking at the situation in theory or practice sequences or by experience. A fair number (14) specifically made a point of saying their preparation and the modeling they observed had been positive influences.

It is of interest that the most negative comments came from those who received advanced preparation outside of nursing. What is not clear is whether it was negativism about nursing that led them to seek outside preparation, or whether they developed a negative nursing identity after obtaining such preparation. Neither is it clear, of course, whether nurses reinforce their positive self-image by over-estimating the positive aspects of their own preparation.

Another important question was related to the effect the women's movement had in their lives. The responses in this category included one nurse who pointed out that she would probably not be in independent practice, without the movement. Others indicated that their own consciousness-raising had led them to major changes in their lives, particularly in the areas of career choices and interpersonal relationships, primarily with men. There were also a number (5) of what might be characterized as "queen bee" responses to this question, such as "I've always done what I wanted with my life, I never needed a movement," and comments that the movement was most useful in helping others be more accepting of their behavior.

A further question dealt with current involvement in the women's movement. It might be argued that in practice, most respondents come closer to doing non-sexist, rather than feminist therapy, based on this category. Since many believe it is the active involvement in changing the social institutions which oppress women that makes one a feminist therapist, the fact that 26 respondents indicated no involvement or only personal change is interesting, and merits further study.

The responses to the question about what therapists saw as important issues in the treatment of women were varied; some addressed therapist assumptions or client variables while others focused on specific interventions. The largest category of responses was related to the therapists' outcome expectations. These were also consistent with the responses to the question about the way in which therapists believed their clients changed following therapy: improved self-esteem, increased assertiveness, greater self-awareness, autonomy/independence, improved coping abilities, and problem-solving skills, with resulting decreases in feeling of depression, helplessness and hopelessness.

Feminist nurse psychotherapists listed (in order of degree) their most effective interventions to include confrontation, alerting clients to process, role-playing, support, empathy, information, interpretation, clarification and problem solving/goal setting. One way the literature differentiates feminist from traditional therapy is in the tendency for feminist therapy to be more active and confrontational. These responses tend to support those findings, as well as those which describe feminist therapy as demystifying the therapy process by discussing theory and process and by providing high degrees of support for the client. It is interesting, however, that transparency or self-disclosure were not among the more commonly indicated processes.

The attitudes which the therapists saw themselves presenting to clients were congruent with those in the Hardin and Durham study, and were also consistent with the points raised in feminist literature about appropriate therapeutic relationships; i.e. supportive, encouraging, warm and caring, understanding, interested, etc. While these may appear to be stereotypically feminine characteristics, it should be noted that social desirability may be a larger factor here than feminist or traditional ideology. This possibility is raised since it has been shown repeatedly in studies that patient improvement is related to high levels of empathy and respect, as well as to self-disclosure and confrontation, and to the therapist relating in a concrete and genuine fashion (Fix & Haffke, 1976). The question which can be raised here, as it was somewhat differently in the Hardin and Durham study, is whether effective modeling of assertive autonomous behavior might relate to perceived intelligence, confidence, and competence. The fact that only two respondents specifically mentioned "egalitarian" as an attitude is difficult to interpret—since egalitarianism may be awkward to define behaviorally in the context of this question.

Another question raised in feminist literature concerns the concept of pathology. This was answered in many ways. Most subjects referred to the usefulness of having a diagnosis. That a diagnosis was seen as most useful for *insurance purposes* may reflect that the nomenclature which exists in the DSM III may be more useful for communicating with other professionals than for formulating a treatment plan. It would be interesting to learn more about the relationship between nursing diagnostic categories and the ways which feminist therapists describe clients' experiences.

I have attempted to address some of the methodological problems and theoretical questions relating to these data as they have been reported. The need to do a more extensive analysis across categories is clear. For the near future, I plan to analyze those questionnaires which were obtained from the Hardin and Durham study and to expand the sample. It would also be desirable to interview many of the subjects to seek clarification of some of the more abstract aspects of the models. Future efforts will compare the findings of feminist nurse psychotherapists with data from non-feminist nurse psychotherapists as well as with feminist therapists who are not nurses. The dimension of practice which seems least apparent from the data obtained thus far is just how the therapists see their nursing backgrounds preparing them to do therapy in ways which differ from non-nurse therapists and from other feminist therapists.

REFERENCES

American Psychiatric Association, (1980). *Diagnostic and Statistical Manual of Mental Disorders (third ed.)*.

Bird, M., Marks, I. M., & Lindley, P. (1979). Nurse therapists in psychiatry: Developments, controversies and implications. *British Journal of Psychiatry, 135,* 321-329.

Brown, C. & Hellinger, M. (1975, July). Therapists' attitudes towards women. *Social Work,* 266-270.

Fishel, A. (1979, June). What is a feminist therapist and how to find one. *Ms.,* pp. 79-82.

Fix, A.J. & Haffke, E.A. (1976). *Basic psychological therapies: Comparative effectiveness.* New York: Human Sciences Press.

Gilbert, L. (1980). Feminist therapy. In A. Brodsky & R. Hare-Mustin (Eds.), *Women and Psychotherapy* (pp. 245-265). New York: The Guilford Press.

Hardin, S. & Durham, J. (1985). First rate: Exploring the structure, process and effectiveness of nurse psychotherapy. *Journal of Psychosocial Nursing and Mental Health Services. 23* (5), 8-15.

Hoeffer, B. (1983). The private practice model: An ethical perspective. *Journal of Psychosocial Nursing and Mental Health Services, 21* (7), 31-37.

Huey, F.L. (1975). *Psychiatric nursing. A report on the state of the art.* New York: American Journal of Nursing Co.

Johnson, M. (1980, Spring). Mental illness and psychiatric treatment among women: A response. *Psychology of Women Quarterly, 4* (3), 363-371.

Kaschak, E. (1981). Feminist psychotherapy: The first decade. In S. Cox (Ed.), *Female psychology: The emerging self* (2nd ed.). New York: St. Martin's Press.

Kjervik, D. & Palta, M. (1975). Sex-role stereotyping in assessments of mental health made by psychiatric-mental health nurses. *Nursing Research, 27* (3), 166-171.

Lego, S. (1973). Nurse psychotherapists: How are we different? *Perspectives in Psychiatric Care, 11,* 144-147.

McGrory, A. (1980, Sept.). Women and mental illness: A sexist trap? Part 1. *Journal of Psychiatric Nursing and Mental Health Services, 18,* 9-13.

McGrory, A. (1980, Oct.). Women and mental illness: A sexist trap? Part 2. *Journal of Psychiatric Nursing and Mental Health Services, 18,* 16-22.

Muff, J. (Ed.) (1982). *Socialization, sexism and stereotyping: Women's issues in nursing.* St. Louis: C.V. Mosby Co.

Orem, D. (1980). *Nursing: Concepts of practice* (2nd ed.). New York: McGraw-Hill.

Peplau, H. (1952). *Interpersonal relations in nursing.* New York: Putnam.

Sturdivant, S. (1980). *Therapy with women.* New York: Springer.

Thomas, S.A. (1977, November). Theory and practice in feminist therapy. *Social Work,* 447-454.

Extramarital Sex:
Good for the Goose?
Good for the Gander?

Christina J. Taylor

Two experiments were carried out to elucidate beliefs about
marital fidelity and extramarital sex by examining how the
social evaluation of extramarital relationships is affected by
three situational factors—sex of the extramarital actor, the actor's physical attractiveness, and the frequency of the actor's
involvement in extramarital affairs (i.e., extramarital experience). Overall, there has been little research on this subject in
social psychology, and what findings do exist (Hartnett, Mahoney, & Bernstein, 1977; Vallacher, 1982) have limited general-
izability because of the youth of the subjects, contrary definitions of extramarital relationships, and contradictory evidence
regarding the double standard.

EXPERIMENT 1

Subjects and procedure. A total of 526 (265 females, 261
males) subjects ($M = 34.7$ years of age) drawn from colleges
and universities in Connecticut and New York responded to a
scenario about a married couple (David and Susan) which had
one of three endings: (a) a husband/wife chose not to become
involved in his/her extramarital affair, (b) a husband/wife became involved for the first time in an extramarital affair, (c) a
husband/wife with a history of several extramarital affairs became involved in another extramarital affair. Photographs pre-
rated for attractiveness portrayed the married couple and the

Christina J. Taylor is Assistant Professor of Psychology at Sacred Heart University, 5229 Park Avenue, Bridgeport, CT 06606.

other man/other woman as either attractive or very attractive. Two sets of photos were used for each attractiveness level.

Dependent measures included the following ratings on 7-point scales: (a) perceptions of the actors on 14 traits, (b) perceived justifiability of the spouse engaging in an extramarital affair, and (c) perceived responsibility of each of the actors and circumstances for the spouse engaging/not engaging in an extramarital affair. Subjects were also asked to state the single most important cause for the extramarital affair.

Results

In preliminary analyses, alpha coefficients for the trait ratings indicated adequate reliability (.70 - .93) for the ratings to be combined into a single social evaluation score. Significant main effects for Physical Attractiveness produced by ANOVAS on the mean physical attractiveness ratings assigned to the husbands, $p < .0001$, the wives, $p < .0001$, the other men, $p < .0001$, and the other women, $p < .02$, indicated that subjects perceived the very attractive group of stimulus persons to be more attractive than the attractive group. Results of separate analyses of the data from the two picture sets were virtually identical so that the data from the two sets were combined.

The main findings of interest from a $2 \times 2 \times 2 \times 3$ (Sex of Subject by Extramarital Spouse by Physical Attractiveness by Character) repeated measures MANOVA performed on the mean social evaluation scores for each actor (see Table 1) demonstrated that spouses were perceived very favorably when they resisted the temptation to become involved in an extramarital affair (husband, $M = 5.68$; wife, $M = 5.69$) and when they stood by a faithful/faithless spouse (husband, 5.45, 5.27, 5.38; wife, 5.61, 5.33, 5.25), $F (4, 1002) = 99.48, p < .0001$. They were perceived less favorably when they were involved in their first affair (husband, 4.11; wife, 4.16) and the least favorably when they had been involved in many affairs (husband, 3.76; wife, 3.65), Duncan, $p < .05$. Most strikingly, no evidence for a double standard was obtained from this analysis.

The perceived justifiability of a spouse engaging in an affair tended to be low across all conditions (husband, $M = 1.87$; wife, $M = 1.77$). And the only significant effect which

Table 1

Mean Social Evaluation Scores for Each Actor by Condition

Actor	Wife as extramarital spouse			Husband as extramarital spouse		
	No affair	First affair	Many affairs	No affair	First affair	Many affairs
Attractive						
Susan	5.59	4.07	3.62	5.59	5.35	5.24
David	5.27	5.31	5.45	5.66	4.03	3.71
Other[a]	5.09	3.80	3.73	5.11	3.58	3.76
$\underline{n}$	41	40	47	45	47	44
Very attractive						
Susan	5.78	4.24	3.68	5.63	5.43	5.26
David	5.62	5.25	5.31	5.69	4.21	3.81
Other[b]	5.29	3.78	3.77	5.48	3.92	3.95
$\underline{n}$	44	42	41	43	43	48
Total						
Susan	5.69_a	4.16_c	3.65_d	5.61_a	5.33_b	5.25_b
David	5.45_b	5.27_b	5.38_b	5.68_a	4.11_c	3.76_d
Other[c]	5.19_a	3.79_b	3.73_b	5.29_a	3.75_b	3.86_b
$\underline{n}$	85	82	88	88	91	92

Note. Means in a given row with dissimilar subscripts are significantly different at the $\underline{p} < .05$ level according to the Duncan Multiple Range Test.

[abc]Other refers to the "Other Man" in the Wife as Extramarital Spouse condition, and to the "Other Woman" in the Husband as Extramarital Spouse condition.

emerged from a $2 \times 2 \times 2 \times 3$ ANCOVA performed on these means, using religiosity as a covariate, identified a tendency, $F (1, 505) \times 5.37, p < .02$, for males to perceive a husband's extramarital involvement $(M = 1.97)$ as more justifiable than a wife's $(M = 1.61)$, Duncan, $p < .05$. The analysis of the causal attribution data helped to explain the truncated nature of the justifiability ratings.

The causes offered for spouses engaging and not engaging in an affair were classified into three categories by two independent judges (92% and 94% agreement respectively)—Marital Dissatisfaction (Marital Satisfaction in the no affair condition), Extramarital Spouse, and Extramarital Partner/Relationship. Marital Satisfaction was the principal attribution made for a wife (63.85%), X $(2, N = 83) = 38.34, p < .001, and husband (70.45%), X (2, N = 88) = 53.46, p < .001$, choosing not to engage in an extramarital affair. In the first affair condition, only 18.68% of the subjects cited Marital Dissatisfaction as the cause of a husband's affair, X $(2, N, c5 91) = 9.38, p < .01$; about a third of the subjects (34.15%) attributed a wife's affair to Marital Dissatisfaction, X $(2, N = 82) = 3.61$, ns. In the many affairs condition, most subjects were found to attribute both a wife's affair (51.72%), X $(2, N = 87) = 16.62, p < .001$, and a husband's affair (55.43%), X $(2, N = 92) = 20.24, p < .001$, to the Extramarital Spouse herself or himself, rather than to Marital Dissatisfaction (wife, 32.18%; husband, 21.73%). These findings thus suggest that subjects did not find an extramarital affair to be very justifiable for either spouse because they perceived them to have a satisfactory marriage.

Analysis of the responsibility ratings through a $2 \times 2 \times 2 \times 3 \times 4$ (Sex of subject by Extramarital spouse by Physical attractiveness by Extramarital experience by Locus of responsibility) repeated measures MANOVA demonstrated that while husbands (5.55, 5.05, 5.21) and wives (5.39, 5.07, 5.27) were rated highly responsible for both engaging/not engaging in an affair, $F (6, 1462) = 3.64, p < .001$, bystanding or faithful spouses were rated significantly more responsible for their spouses not engaging in an affair (husband, 4.16 vs. 2.73 and 2.98; wife, 3.81 vs. 2.90 and 2.88) than they were for their spouses engaging in one, Duncan, $p < .05$. Of further note, the very attractive wife in the many affairs condition was rated significantly more responsible (5.71), $F (6, 1462) = 2.69, p < .02$, for engaging in an extramarital affair than her attractive counterpart (4.89) in the many affairs condition, Duncan, $p < .05$.

EXPERIMENT 2

Subjects and procedure. A total of 94 (56 females, 38 males) subjects ($M = 38.3$ years of age) viewed one of two videotapes of a Hollywood film about an extramarital affair between a married woman and married man. In one, information that the female character had a previous extramarital affair was included, in the other, this information was deleted by editing the film. Dependent measures were similar to those in Experiment 1.

Results

The results of a 2 (Sex of Subject) × 2 (Extramarital Experience) × 2 (Character) repeated measures ANOVA, with repeated measures on the last factor, showed that the woman's ($M = 4.33$) extramarital involvement was perceived as more justifiable than the man's ($M = 2.83$), $F(1, 92) = 88.58, p < .0001$, and that their extramarital affair was perceived as more justifiable when it was believed to be the woman's first extramarital involvement ($M = 3.83$ vs. $M = 3.34$), $F(1. 92) = 9.22$, $p < .003$.

The causal attributions for each actor's extramarital involvement were coded with 94% agreement by two judges into four categories—Marital Dissatisfaction, Ego Enhancement, Need Frustration, and Physical/Emotional Attraction. Subjects were overwhelmingly more likely to attribute the woman's affair to Marital Dissatisfaction (71.41%) than to other causes, X $(3, N = 94) = 29.92, p < .001$. In contrast, no one cause was cited more often than any other in accounting for the man's affair, X $(3, N = 93) = 2.31$, ns. Thus, in a comparison between an unhappily married woman's affair and a happily married man's, subjects' judgments about the justifiability of their extramarital involvement were less affected by the double standard than they were by the quality of the actors' marriages.

CONCLUSIONS

The pattern of findings from both studies showed that marital dissatisfaction is generally regarded as the only justifiable reason for engaging in an extramarital affair. Most remarkably, perhaps, the results provided little support for a differential evaluation of husbands' and wives' extramarital activities. The observers of this study thus appeared to hold a contractual view of marital fidelity whereby extramarital sex is proscribed for *both* husbands and wives for as long as and until the marriage itself remains reasonably satisfactory. It is a distinctly modern belief, but one which is very much in keeping with serial monogamy and the impermanence of the marriage vows. It also represents a transformation of traditional normative beliefs about marital fidelity and signifies a radical departure from the traditional code of sexual ethics which condemned the participation of married women in extramarital affairs while condoning the same behavior for married men.

The equality women have achieved in the domain of marital fidelity must be interpreted with caution because the overall results of this investigation revealed a fairly traditional and conservative portrait of extramarital affairs. Given the circumstances of what appeared to be a happy marriage, social observers were not inclined to find an extramarital affair very acceptable for either marital partner. Tolerance of extramarital affairs thus occurs within very circumscribed boundries. What is new is the fact that those boundaries appear to constrain men and women equally. The favorable evaluations of spouses who remained faithful to their mates despite a strong extramarital attraction and the opportunity to engage in an affair cogently illustrates this point. Herein, a husband who demonstrated this type of staunch fidelity was actually evaluated more favorably than in any other condition (see Table 1). This is an interesting twist on the double standard according to which a husband's social standing is enhanced by his participation in extramarital affairs. Thus, contrary to what may be an outdated stereotype of the "macho" male, these findings demonstrated that a husband's image was enhanced by *avoidance of,* rather than an *involvement in* an extramarital affair.

/In sum, these results showed that the ethic of marital fidelity is alive and well in the minds of ordinary social observers. At the same time, however, the findings indicated that there has truly occurred a rejection of sexist and rigidly absolutist marital mores. To reiterate the central finding in this regard, the new "ethic" of marital fidelity appears to be a conditional one wherein it is expected of a spouse for as long as the marriage remains fulfilling. There are two principal implications of this new ethic. First, when they are caught in a bad marriage, it is now legitimate for women and men to pursue emotional and sexual fulfillment outside the marriage. To do so more than once is, however, not as acceptable or justifiable. Second, the social pressure on wives to accept, rationalize, and/or ignore their husbands' involvement in extramarital sexual activities should be diminished. In other words, women should no longer be expected to play the role of the long-suffering wife who must tolerate a husband's affairs. Correlatively, men should receive less social support for engaging in extramarital affairs that are not motivated by marital dissatisfaction.

This investigation explored and analyzed the network of factors which determine how social observers process and assimilate knowledge of extramarital involvements. The findings clearly bespeak the currents of social change which are moving us toward new definitions of acceptable conduct in this area of socio-sexual behavior. Whether and how our thinking about extramarital sexuality will evolve must continue to be a subject of social and research concern.

REFERENCES

Hartnett, J., Mahoney, J. & Bernstein, A. (1977). The errant spouse: A study in person perception. *Perceptual and Motor Skills, 45,* 747-750.
Vallacher, R.R., The double standard in extra-marital relations: A social cognitive analysis. *Paper presented at the meeting of the American Psychological Association,* Washington, D.C., August, 1982.

Marching to a Different Drummer? Sex Roles of Asian Indian Women in the United States

Shamita Das Dasgupta

Studies of the Asian population in the United States have generally focused on immigrant groups from the far East. Asian Indians, as a community, have not yet received much research attention. The reason for this neglect is probably the insignificance of their number in this country, until quite recently. Though the history of Asian Indian immigration to the United States can be traced back to the early 1800s, the major influx did not occur till the mid-1960s. According to the 1980 census, 387,000 Asian Indians live in the United States today. The constitutency is still less than 1% of the total population, but its growth rate since 1970 has been phenomenal. Unlike the early immigrants from India, who arrived around the turn of the century and were mainly farmers, the new population consists of well-educated professionals who are economically quite well-off.[1] It is possible that in the near future this community will also become a significant political and social force. The profile of Asian Indians that emerges from the statistics is as follows: (a) it is an urban community (91% reside in metropolitan areas); (b) it is a comparatively young community (median age in 1980 was 28.7 years); (c) the majority of the population was born outside the United States (70% are foreign born); (d) the community is well-educated (80% are at least college educated); (e) most of the community may be categorized as middle class (median income in 1979 was $24,993; only 9.9% were considered poor); (f) most families are traditional; that is, males head most households (only 6% of families were headed by women); and (g) 47% of

Shamita Das Dasgupta is at the Department of Psychology, Newark College of Arts and Sciences, Rutgers University.

the Asian Indian women in this country participate in the labor force.

The Asian Indian immigrants to this country bring with them a strong sense of their native culture and customs. In their adopted land they are still struggling to retain their identity as Indians and to maintain close relationships with their natal country (Nandi, 1980). An important aspect of maintaining this identity is to promote and perpetuate the traditional Indian culture. Central to the Indian culture is a set of beliefs about men and women that have their endorsement from the mythology and philosophy of the country. These beliefs have given rise to appropriate sex role expectations and behaviors that are unambiguous and well defined. The present study examines the sex role attitudes of Asian Indian women in the United States. It investigates the relationship between these women's occupational roles and sex-role attitudes, and scrutinizes the latter's relationship to influences of acculturation. A secondary goal of this study is to assess the attitude of these women towards western feminism.

Gender dichotomy in the Indian culture is quite definite, thus, the resultant sex roles are also rigorously bipolar. Women and men are delegated different roles in the society; one is in charge of home maintenance and providing emotional support, and the other is charged with the maintenance of the world without. Socialization practices in India firmly teach children these sex assigned behaviors and attitudes. This patriarchal world order is well accepted in society and is supported strongly by various Indian media.

BACKGROUND

Indians who leave their country in search of opportunities do not necessarily shed their traditional cultural beliefs simultaneously with their residences. Solanki (1973) found that his Colorado sample of Asian Indians was only marginally acculturated to the United States culture. In this sample most adaptation had occurred in superficial behavior such as clothing, and least in deeper beliefs such as religion. Another study with East Indian and Pakistani women residing in Canada found that the women maintained traditional values concerning home, family, children, religion and marriage (Naidoo, 1984). These studies, though few in number, have not tried to probe the relationship between women's sex role attitudes and occupational behaviors. Since occupational behavior is a major part of one's role in society, it can be assumed that it is affected, and in turn affects an individual's sex role attitude.

Gender dichotomy in society has not only relegated women to the confines of a restrictive role, it has provided strong biases when women do decide to enter the nontraditional world of occupations. Strong sex-labelling has indeed limited women's choices in this realm. Jobs that require care-giving and dealing with young children and people, have generally been considered women's forte, as these are supposed to exploit their affiliative tendencies. Occupations that require leadership, intellectual competence, scientific and technical knowledge, are considered beyond women's abilities (Albrecht, Bahr, & Chadwick, 1977; Gettys & Cann, 1981; Horner, 1972; Panek, Rush, & Greenwalt, 1977).

There is some evidence that an individual's choice of occupation, especially the choice of a male-dominated one, is related to one's personal feeling of masculinity and femininity. Individuals possessing masculine gender identity seem to choose occupations and major subjects of study in college that are predominantly assigned to men (Tyer & Erdwins, 1979; Wolfe & Betz, 1981; Yanico & Hardin, 1981). Choice of a female-dominated or neutral occupation does not seem to follow a corresponding trend. Dasgupta (1983) found a positive relationship between nontraditional sex role attitudes and participation in male-dominated occupations in women who were white-collar workers. No such relationship seemed to exist in blue-collar working women. In a college-student sample in India, choice of nontraditional major subjects was found to be related to nontraditional attitudes towards women's roles (Kazi & Ghadially, 1979). Egalitarian attitude was also related to more westernized educational background and higher level of education (Ghadially & Kazi, 1979; Gupta, Shah, & Beg, 1982).

From this generally mixed bag of evidence only a few conclusions may be drawn. First, there seems to be a positive relationship between choice of male-dominated occupations and masculine gender identity. Second, this relationship may hold true only for women working in white-collar jobs. Cross-cultural studies from India seem to corroborate these claims to a certain degree.

Purpose of Study and Hypotheses

The present study examines the relationship between occupation and sex role attitude in a special group of women, namely, the Asian Indian women in the USA. It also tries to assess the part that acculturation, as indicated by the length of stay and attendance at educational institutions in the United States, plays in this relationship. As a secondary goal, these women's opinions and attitudes toward the contemporary feminist movement are explored.

It is hypothesized that there will be no statistically significant difference in sex role attitudes between women who have retained the traditional role of home-maker and women who work outside their homes. The density of women engaged in any particular occupation is not anticipated to affect sex-role attitudes in any way. The latter hypothesis contradicts most of the previous studies (Dasgupta, 1983; Gupta et al., 1982; Tyer & Erdwins, 1979; Wolfe & Betz, 1981; Yanico & Hardin, 1981). However, based on the findings of Naidoo (1984) that South Asian immigrant women tend to adhere strongly to traditional values regardless of career orientation, it is hypothesized here that Asian Indian women participating in the present study will also view occupational roles and sex roles as independent dimensions.

METHOD

Sample. Asian Indian women who are residing in the United States at present, and are at least 18 years of age, were approached to voluntarily participate in the study. Though the majority of the women in the sample were from the East Coast, some were from the Mid-West, the West Coast, and the southern states. Each participant responded to a set of questionnaires consisting of questions seeking particulars about the subject's educational background, present occupation, length of stay in the United States, etc., and a measure of sex role attitude, namely, the Index of Sex Role Orientation (ISRO) (Dreyer, Woods & James, 1981). Each woman was also asked whether she belonged to any women's organizations, and to express her opinion about the contemporary western feminist movement. All subjects were asked to state their extent of agreement with the same movement by choosing one of five statements that ranged from "I disagree with it strongly" to "I agree with it strongly." Most women completed the questionnaires at their own convenience and mailed them back to the investigator.

Procedure. Approximately 200 questionnaires were distributed and 92 (46%) completed sets were returned. According to the subjects' occupations these were then divided into four groups. Since all the working women were engaged in white-collar occupations only, the divisions were made within this stratum (Rifkin & Rifkin, 1979). The first group comprised women who were working in occupations that had 30% or less females employed in them. This was considered to be the male-dominated occupational group (ML). Computer scientists (density of females employed [DFE] = 28.5%), engineers (DFE = 5.7%) and physicians (DFE = 14.6%) fell into this category (Statistical Abstract of the United States: 1984, 1983). Conversely, women engaged in occupations where the density of female employees was 70% or more, constituted the female-dominated occupational group (FL). Registered nurses (DFE = 95.6%), bank tellers (DFE = 92%), bookkeepers (DFE = 91.8%), cashiers (DFE = 86.8%), librarians (DFE = 80.7%), school teachers (DFE = 70.7%) and sales clerks (DFE = 70%) were categorized as such (Statistical Abstract of the United States: 1984, 1983). Women who declared their occupations as college professors (DFE = 35.4%), social scientists (DFE = 38%) and students were grouped together in the third or neutral category (NL), where the percentage of women working was greater than 30 but less than 70. The fourth group in this study was made up of home-makers (HM).

RESULTS

In the three occupational groups, 18 women in ML, 20 in FL, and 30 in NL categories responded to the questionnaires. Twenty-four homemakers also participated in the study. The

Socioeconomic Index (Duncan, 1961) was used to quantify the socioeconomic status (SES) of the subjects. In the case of married subjects with both partners working, the higher SES index was included in the analyses. Each subject's marital status, age, SES, educational level, years of education in the United States, length of occupational life in the United States, length of stay in the United States, length of occupational life in India, membership in women's organizations, overall opinion about feminism and sex role attitude were used as variables of this study. (See Table 1.)

All four groups were included in a stepwise discriminant analysis with the previously mentioned variables. The most statistically significant function consisted of years of education in the United States, which had a standardized Discriminant Function Coefficient (DFC) of .608. The second function, which was also statistically significant, identified marital status as the major negative contributor to this function (DFC = -.520). Neither function clearly isolated one or more major variables on which these groups were distinct. Rather, the two dimensions that distinguished the four groups were made up of the variables of marital status, general educational level, years of education in the United States, length of working life in the United States, length of stay in the United States and ISRO. To test the set of hypotheses, only these variables were included in further analyses.

A oneway analysis of variance of the four groups (ML, FL, NL & HM) by length of stay in the United States found no statistically significant differences between them ($F = 2.02, p < .1ed2$). Therefore, this variable was eliminated from further analyses. On the variable of marital status, though the groups were significantly different from each other ($F = 4.226, p < .01$), the variance seemed to be confined to two pairs. Posteriori pairwise contrasts of the four means by the Scheffé procedure showed that the male-dominated occupational group was significantly different from the neutral occupational group, and the latter was significantly distinct from the homemakers' group (Scheffé criterion for the .05 level = 4.03). All other pairs were not statistically significantly different from each other.

To test whether there was any difference between the four groups on ISRO, a oneway analysis of variance was per-

Table 1

Correlation Coefficients of All Variables with ISRO

Variables	N	Corr. Coefficient	Significance
Marital Status	92	.170	.052
Age	87	-.155	.076
SES	92	.247	.009
Education	92	.313	.001
US Education	92	.471	.0001
US Work-life	92	.109	.150
Stay in USA	92	.253	.007
Work-life, India	92	-.160	.064
Membership in			
Women's Org'n	92	-.165	.058
Opinion/Feminism	89	.229	.015

formed. The results showed that the four groups were significantly different on this variable ($F = 14.464$, $p < .00001$). Posteriori pairwise contrasts by the Scheffé procedure identified the following pairs to be statistically significantly different from each other (Scheffé criterion for the .05 level = 4.03):

(a)ML was significantly more nontraditional than HM;
(b)ML was significantly more nontraditional than FL;
(c)NL was significantly more nontraditional than HM; and
(d)NL was significantly more nontraditional than FL.

For more precision in analysis, the above mentioned pairs were further submitted to an analysis of covariance. With the covariates of general educational level, years of education in the United States, and length of occupational life in the United States partialled out, the male-dominated occupational group was no longer significantly different from the homemakers' group ($F = 1.17$, $p < .29$). With the same covariates partialled out, the second pair of extreme occupational groups, ML and FL, remained statistically different ($F = 8.212$, $p < .01$). The third pair that was identified as significantly different, NL and HM, remained so even after the same covariates and an additional one, marital status, were partialled out ($F = 8.964$, $p < .004$). Marital status was introduced as an extra covariate in this pair, because it had already been established as a variable that significantly differentiates these two particular groups. NL remained significantly different from FL after the same variables (with the exclusion of marital status) were partialled out ($F = 12.791$, $p < .001$). In summary, after the relevant covariates were partialled out, the following relationships emerged;

(a1)ML did not possess significantly more nontraditional sex role orientation than HM;
(b1)ML remained significantly more nontraditional in sex role orientation than FL;
(c1)NL remained significantly more nontraditional in sex role orientation than HM; and
(d1)NL remained significantly more nontraditional in sex role orientation that FL.

To test the main hypothesis that no difference existed between Asian Indian working women and homemakers on sex role orientation, the three occupational groups were collapsed into one. With the variables of marital status, general educational level, years of education in the United States, and length of work-life in the United States partialled out, the difference between the working and homemakers' groups did not reach statistical significance.

To examine whether there was any relationship between sex role orientation and other variables, correlations were drawn between ISRO scores, age, SES, general educational level, years of education in the United States, length of work-life in the United States, length of stay in the United States, length of work-life in India, whether the subject was a member of any women's organization, and her general opinion about the feminist movement. Nontraditional sex role orientation was significantly and positively related to SES, general educational level, length of education in the United States, length of stay in the United States, and general opinion about feminism.

All the subjects were asked whether they were feminists, and whether they belonged to the National Organization for Women (NOW). In the homemakers' group, only 2 (8.33%) declared themselves to be feminists and none were members of NOW. In the FL group 2 (10%) asserted that they were feminists, 2 (10%) were members of NOW, and only one (5%) person belonged to NOW and was also a feminist. Six (33.3%) women were feminists in ML, one (5.56%) was a NOW member, and one (5.56%) was both a feminist and a NOW member. In the NL group 15 (50%) considered themselves to be feminists, 5 (16.67%) women were NOW members and 5 (16.67%) were both.

DISCUSSION

The major objective of the study was to investigate the relationship between occupational role and sex roles of the Asian Indian women in the United States. An attempt was made to focus on what part acculturation plays in liberalizing the sex role views of the subjects. A secondary goal of the study was to assess the opinion Asian Indian women held about feminism.

The main hypothesis of the study, that there is no difference between Asian Indian working women and homemakers in sex roles was supported. When the working women's group was separated into three subdivisions according to the density of women working in each, some interesting differences surfaced. In sex roles, the male-dominated occupational group was significantly different from the female-dominated occupational group and homemakers. On the same variable, women working in neutral occupations were also significantly different from women working in female-dominated occupations and full time homemakers. With pertinent covariates partialled out only three differences remained statistically significant; that between the male-dominated and female-dominated occupational groups, between the neutral occupational group and homemakers, and between the female-dominated and neutral occupational groups. In the three cases, the male-dominated occupational workers and the neutral group were more nontraditional than the other groups. Density of women in occupations, apparently, does have some relationship to sex roles.

The relationship between choice of cross-sex occupation or major subject of study in college and nontraditional view of the sex roles has already been demonstrated (Dasgupta, 1983, Ghadially & Kazi, 1979; Kazi & Ghadially, 1979). The finding of a statistically significant difference between the more extreme occupational groups corroborates those results. However, it was also found that no significant difference exists between women who have chosen male-dominated careers and homemakers on sex roles. This is a more surprising finding. Previous research and part of the present findings would indicate the differences to be strongest between these two groups. Why has the relationship between sex roles and cross-sex occupational role not carried over in these two groups?

The greater variance within the homemaker's group is obviously responsible for the contradictory relationships between HM, ML, and FL. An explanation of this apparently aberrant relationship may lie in the commonality in their reference groups. Both the homemakers and the women working in male-dominated occupations live in a world that is dominated by men. Thus, both groups have many opportunities to realize the social stereotypes and the limitations of their roles. Recognition of their own positions and dealing with the injustices and thwartings of a patriarchal world on a day-to-day basis, may be antecedents to similar sex roles in both groups. Perhaps women who are working in female-dominated occupations do not come face-to-face with similar discriminations as much. The latter group is fulfilling its own need to achieve in the working world to a certain degree, without overstepping the sex role boundaries. Thus, workers in female-dominated occupations are avoiding the day-to-day frustrations of a home-maker's life, but not incurring societal wrath by totally breaking the sex role barrier. Both the home-makers and the workers in male-dominated areas are perhaps unsuccessful in achieving this enviable middle-of-the-road position.

Interestingly, though the male-dominated occupational group was significantly more nontraditional in sex roles than the female-dominated occupational group, no such difference existed between the homemakers and the women in the female-dominated occupational group. Since both these groups have remained in relatively more sex-appropriate roles, the similarity in these roles is not unexpected. Another contributed factor to this similarity may be their equivalent general educational backgrounds. Summarizing this set of results, it may be said that the Asian Indian home-makers in this study are not statistically significantly different from women working in male-, as well as in female-, dominated occupations. Contrarily, the latter two groups do emerge as significantly different from each other. Some possible explanations of the relationships between the pairs, that is, the male-dominated occupational and homemakers' groups, and the female-dominated and homemakers' groups, have already been presented. An alternate explanation for the relationship may lie in the role that is dominant in the home-makers' lives during the present time. It is quite likely that the homemakers of this study have young children at home. Thus, their present role may be due to the parental imperatives, rather than any personal choice or traditional outlook. In their life course, the homemaker status may be only a temporary position. Thus, it is of small surprise that greater within group variability can be observed in sex roles, and the consequent nonsignificant difference form the other two groups. Since no data on the number of children each subject had, nor the children's ages were collected, no support can be provided for this hypothesis. Certainly, this is an area that needs further scrutiny. The high educational level of the home-makers' group supports the contention, that the homemaker status of these women may only be temporary as a result of parental duties and obligations.

The findings, however, provoke concern about the situation of Asian Indian homemakers in the United States. Obviously, these women are in a severe pressure situation: choosing or being forced to remain in the traditional homemaking role yet feeling the inequalities inherent in it. Clearly unique, these results may hardly be generalizable, even to a similar sample in India. The immigrant women may have undergone changes and pressures that are only peculiar to their situation.

The women in the neutral occupational group, which included mainly social scientists and women in academia, were significantly more nontraditional in sex roles than the female-dominated occupational group and the homemakers. The neutral groups' consciousness about women's issues is, perhaps, responsible for these differences. Their superior knowledge about feminism as a social movement and philosophy was evident in the fact that 21 (70%) responded to the question "please write a few lines about your understanding of feminism." Five (25%) women in the female-dominated, 9 (50%) in the male-dominated occupations, and 4 (16.7%) home-makers responded to the same. Fifty percent (15) of the women in the neutral occupational group also identified themselves as feminists, whereas, 33% (6) in the male-dominated, 10% (2) in the female-dominated occupations, and 8.33% (2) in the homemakers' group identified themselves as such. It much be mentioned here that in the questionnaires no attempt was made to define feminism. It was assumed that most women in today's world are conscious of a global definition of feminism, if not its subtle within group variations. In general the educational level and number of years of education and work in the United States of the neutral group was significantly higher than the female-dominated occupational group and the home-makers. Possibly, these variables gave rise to a general awareness and familiarity with relevant social issues; which in turn generated a more egalitarian world view in these women. Again, the neutral group was not significantly different from the male-dominated occupational group. This result is, perhaps, inevitable, as both groups are obviously aware of women and their role in society. The consciousness about women's conditions and actual experience that the two groups have may be the reason why they do not possess significantly different sex roles.

SES and general level of education were both found to be significantly and positively correlated to sex roles. This finding supports some previous studies conducted in the United States and India (Dasgupta, 1983; Dreyer et al., 1981; Ghadially & Kazi, 1979; Kazi & Ghadially, 1979). Acculturation, as indicated by number of years of education and stay in the United States, was also a significant correlate of nontraditional sex roles. Interestingly, the single most important factor in nontraditional sex roles seems to be the number of years an individual has gone to school in the United States. Apparently, not just the length of stay in the United States, but the actual length of participation in the Western educational system is related to egalitarian feelings in this sample of Asian Indian women. Western educational background was also found to be related to egalitarian attitudes in a native Indian sample (Ghadially & Kazi, 1979).

Even though there were differences in mean scores of ISRO among the four groups in this study, not one of them can be considered truly traditional in their view of the sex roles. The possible range of scores on the measure ISRO varies from 16 to 80, with high scores indicating nontraditional sex roles. A score of 48, which is the midpoint, would denote neutral sex roles. A score of 50 may, thus, be considered the lower limit of nontraditional sex roles. All four groups of Asian women scored well above this limit. The lowest score, that at the homemakers, was 56.29.

Although all the Asian Indian women in the sample should be considered nontraditional in their sex role attitude, only 25 (27%) identified themselves as feminists. An overwhelming number of the women viewed the western feminist movement as not sensitive to the needs and plight of Asian Indian women. The apparent gap between attitude and behavior, therefore, is perhaps due to this perception of difference between the problems facing the Indian woman and her American sister.

The findings of this study show that Asian Indian immigrant women, as a group, are definitely egalitarian in their view of the sex role. Whether working outside their homes or within, Asian Indian women are similar in their sex roles. But when working women were divided in groups according to the number of women working in the occupations, differences in sex roles emerge. Women who are working in traditionally feminine occupations seem to be significantly more traditional in their view of the sex roles than women who are working in cross-sex and neutral occupational areas. But this relation between sex roles and density of women in occupational areas does not hold true when homemakers are compared. This latter group seems not to be significantly different from both the male- and female-dominated occupational groups, due to higher within group variance. Asian Indian homemakers in the United States seem to be under contradictory pressures. They seem to be adhering to the traditional role, yet are conscious of the inequities in it. There also seems to be a pull towards adapting to this role, in spite of this awareness. The majority of the women in the sample expressed skepticism about the women's movement and its sensitivity to the needs of women of Indian heritage.

The findings of this study might be cautiously generalized. The Asian Indians in this sample are a highly educated and affluent immigrant group. It is quite likely that the different factors affecting them are peculiar to their group only. The Asian Indian women with their educational background and access to economic resources are emerging as a potentially influential community in the United States. There is sure to be mutual gain if this group participates actively in the feminist movement. Whether the western feminist movements will make an effort to bring them into the ranks of active participants in the future is, of course, an open question.

REFERENCE NOTE

1. The population of Asian and Pacific Islanders has increased 142% between 1970 and 1980. The magnitude of this growth can be appreciated if it is contrasted to the growth rate of other ethnic populations. For example, the American Indian, Eskimo, and Aleut population increased 71%, people of Spanish origin 61%, and the Black population increased only 17% during the same period.

Most Asian Indians are involved in technically oriented jobs. 27.5% of Asian Indians hold managerial-professional jobs in the United States, 41.6% hold technical, sales, and administrative support jobs and 30.9% are engaged in service work, production and industrial labor.

REFERENCES

Albrecht, S. L., Bahr, H. M., & Chadwick, B. A. (1977). Public stereotyping of roles, personality characteristics, and occupations. *Sociology and Social Research, 61,* 223-240.

Dasgupta, S.D. (1983). *Relations between women's gender identities and gender-associated activities in crime and occupation.* Unpublished doctoral dissertation, The Ohio State University, Columbus, Ohio.

Dreyer, N. A., Woods, N. F., & James, S. A. (1981). ISRO: A scale to measure sex-role orientation. *Sex Roles, 7,* 173-182.

Duncan, O. D. (1961). A socioeconomic index for all occupations. In A. J. Reiss, Jr. (Ed.), *Occupations and social status.* N.Y.: Free Press.

Gettys, L. D., & Cann, A. (1981). Children's perceptions of occupational sex stereotypes. *Sex Roles, 7,* 301-308.

Ghadially, R., & Kazi, K. A. (1979). Attitudes toward sex-roles. *Indian Journal of Social Work, 40,* 65-71.

Gupta, S., Shah, M. A., & Beg, M. A. (1982). Education and socioeconomic status as determinants of Indian women's attitudes towards equality of women. *The Journal of Social Psychology, 118,* 139-140.

Horner, M. S. (1972). Toward an understanding of achievement-related conflicts in women. *Journal of Social Issues, 28,* 157-175.

Kazi, K. A., & Ghadially, R. (1979). Perception of the female role by Indian college students. *Sociological Bulletin, 28,* 59-70.

Naidoo, J. C. (1984, August). *Multiculturalism and identification crises for South Asian women in Canada.* Paper presented at the Annual convention of American Psychological Association, Toronto, Canada.

Nandi, P. K. (1980). *The quality of life of Asian Americans.* Chicago, Illinois: Pacific/ Asian American Mental Health Research Center.

Panek, P. E., Rush, M. C., & Greenwalt, J. P. (1977). Current sex stereotypes of 25 occupations. *Psychological Reports, 40,* 212-214.

Rifkin, B., & Rifkin, S. (1979). *American Labor Sourcebook.* N.Y.: McGraw-Hill Book Co.

Solanki, R. (1973). *Americanization of immigrants: A study in acculturation of Asian-Indians in the state of Colorado and the educational implications thereof.* Unpublished doctoral dissertation, University of Denver, Colorado.

Tyer, Z. E., & Erdwins, C. J. (1979). Relationship of sex role to male- and female-dominated professions. *Psychological Reports, 44,* 1134.

U.S. Bureau of the Census. (1984). *A statistical profile of selected racial/ethnic groups.* Washington, DC.

U.S. Bureau of the Census. (1983). *Statistical Abstract of the United States: 1984,* (104th. edition). Washington, DC.

Wolfe, L. K., & Betz, N. E. (1981). Traditionality of choice and sex-role identification as moderators of the congruence of occupational choice in college women. *Journal of Vocational Behavior, 18,* 43-55.

Yanico, B. J., & Hardin, S. I. (1981). Sex-role self-concept and persistence in a traditional vs. nontraditional college major for women. *Journal of Vocational Behavior, 18,* 219-227.

Relationships Between Stress and Marital Satisfaction Among Dual-Earner Couples

Sara Yogev

Stress or role overload and marital satisfaction are both issues of concern to family researchers studying dual-earner couples. However, these researchers have given little attention to the interaction between these two issues. The purpose of this paper is three fold: (1) to study the relationships between perceptions of stress and marital satisfaction; (2) to compare the degree of stress reported by spouses in dual-earner marriages; and (3) to investigate the relationships between stress and two main potential contributors, involvement in work role and involvement in family roles.

The increase of dual-earner couples in the general population in the last two decades resulted in a surge of research focusing on this family pattern. For example, traditional expectations about the division of roles and labor in the family led researchers to wonder how this new pattern would affect family life and if it would disrupt it. Several researchers were concerned about the various problems occurring when men and women combined work and family (Holohan & Gilbert, 1979; Keith & Schafer, 1980). Depression, role strain, stress and psychological well-being are some of the issues researchers examined under the assumption that these might be the areas of disruption. Other researchers were concerned that role overload, role conflict, role strain and/or stress would occur among dual-earner couples (Burke & Weir, 1976; Rapoport & Rapoport, 1969). However, the results showed discrepant and inconsistent findings.

The stress experienced by dual-earner couples has typi-

Sara Yogev is Assistant Professor at the Center for Urban Affairs and Policy Research, Northwestern University, 2040 Sheridan Road, Evanston, IL 60201.

cally been conceptualized within a framework of time demand (Berk & Berk, 1979; Keith & Schafer, 1980; Rapoport & Rapoport, 1969). The impact of this stress and role overload has been found by some researchers to be related among women to depression (Radloff, 1975; Wright, 1978) and symptoms of distress (Woods & Hulka, 1979), while other studies found that women combining paid employment with family roles have better mental health (Kessler & McRae, 1981; Sales & Frieze, 1984). Among dual-earner men the same inconsistent results appear. Several studies found husbands of employed women in poorer mental health than husbands of homemakers (Burke & Weir, 1976; Keith & Schafer, 1980; Kessler & McRae, 1981). Booth (1979) found that husbands of homemakers were in worse mental health than husbands of women employed outside the home. Furthermore, Kessler & McRae (1981) found that there is no evidence that objective burdens associated with increased family work play a part in the elevated rate of distress among dual-earner husbands.

Yogev (1982) noted that, in many of the studies reporting stress and role overload, it is not always clear whether the subjects themselves reported that they feel overworked or whether the researchers assume this was a consequence of their subjects' lifestyles. A distinction was suggested between objective-quantitative perception of role load and subjective-qualitative perception. This distinction might be helpful when considering the inconsistent results about the impact of stress and role overload on psychological well-being. Indeed, Barnett and Baruch (1982) found in a study of multiple role strain and psychological well-being that qualitative and structural aspects of one's experience in a role are more salient to multiple role strain than merely occupying the role. Thus the same situation might be perceived as stressful to one individual but satisfying to another.

In summary, an important conclusion drawn from the accumulated literature about stress and mental health or psychological well-being, is that the individual's interpretation of his/her own situation is very important and crucial for his/her perception of stress.

While there are many studies comparing marital satisfaction among dual-earner versus single-earner couples (Burke

& Weir, 1976; Orden & Bradburn, 1969) there are no studies correlating role overload or stress with marital satisfaction. However, a few studies found a relationship between marital satisfaction and the husband's greater participation in family work. Dual-earner couples who perceive their spouses as doing their share of family work, reported higher level of marital satisfaction than those who perceive their spouses as doing less than their share (Pleck & Lang, 1978; Yogev & Brett, 1985). Similarly, Bailyn (1970) found, in a British sample, that employed wives performing more family work were experiencing lower marital happiness than those performing less family work.

On the basis of the data generated from the relationship between stress and mental health on one hand, and marital satisfaction and division of family work on the other, it was expected that a negative correlation would be found between stress and marital satisfaction. Thus, dual earner individuals who report higher levels of stress should also report lower levels of marital satisfaction.

Hypothesis 1: The higher scores on the stress scale will be correlated with lower scores on marital satisfaction for both men and women.

Since studies focusing on the division of family work among dual-earner couples found that role overload and stress are particularly common among the wives because they still carry the lion's share of family work (Pleck, 1983), it was expected that a higher overload level would be found among the dual-earner wives.

Hypothesis 2: Dual-earner wives will report higher stress scores than dual-earner husbands.

Much of the research on stress and role overload among dual-earner couples focused on time demands (as reviewed earlier). Moen (1982) noted that the relationships between work time and family time are complex and under-researched. Treating time in simplistic fashion (e.g., more time at work → less time for family or more time at work and more time for family → stress) may well obscure as much as it reveals. She emphasized the importance of commitment and energy as psychological constructs contributing to our understanding of dual-earners' lifestyle.

According to role theory, role overload will occur when

conflicting and competing expectancies are perceived from two or more roles enacted by an individual. Thus a conceptual framework allows for the direct focus on the importance of life roles seemed particularly appropriate to the study of stress among dual-earner couples. The two main sources of role overload among dual-earner couples are, of course, work and family. "It is possible for dual-earner parents to rate themselves as highly committed to both parenting and employment. It is in this instance that the strains produced by the two roles are likely to be most pronounced" (Moen, 1982: p. 405).

Since the person's experience of his/her situation was found to be more important to role strain and distress than the actual role (Barnett & Baruch, 1982), information was gathered on these two main sources of role overload by using the person's report of his/her work involvement and family involvement. It was expected that highest stress levels would be experienced by individuals who report high level of involvement in both their work and family roles; lowest stress levels would be experienced by individuals who report low level of involvement in both work and family roles, and average stress levels would be experienced by individuals who report high involvement in only one role and low involvement in the other.

Hypothesis 3: There will be significant differences in stress scores according to involvement scores.

METHOD

Sample

Data were collected from a sample of male and female employees of a large midwestern, high technology organization and their spouses. The sample was selected in the following way. All Chicago area employees received a mailing which included both a letter from the firm's president encouraging employees to cooperate with a university study of work life and family life and a letter from the researchers. The researchers' letter stated that married couples with children living at home were being sought for the study. Couples interested in participating were asked to return a postcard to the researchers. Approximately 650 postcards were returned. From this group, 376 families were considered eligible for the study. Eligibility requirements included: that the couple be married and living together; that either both spouses be employed, or that if only one spouse is employed it be the husband; that there be children living in the home under the age of 18; and that no member of the immediate family for whom the adults in the household provide daily care or have ongoing responsibility, suffer from a chronic disease, impairment or handicap. Childless couples (177), couples with a sick/handicapped family member (67), and couples who were not married or in which the husband was unemployed (31) were excluded.

Identical questionnaires, one for the husband and one for the wife, were sent to each of the 376 eligible couples. The response rate was 64 percent. The resulting file consisted of 239 couples. In 103 of these couples, only the husband was employed, and in 136 couples, both spouses were employed. The 136 dual-earner couples were the subjects for this study.

The demographic characteristics of the sample were as follows: the average male was 41 years old and had some college experience but not a college degree, had been in the work force for almost 23 years, and spent on the average of 51.5 hours per week working and commuting. His earnings were between $26,000 and $31,000 per year. Twenty-seven percent of the men had blue-collar occupations; 40 percent were in sales and management and 28 percent were in other white-collar and clerical occupations. The average woman in the sample was 38 years old, had at least a high school degree but no college and had been in the work force for 13 years. She spent on the average of 43.9 hours per week working and commuting. She earned between $11,000 and $15,000 per year. Nine percent of the women were in blue-collar jobs. Seventeen percent were in sales and management, 46 percent held clerical positions and 27 percent were teachers or held other white-collar jobs.

Measures

Marital satisfaction was measured by the Spanier (1976) dyadic satisfaction scale. In this study, the dyadic satisfaction mean was 40.53, the standard deviation 5.81, the range from 13–50 and the coefficient alpha .87.

Job involvement was measured with the instrument developed by Lodahl and Kejner (1965). This is a Likert-type scale using a 5-point response format from strongly agree to strongly disagree. In this study, the job involvement mean was 58.47, the standard deviation 7.69 and the coefficient alpha .80.

Dual-earner men and women were placed in high/low work involvement group on the basis of whether their own scores were higher/lower than the mean. The mean work involvement score for the men was 60.02 and the mean for the women was 55.65.

Family involvement was measured with an instrument developed particularly for this research. The instrument was modeled after the Lodahl and Kejner (1965) job involvement instrument with eleven items on a 5-point response format. It focused on two family roles: spouse and parent. In this study, the family involvement mean was 42.66, the standard deviation 5.76, and the coefficient alpha .80 (see Appendix A, Family Involvement Scale).

Individuals were placed in high/low family involvement groups on the basis of whether their scores were higher/lower than the mean. The mean family involvement score for the men was 42.58 and the mean for the women was 43.0.

Stress or overload was measured by an instrument developed specifically for this research. It consisted of the following three items: how often do you feel overloaded or stressed because of your work responsibilities? How often do you feel overloaded or stressed because of your family responsibilities? How often do you feel overloaded or stressed because of your work and family responsibilities?

Answers were on a 5-point Likert-type scale ranging from never to almost all the time. In this study the stress scale mean was 8.53, the standard deviation 2.32 with a coefficient alpha of .78.

RESULTS

Table 1 presents the results testing the relationship between marital satisfaction and perceived stress. These correlations were significant for both husbands and wives in dual-earner marriages. The direction of this correlation was: the more

Table 1

Correlations between marital Satisfaction and Stress for Dual-Earner

Couples

	N	r	p
Dual earner husbands	135	-.23	.003
Dual career wives	133	-.44	.001

stress—the less marital satisfaction. Thus our first hypothesis was confirmed.

Table 2 presents the differences in perceived level of stress among husbands and wives. Again, our hypothesis was confirmed. Dual-earner wives' levels of stress were significantly higher (F = 5.917 p ≤ .0006) than their husbands' reported levels of stress (9.04 and 8.02) respectively.

Table 3 presents the results of the regression predicting stress by entering work involvement and family involvement. For the dual-earner wives, involvement in these two important roles predicted level of stress. This multiple correlation was significant at the .01 level. Each of these involvements was also separately significantly correlated with stress (Work involvement − R^2 = .16 p ≤ .03, Family Involvement R^2 = .19 p ≤ .01). However, for dual-earner men neither involvement in work role, family role nor both roles were significantly related to stress. Thus, our hypothesis was only partially confirmed. Only the dual-earner women showed the predicted correlation between stress and involvement in family and work roles.

Table 4 presents the difference in stress level when dual-earner couples were grouped into one of three groups according to their scores on the involvement levels. The three groups were: (1) high in both work and family involvement; (2) low in both work and family involvement; and (3) high in one involvement and low in the other involvement. There were no significant differences between the three groups on the stress scale, neither for women or for men. However, the scores on the stress scale for both men and women did show the expected tendency, (i.e., group 1 people who are high in both involvement levels did score the highest on the stress; group 2—low in both involvement scores scored the lowest on the stress scale; and group 3—high only in one involvement was intermediate but these differences did not reach a significant level.

DISCUSSION

This study found a significant negative relationship between perceived level of stress and marital satisfaction among dual-earner couples. These results support other studies which

Table 2

Differences on Reported Stress among Dual-Earner Couples

	N	Mean	SD	F	P
Dual-earner husbands	134	8.02	2.08		
Dual-earner wives	135	9.04	2.45	5.197	.0006

Table 3

Regression Predicting Stress by Work Involvement and Family
Involvement

	R^2	F	P
Dual-earner husbands	.13	1.08	NS
Dual-earner wives	.26	4.51	.01

Table 4

Differences on Stress among Groups Based on Work and Family
Involvement

	Wives			Husbands		
	Mean	S.D.	N	Mean	S.D.	N
High on both Work and Family						
Involvement	9.14	2.40	41	8.42	1.93	4
Low on both Work and Family						
Involvement	8.57	2.22	21	7.72	1.96	36
High on one and low on other	9.10	2.55	73	7.93	2.23	58
	F = .44 NS			F = 1.22 NS		

found that stress was significantly correlated with depression (Radloff, 1975; Wright, 1978). While Bailyn (1970) found that among employed women, performance of more family work (which we can assume might contribute to stress) was associated with lower marital satisfaction, this study found that the negative impact of stress on marital satisfaction did not spare the husbands. Thus, both spouses experienced lower levels of marital satisfaction when they reported high levels of stress.

A possible explanation for the correlation between marital satisfaction and stress is based on my clinical experience with dual-earner couples in my practice for marital therapy. With some couples, one spouse sometimes responds to the other's needs, and changes his/her behavior. If this change does not bring much improvement in the overall marital situation, the result often is despair, a sense of inadequacy as a spouse and lower marital satisfaction.

Some studies indicate that dual-earner husbands have recently increased their level of family work (Hofferth, 1981; Pleck, 1983) and that there are significant relationships between marital satisfaction and perceptions of the distribution of family work. Higher marital satisfaction has been associated with more family work done by husbands (Pleck & Lang, 1978; Yogev & Brett, 1985). On the basis of these two general findings in the literature and my clinical observation I think it possible that if, in spite of the husband's increased participation in family work, both spouses still experience role overload and stress, they might be feeling they are not capable of coping effectively with the demands of their family situation. This possible sense of inadequacy or failure might make them doubt the success of their marital team and lower their marital satisfaction.

I do not mean to imply causality about the relationships between marital satisfaction and stress. It is possible that coping successfully as a team with work and family demands contribute to marital satisfaction or, the opposite phenomenon, marital satisfaction may make it easier to create an efficient lifestyle which reduces stress. Whichever the causal direction, the important result of this study is its demonstration of relationships between marital satisfaction and stress for both spouses.

Our finding that dual-earner wives reported higher levels of stress is in accordance with other studies which found that dual-earner wives still carry the lion's share of family work (Pleck, 1983).

The second interesting finding of this study is that involvement levels in work and family roles predict levels of stress among women, but not among men. On the basis of the results which found a significant positive correlation between work involvement and time devoted to work (Lawler & Hall, 1970), we can assume that, for women, higher involvement scores on work and family scales mean more time and energy devoted to these roles thus resulting in stress.

The picture is different among the men, however. While a significant negative correlation between marital satisfaction and stress was found among dual-earner couples, it was not found that the husbands' work involvement and family involvement predicted their levels of stress, unlike dual-earner wives for whom work involvement and family involvement do significantly predict levels of stress.

There are two possible explanations for these findings. The preponderance of data indicate that even though husbands' participation in family chores has indeed increased somewhat over time and that dual-earner men clearly perform a higher proportion of the couple's total family work, employed wives continue to do the bulk of family work (Pleck, 1983). It is possible that since dual-earner husbands do not participate in family work as much as their wives, they do not feel overloaded or stressed because of their combined level of involvements. The significant higher stress scores of the wives support this agreement. The husbands might be very psychologically involved in their family but do not translate this higher involvement into actual behavior and do more family work. Indeed Yogev and Brett (in press) found that men married to housewives reported higher levels of psychological involvement in the family than men married to employed women. Thus it might be that, since family involvement does not necessarily lead to actual greater participation in family work among men, their combined levels of involvement in family and work roles are not related to stress.

Another possible explanation for the lack of relationship

between work, family involvements and stress among these men, might be sex role stereotyping. Early socialization and continued reinforcement of the expected feminine role in our society, make it easier for women to express anxiety, uncertainty, nervousness and helplessness (Freeman, 1974) Men, however, are expected to be strong, independent and self sufficient, even individuals who do not share feelings—particularly negative ones. Self-report which conflicts with such an idealized self-image might be distorted and adjusted to conform to beliefs about gender stereotypes (Spence, Helmreich & Stapp, 1975). Asking men to report feelings of stress and overload may conflict with their masculine self-images, and expressions of such feelings may be dissociated accordingly. Thus, they are able to report involvement in work and in their families since these involvements do not conflict with masculine self-concept and are socially desirable. However, men may tend to minimize or omit reports of their own levels of stress since such reports conflict with ideas about positive masculine self-concept and may not be socially desirable. The trend that we see in Table 4 (high stress scores for men who show high involvement in both work and family roles and lowest stress scores for men who are low in both roles) might support this argument, even though it is not significant.

Future Implications

The results of this study have implications for future clinical work as well as for future research. Clinicians and family therapists should be aware of the relationship between stress and marital satisfaction among dual-earner couples. Yogev (1983) in a paper about marital therapy with dual-earner couples, noticed that "most therapists tend to focus on internal-identity conflicts and often fail to realize the crucial role that external demands play in the dual-earner lifestyle" (p. 40). The link was emphasized between unsuccessful and unresolved marital conflicts. The results of the present study confirm this link. Coping mechanisms which might reduce the level of stress and focus attention on strategies to manage external demands, can further subsequent therapeutic work on internal issues. People cannot experience intimacy when their basic needs for stress reduction are not met. Perceiving oneself as stressed or awareness of overloading for one's spouse can affect an individual's perceptions of his/her successful role as spouse and can enhance or reduce the level of marital satisfaction.

It is quite possible that, similarly to the curvilinear relationship between role demands and mental health (Sales & Frieze, 1984) there is a curvilinear relationship between stress and marital satisfaction. Cooke and Rousseau (1984) found that work overload and role conflict contribute to physical strain. Family roles can both induce and reduce physical symptoms of strain. They conclude that future research on health seemed warranted, particularly on subjective measures of support associated with family roles. Marital satisfaction as a part of family roles can have a similar impact on psychological stress. More studies focusing on this relationship are needed. The difficulty is that each topic is researched by a different discipline: stress is usually investigated by physiologists and industrial psychologists, marital satisfaction by family therapists and marital therapists. In order to better understand the relationship between marital satisfaction and stress, more cross-disciplinary studies are needed.

The discussion of stress and marital satisfaction, while based on empirical knowledge, should be viewed as somewhat speculative and limited by crucial problems in interpretation. There are a variety of measures currently used as indicators of stress. Yogev (1982) noticed that in studies about professional women, it is not always clear whether the subjects themselves reported that they feel stressed or whether the authors concluded that overwork was a consequence of their subjects' life style. She suggested clarifying the overwork and stress issues by distinguishing between objective-quantitative and subjective-qualitative perceptions of role load. Even within the objective measures there is a great variety of measures as indicators of stress. Some authors used physical-physiological symptoms and medical records while others considered use of medications and health care services, while still others used number of hours of work or number of tasks in family work or number of certain life events. Thus, before generalizing about the relationship between stress and marital satisfaction, a clear distinction is needed about which aspects of stress we mean.

A second problem relates to the influence of other factors in one's life on marital satisfaction. We know that marital satisfaction varies with regard to socio-economic status, age, family stage, and age of children. Before we conclude that marital satisfaction is beneficial we must control other variables that may be the actual source of these benefits.

A third, and perhaps a crucial interpretive dilemma, is that personality has a strong impact on stress resistance and coping mechanisms. The hardy personality can be a moderator of stressful life events (Maddi, 1980). Individuals differ with regard to the degree to which situations in one's life are appraised as stressful (Cohen, Kamarck & Mermelstein, 1983). Future studies should control for this variable as well.

With such directions for study, the results of future research may provide a foundation for guiding policy decision makers, corporations, therapists and individuals in designing and structuring lifestyles which are conducive to health, job performance, family life and personal life satisfaction.

REFERENCES

Bailyn, L. (1970). Career and family orientations of husbands and wives in relation to marital happiness. *Human Relations, 23,* 97–113.

Barnett, R.C. and Baruch, G.K. (1982). On the psychological well-being of women in the mid years. Working Paper No. 85, Wellesley College, Center for Research on Women, Wellesley, MA 02181.

Berk, R.A. and Berk, S.F. (1979). *Labor and leisure at home.* Beverly Hills, CA: Sage.

Booth, A. (1979). Does wives' employment cause stress for husbands? *The Family Coordinator, 28,* 445–49.

Burke, R.J. and Weir, T. (1976). Relationship of wives' employment status to husband, wife and pair satisfaction and performance. *Journal of Marriage and the Family, 36,* 279–287.

Cohen, S., Kamarck, T. and Mermelstein, R. (1983). A global measure of perceived stress. *Journal of Health and Social Behavior, 24,* p. 385–396.

Cooke, R.A. and Rousseau, D.M. (1984). Stress and strain from family roles and work-role expectations. *Journal of Applied Psychology, 69,* 252–260.

Freeman, J. (1974). Women In Society. In A. Skolnick and J. Skolnick (Eds), *Intimacy Family and Society,* (pp. 201–236). Boston: Little Brown.

Hofferth, S. (1981). *Effects of number and timing of births on family well-being over the life-cycle.* Washington, D.C.: Urban Institute.

Holahan, C.K. and Gilbert, L.A. (1979). Interrole conflict for working women: Careers versus jobs. *Journal of Applied Psychology, 64,* 86–90.

Keith, P.M. and Schafer, R.B. (1980). Role strain and depression in two-job families. *Family Relations, 29,* 483–488.

Kessler, R.C. and McRae, J.A. (1981). Trends in the relationship between sex and psychological distress: 1957–1976. *American Sociological Review, 46,* 443–52.

Lawler, E.E. III and Hall, D.T. (1970). Relationship of job characteristics and job involvement. *Journal of Applied Psychology, 54,* 305–311.

Lodahl, T.M. and Kejner, M. (1965). The definition and measurement of job involvement. *Journal of Applied Psychology, 49*, 24–33.

Maddi, S.R. (1980). *Personality as a resource in stress resistance: The hardy type.* Paper presented at the American Psychological Association Convention, Montreal, Canada.

Moen, P. (1982). The two-provider family: problems and potentials. In M. E. Lamb (Ed.) *Nontraditional Families* (pp. 397–427). New York: L. Erlbaum.

Orden, S.R. and Bradburn, N.M. (1969). Working wives and marriage happiness. *American Journal of Sociology, 74*, 362–407.

Pleck, J.H. and Lang, L. (1978). Men's family role: Its nature and consequences. Working Paper, Wellesley College Center for Research on Women, Wellesley, MA.

Pleck, J. (1983). Husband's paid work and family roles: Current research issues. In H. Lopata & J. Pleck (Eds.), *Research in the interweave of social roles: Families and jobs,* (pp. 251–321). Greenwich, CT: JAI Press:

Radloff, L.S. (1975). Sex differences in depression: The effects of occupation and marital status. *Sex Roles, 1*, 249–65.

Rapoport, R. and Rapoport, R. (1969). The dual-career family: A variant pattern and social change. *Human Relations, 22*, 3–30.

Sales, E. and Frieze, I.H. (1984). Women and work: Implications for mental health. In E. Walker, *Women and Mental Health Policy*, 229–246. Beverly Hills, CA: Sage.

Spanier, G.B. (1976). Measuring dyadic adjustment: New scales for assessing the quality of marriage and similar dyads. *Journal of Marriage and the Family, 38*, 15–28.

Spence, J., Helmreich, R. and Stapp, J. (1975). Ratings of self peers on sex role attributes and their relation to self-esteem and conceptions of masculinity and femininity. *Journal of Personality and Social Psychology, 32*, 29–39.

Woods, N.F. and Hulka, B.S. (1979). Symptom reports and illness behavior among employed women and homeworkers. *Journal of Community Health, 5*, 36–45.

Wright, J.P. (1978). Are working women really more satisfied? Evidence from several national surveys. *Journal of Marriage and Family, 40*, 301–313.

Yogev, S. (1982). Are professional women overworked: Objective versus subjective perception of role loads. *Journal of Occupational Psychology, 55*, 165–169.

Yogev, S. (1983). Dual career couples: Conflicts and treatment. *The American Journal of Family Therapy, 11/12*, 38–44.

Yogev, S. and Brett, J., 1985. Perceptions of the division of housework and childcare and marital satisfaction. *Journal of Marriage and the Family, 47*, 609–618.

Yogev, S. and Brett, J. (in press). Patterns of work and family involvement among single and dual earner couples. *Journal of Applied Psychology.*

Appendix A

Family Involvement Scale

1. A great satisfaction in my life comes from my role as a parent.
2. A great satisfaction in my life comes from my role as a spouse.
3. Quite often I plan ahead the next day's family activities.

4. For me, days at home really fly by.
5. I am very much involved personally with my family members' lives.
6. I would be a less fulfilled person without my role as a spouse.
7. The most important things that happen to me are related to my family roles.
8. If I had to do all over again I would not have married my present spouse. (Reversed scored.)
9. I would be a less fulfilled person without my role as a parent.
10. Nothing is as important as being a spouse.
11. I enjoy talking about my family with other people.

All items were measured on the following scale:

1	2	3	4	5
Strongly disagree	Disagree	Neither agree nor disagree	Agree	Strongly agree

Sex Differences in the Perception of Street Harassment

Jaclyn Packer

For some women, being approached by male strangers on the street is considered an inconvenience, a momentary distraction from other thoughts, sometimes even a compliment. For others, however, it is a major intrusion into one's personal space, an encroachment that *demands* attention, a humiliating experience, and occasionally a situation potentially fraught with danger.

While sexual harassment of women in employment situations has been given a lot of attention lately in sociological and psychological literature, street harassment has been virtually ignored, except in feminist literature. While working on this paper, I reviewed what little research I could find on the topic and also talked to many women about their personal experiences. Many street harassment situations appear to have certain characteristics in common. For instance, many men who harass do it to impress their buddies—women seem to be harassed more often by men in groups than by men alone. An informal study (Benard and Schlaffer, 1981) was conducted in Germany by two women who stopped every man on the street who harassed them, and asked them to fill out a questionnaire. The authors found that many men would not engage in this behavior when alone and stated that the finding "supports the explanation that the harassment of women is a form of male bonding, of demonstrating solidarity and joint power." Another characteristic seems to be that many men do not think it is worth harassing a woman unless she is aware that she is the object of the attention. One woman I spoke to, who is often harassed, told me that she

Jaclyn Packer is a Graduate Research Assistant and student in the Doctoral program in Social/Personality Psychology at the Graduate Center, City University of New York.

made the discovery that when she is carrying her "walkman" radio and is wearing the earphones, men don't make comments to her (apparently because they believe she cannot hear them). She now makes a deliberate effort to carry her walkman with her wherever she goes, whether she actually turns the sound on or not. One more important characteristic of these situations seems to be that men will almost never harass a woman who is in the company of a man. I was told a story about a woman who appeared to be alone—her boyfriend had stopped to tie his shoes and she was walking ahead of him. Several men started whistling at her and making comments. When her boyfriend caught up with her, the harassers apologized to *him,* saying that they were sorry, but they didn't realize that "she was his."

In an article by Gardner (1980), she says:

> There is no sure way for a woman to pass down the street alone and not be commented upon. Accompanied by a man or a child, she furnishes evidence of proper in-role standing. But if she is alone, that standing is always in doubt and may be metaphorically spoken to by men.

She suggests that indirect evidence of *having* a man, such as wheeling a baby carriage or being pregnant, will often prevent men from bothering a woman on the street. An additional point that is important to note here is that street harassment probably happens most often in large cities, where there is more anonymity between people, and where men can take less responsibility for their actions.

Women's reactions this type of harassment vary from situation to situation. There are some harassment situations in which women say that they feel somewhat complimented. These appear to be situations where the woman feels free from any danger of physical harm (ususally when she is in a well-lit area where there are many other people around) and where the man is someone who she feels is attractive. Some women feel more complimented by street harassment when they are not feeling good about their own appearance. For instance, a 66-year-old woman told me that she was extremely complimented by a beggar on the street who, after she refused to give him money, said that she sure was pretty for someone who was fifty years old. It is unfortunate that our culture is so agist that this woman needed to have a beggar on the street tell her that she looked younger in order to feel good about herself.

In most cases, the women I talked to felt angry about being approached on the street. One woman said that she was angry that she never had any privacy on the street. She would often take alternate routes traveling to and from work, in order to avoid the particular streets where the harassment was worse.

An article in *Glamour* magazine (1983) suggested that women should answer men back in situations where they feel safe. They suggest that women do whatever they need to do in the situation, in order to feel in control. One idea is to say something such as "Would you like it if another man made that comment to your wife or girlfriend?" One of the experts they quoted said that women think of good retorts for different situations, and then practice them until they feel comfortable with saying them. This is a sad comment on our society that women might waste what precious personal time they have at home preparing to defend themselves verbally on the street. (I wonder if the street harasser goes home and practices—or if it just comes naturally to him.)

A woman I spoke to said that she formerly would try to educate the men on the street who bothered her. She would use similar techniques to those suggested in the *Glamour* magazine article. After years of doing this, she now just tries to ignore it as much as possible, otherwise, she says, "It just ruins your whole day."

The present study is a first step in trying to ascertain how men and women feel about street harassment of women. For the purposes of this study I defined street harassment as a situation in which a man responds to a female stranger on the street by an action such as whistling at her, commenting on her appearance, or making a sexual comment to her.

This study examined sex differences on three separate issues:

— how subjects think a woman feels in this situation;
— how subjects think the harasser *intends* for her to feel in this situation;

— subjects' impressions of how *often* women are typically harassed.

Seventeen male and seventeen female subjects were given a questionnaire to fill out, which contained several rating questions. The first part asked subjects to rate, on a scale from 1 to 5, how complimented, offended, pleased, angry and safe a woman feels in a harassment situation. (Note that the word "harassment" was never used in this questionnaire. The harassment situation was operationally described as mentioned previously—whistling, a comment on appearance, or a sexual comment.) The next part of the questionnaire asked how complimented, offended, pleased, angry and safe the man intends for her to be by his actions. Finally, subjects were asked to guess how many times per week the average woman in New York City is approached in this manner by a male stranger on the street.

Subjects worked for a social service agency, in a variety of occupations, ranging from blue collar to PhD professional level positions. Subjects' ages ranged from 18 to 65 years, with a mean age of 35.

It seemed to me that the questionnaire was straightforward, and I was fairly sure I knew what I would find—that women generally feel negatively about street harassment, while men think women like it; and that women think harassers engage in the behavior in order to provoke them, while men think harassers do it to be complimentary. My latter assumptions turned out to be incorrect.

In the first part of the questionnaire, where male and female subjects rated how a harassed woman feels, a consistent sex difference emerged. Overall, female subjects thought women were significantly less complimented, less pleased, more angry and more offended than male subjects thought. Female subjects also thought that victims of harassment felt significantly less safe in the situation than male subjects thought.

Surprisingly, in rating the intentions of the harasser, male subjects thought that the harasser intended to be significantly less complementary and more anger-provoking than the females thought. While results were not significant for the other three adjectives, the trend was in the same direction for two:

the males thought harassers intended to be more offending and less pleasing to the women. (See Table 1 for results.) (Note that while seven out of ten items obtained significant differences, it does not imply that men and women rated each item at the *opposite ends* of the ranks. For instance on the item regarding how complimented women feel, the mean for

Table I

Mean ratings* and significance levels of men and women subjects' responses to questions regarding a woman's feeling and a man's intentions in a street harassment situation.

	Woman Ss	Male Ss	Sig. Level
woman victim's			
feeling			
complimented	1.65	3.00	p<.001
offended	4.00	3.12	p<.02
pleased	1.35	3.00	p<.001
angry	3.70	2.88	p<.05
safe	2.53	3.24	p<.05
male harasser's			
intention			
complimented	4.29	3.53	p<.05
offended	1.89	2.29	N.S.**
pleased	4.35	3.59	N.S.**
angry	1.59	2.53	p<.01
safe	2.76	3.40	N.S.**

*ratings are on a scale from 1 (not at all) to 5 (very).

**not significant at the .05 level.

women was 1.65 on a 5 point scale, and for men it was 3.0. While there were men who checked the "complimented" choice, there were others who checked "not complimented at all." There was a wide range of responses for both sexes, but strong consistent differences emerged, nevertheless.)

These results seem to indicate that women dislike being harassed on the street—it offends them and makes them angry; yet, at the same time, they give the harasser the benefit of the doubt, and assume he means no harm by his actions. The conclusion here, for many women, may be that since men don't know that women don't like this behavior, it's really not their fault.

For males, even though they seem to feel that the harasser's intentions are malevolent, they also believe that women really like to be the focus of this negative energy. The conclusion here, for many men, may be that since women like it, the men aren't really doing anything wrong. No matter which of these conclusions one comes to, the harasser does not have to take responsibility for his actions.

In regard to the question of how often women are typically harassed in New York City per week, there was, surprisingly, little overall difference between men's and women's responses. In fact, the men tended to guess slightly *larger* numbers. The median number of times per week mentioned by women was 7, and for men it was 10. I analyzed these answers by comparing responses of older and younger women, and by comparing older and younger men. While there were no differences in the two male age groups, there was a signicant difference between the older and younger women. On the average, older women guessed street harassment happened less often than did younger women. This may well be a reflection of personal experience, since older women typically do not fit the stereotype of beauty in our culture, and are therefore probably subject to less harassment. It's important to mention here though, that street harassment, like rape, can happen to any of us. Because there is hostility at the root of much street harassment and not "mere physical attraction" all women are subject to this treatment.

I recently replicated my study with a larger sample. The sample I chose turned out to be a younger group (mean age 29) and since I conducted it near New York University, many of the subjects were probably students. It turned out that there were almost no differences in the means between men and women, although there were some non-significant trends in the same direction as the previous study. Interestingly, the mean for the female subjects' ratings of how harassed women feel, was almost identical to the females' mean in the earlier sample, but the males' ratings this time moved closer to the females. The reversed happened for the data on the harasser's intentions—the females' ratings moved closer to the males. In other words, the younger, probably more well-educated sample, male and female alike, felt that women have negative feelings about street harassment, and this sample felt that men have more negative intentions toward the women they harass than did the previous sample.

This study is only a start in examining people's reactions to this type of behavior. I'd like to point out three main problems with this study. The first problem was that I combined three different types of street harassment, and asked for a single rating. It may be the case that people react very differently to a whistle than to a sexual comment. In further research, these should be separated out. The second problem is that the questionnaire asked about "a man" or "an average woman," and that is clearly going to mean different things to different people. When one is asked how complimented "a woman" is, what type of woman is being referred to, and what type of man is approaching her? Future research might make use of videotaped scenes of street harassment, where subjects would be witnessing a more objective portrayal of the situation. It would be interesting to vary factors such as how the woman is dressed or whether she averts her eyes when being spoken to. Additional factors that might be manipulated are the characters' race, and where the harassment occurs (e.g., urban versus rural, crowded versus deserted street, day versus night).

Whether women miss opportunities in order to avoid harassment should also be explored in relation to street harassment. Gardner (1980) says that some women avoid, "sometimes for years, the place where a particularly offensive remark has occurred." She says that women also avoid certain activities, such as bike riding, during which they are likely to be harassed.

One final problem with the present study is that while most

of the female subjects in my study have probably been harassed many times in their lives, the sample of men may or may not have included men who themselves harass women on the street. As a result, while I can legitimately use my data to show that women don't like to be harassed, I cannot use it to show that men *actually* intend to be anger-provoking and offensive. The best way to attempt to demonstrate this would be to talk to the harassers themselves (using a similar study to the one done in Germany, but conducted in a more systematic manner). Such a study might actually help to educate some of the harassers along the way.

While street harassment is not as serious as major physical threats against a woman, such as rape, nor as overwhelming as job harassment, where a woman's personal and financial situation is in jeopardy, it still lies somewhere along the *same* continuum. Street harassment continues to be one of the "inconveniences" that women, as a group, suffer because of our devalued status in society. Until women can be regarded as equal human beings to men, with the freedom to move wherever we want, whenever we choose, women will continue to be free game for any male on the street.

REFERENCES

Benard, C. & Schlaffer, E. (1981, May). The man in the street: Why he harasses. *Ms.*, pp. 18–19.
Gardner, C. (1980). Passing by: Street remarks, address rights, and the urban female. *Social Inquiry, 50*, (3-4), 328–356.
Glamour Magazine. (1984, February). Verbal abuse on the street: How to talk back.

Index